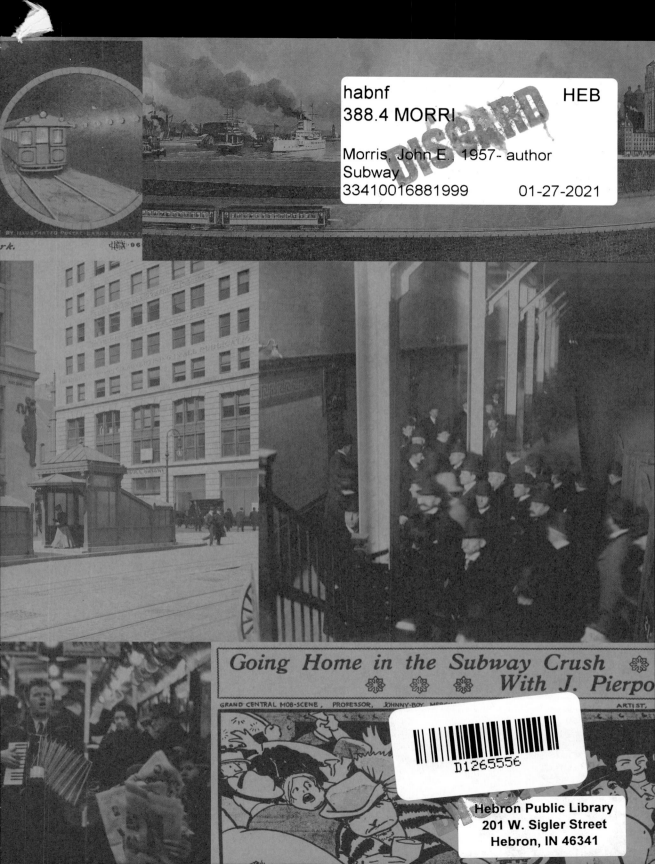

Going Home in the Subway Crush

With J. Pierpo

GRAND CENTRAL MOB-SCENE,   PROFESSOR,   JOHNNY-BOY   MERC   ARTIST.

Subway

Subway

The Curiosities, Secrets, and Unofficial History of the New York City Transit System

JOHN E. MORRIS

BLACK DOG
& LEVENTHAL
PUBLISHERS
NEW YORK

Black Dog & Leventhal Publishers
Hachette Book Group
1290 Avenue of the Americas
New York, NY 10104
www.hachettebookgroup.com
www.blackdogandleventhal.com

First edition: October 2020

Black Dog & Leventhal Publishers is an imprint of Perseus Books, LLC, a subsidiary of Hachette Book Group, Inc.
The Black Dog & Leventhal Publishers name and logo are trademarks of Hachette Book Group, Inc.
The publisher is not responsible for websites (or their content) that are not owned by the publisher.
The Hachette Speakers Bureau provides a wide range of authors for speaking events.
To find out more, go to www.HachetteSpeakersBureau.com or call (866) 376-6591.

Additional copyright/credits information is on page 248.
Print book interior design by Susan Van Horn

Library of Congress Cataloging-in-Publication Data
Names: Morris, John E., 1957- author.
Title: Subway / John E. Morris.
Description: First edition. | New York: Black Dog & Leventhal Publishers, [2020] | Includes bibliographical references and index. | Summary: "New York wouldn't be New York without the subway. This one-time engineering marvel that united and expanded the city has been a cultural touchstone for the last 114 years. Somehow though, there has never been a book that celebrates the subway from the scars it left on the city's fabric to the romantic fantasies it unleashed. Subway will convey a sense of wonder and fun about the world's largest transit system. The book will include a complete, concise history of the subway beginning with the technical obstacles and corruption that impeded plans for an underground rail line in the late 1800s, and the visionary and sometimes wacky schemes put forward in that era for subterranean and elevated transport. It will also tell how additional lines were built and how three independent subway systems were merged, creating the mishmash of numbered and lettered lines we have today. Interspersed throughout will be sidebars and stand-alone sections including profiles of characters that helped make the subway what it is (including the mostly forgotten August Belmont Jr., a flamboyant financier who bankrolled the first subway); graphics and imagery showing the evolution of subway cars, tokens and MetroCards, graffiti, and even subway etiquette ads; how the subway has been characterized in movies, television, and music; a look at abandoned cars and stations and more. Packed with compelling stories, fascinating facts and anecdotes, vivid portraits of the people who made the subway and those who saved it, all supplemented with engrossing imagery and a dynamic design, Subway will be a visual feast and must-have gift book, perfect for any coffee table"—Provided by publisher.

Identifiers: LCCN 2019037942 (print) | LCCN 2019037943 (ebook) | ISBN 9780762467907 (hardcover) | ISBN 9780762467891 (ebook)
Subjects: LCSH: Subways—New York (State)—New York—History.
Classification: LCC TF725.N5 M67 2020 (print) | LCC TF725.N5 (ebook) | DDC 388.4/2097471—dc23
LC record available at https://lccn.loc.gov/2019037942
LC ebook record available at https://lccn.loc.gov/2019037943
ISBNs: 978-0-7624-6790-7 (hardcover); 978-0-7624-6789-1 (ebook)

Printed in China

1010

10 9 8 7 6 5 4 3 2 1

Contents

Introduction

An Underground Microcosm of the City

The story of the subway is the story of the city, with all its energy and dysfunctions.

The New York subway is crowded and decrepit. Chunks of concrete fall from station ceilings with alarming regularity. Rats no longer just scurry along the tracks. They climb up sleeping passengers and drag pizza slices through stations. Then their videos go viral. Passengers suffer long, unexplained delays. Something always seems to be going wrong.

But the subway is also a marvel. It's extraordinarily efficient at moving millions of passengers a day. When the first line opened in 1904, it was the most advanced in the world, and a source of enormous civic pride. Its express tracks were unique. The project was a bid to put New York on the same footing as London, Paris, and Berlin, a symbol of the young nation's aspirations.

Overnight, the subway became an essential function, and an essential part of New Yorkers' state of mind. It inspired dance tunes and movies. Duke Ellington made the A train famous. Nearly a century after the subway's debut, whole *Seinfeld* episodes revolved around it.

The subway is also the great leveler, forcing New Yorkers and visitors of all classes and colors to mingle elbow to elbow. It's mandatory that mayors be photographed on a train, even if they rarely ride the subway. To be a New Yorker is to take the train, to celebrate it, and to grumble or joke about it.

The history of the subway and the city are so intertwined that you can't understand one fully without understanding the other.

The city's raucous politics have been at the center of the subway saga in every era. Battles over the subway's creation in the 1800s pitted street-car owners and public officials on the take against businessmen and social reformers who aspired to improve the city and society through better transit. William "Boss" Tweed, the city's legendarily corrupt power broker in the mid-1800s, once planned to send a mob to tear down the first elevated line because it competed with his own transit ventures. In modern times, subway politics have too often been driven by photo opportunities. Mayors and governors repeatedly staged groundbreakings (cue the pickax, cue the jack-hammer!) for a Second Avenue subway that didn't materialize for decades.

The subway was a response to the needs of a city whose streets were clogged and whose slums were dangerously crowded. The city, in turn, was forever shaped by the subway—which neighborhoods got subway lines and which didn't.

The subway has always brought the city together. This 1913 cartoon shows America's most powerful banker, J. P. Morgan Jr., on the right, wedged in with a chorus girl, a messenger, a "johnny-boy," and a professor, each identified. He was nearly poked in the eye by the feathers in a well-dressed lady's hat.

THE EVENING WORLD, SATURDAY, FEBRUARY 1, 1913.

Going Home in the Subway Crush ❀ ❀ ❀ ❀ ❀ ❀ With J. Pierpont Morgan Jr.

GRAND CENTRAL MOB-SCENE , PROFESSOR, JOHNNY-BOY, MERCHANT, CLERK, CHORUS GIRL, ARTIST, LABORER, J.P. MORGAN, JR.

MRS. UPPER-EAST-SIDE, MRS. WEST-END-AVENUE , BUSINESS MAN . STENOGRAPHERS. MESSENGER - BOY

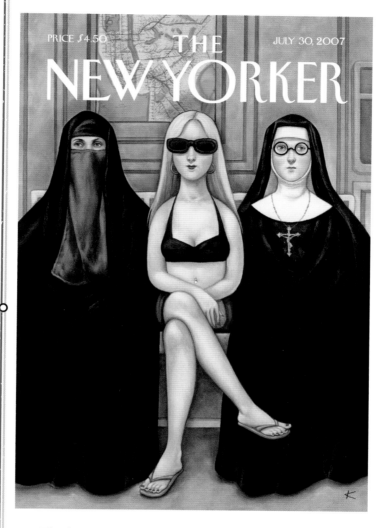

PRICE $4.50   THE NEW YORKER   JULY 30, 2007

The theme of diverse characters pressed together on the subway has been a theme for *New Yorker* magazine covers since the 1930s.

The five men most responsible for making the subway system a reality in the early 20th century are also a window onto the society and social forces of their time. Each is an archetypical American character.

The master contractor for the first line, John B. McDonald, was a no-nonsense, Irish-born immigrant who helped build some of the most difficult rail tunnels of his era. He was snubbed by August Belmont Jr., the wealthy banker and horse breeder who financed and controlled the first subway. But Belmont himself was just one generation further removed from Europe. His father was a German-Jewish immigrant who made a fortune in the 1830s,

Fish have taken to old subway cars dumped into the Atlantic.

married into a prominent Protestant family, and assimilated into the city's elite. The patrician bearing of the gifted chief engineer, William Barclay Parsons, reflected his descent from wealthy colonial landowners and his private school education in England.

George McAneny, the reporter turned politician who brokered the major subway expansion in the 1910s, dedicated his life to civic causes: rooting out corruption, better public transit, city planning, and historical preservation. His frequent nemesis, John Hylan, the mayor who initiated the city-owned Independent Subway System (IND) in the 1920s, grew up dirt-poor on a farm in the Hudson Valley and put himself through law school while working on elevated trains in Brooklyn. The chip always remained on his shoulder.

The 10,000-odd workers who performed the hard labor, many of them fresh immigrants, likewise, were part of the American story.

Much of the subway story has been lost with time. Take Belmont and Parsons. They were prominent figures in their day, but there are no biographies of either in library catalogs or on Amazon.com. William Gibbs McAdoo, the lawyer who built the PATH subways to New Jersey, likewise, is largely forgotten, but this modest, able, likeable character had a colorful side and earned himself a chapter here.

Another chapter of the subway story is the what-ifs, the unfulfilled plans for new lines crisscrossing Manhattan and others spreading to the far corners of the outer boroughs. What would Staten Island be like now if it had been linked to Brooklyn by a much-promised subway tunnel across the Verrazzano Narrows? Would Downtown Williamsburg be a cluster of high-rise apartments or office towers if a 1929 plan had come to pass for two lines from Manhattan to intersect at a massive junction there?

Beyond the politics, personalities, and urban history, the subway is also a feast for trivia lovers. Did you know that tunnel light bulbs have reverse threads so they won't be stolen? Or that old subway car shells dumped off the Atlantic seaboard are home to large schools of fish? Or that the director of *The French Connection* bribed a transit official to film a train hijacking on a real train running on regular tracks?

For those who love the city, the subway isn't just infrastructure or a way to get to work. It's a New York experience. In what other city could you hear a perturbed conductor bark, "Now listen up, folks!" and threaten to take the train out of service if passengers don't remove the belongings obstructing the doors? ("Yeah. Right. He's going to take the train out of service." You can read the minds of your fellow passengers in such situations.)

Like the city, the subway frequently makes you laugh when it doesn't make you want to scream. It is awe-inspiring when it isn't exasperating.

AUTHOR'S NOTE: When referring to particular locations, I've frequently indicated in parentheses the lines currently running there, but those were not always the lines running there at the time of the events described.

The government entities overseeing the subways were created, reformed, renamed, and replaced repeatedly between the 1880s and 1953 (see chapter 8). I've used the contemporaneous names, so sometimes it's a board, other times a commission or authority. Since 1953, when the New York City Transit Authority was established, I've generally used Transit Authority or TA as shorthand, and at other times, when it seemed appropriate, MTA (for Metropolitan Transportation Authority), the Transit Authority's parent since 1968.

Horse-Drawn Gridlock and Dreams of a Subway

1

G OF THE BROADWAY OMNIBUS RACING SEASON OF 1884.

A BLOCKADE ON BROADWAY.—Drawn by Taylor and Meeker.—[See Page 844.]

Corruption and technical obstacles delayed better transit for decades.

When the Civil War ended in 1865, New York was America's largest city, with roughly 900,000 residents jammed into the lower parts of Manhattan. Its streets were clogged. Large urban stagecoaches, known as omnibuses, and horse-drawn streetcars on rails ran bumper-to-bumper at peak times, making it dangerous for pedestrians to cross the street. By the 1850s, an omnibus passed the corner of Broadway and Chambers Street every 15 seconds in each direction for 13 hours, according to someone who kept count.

By 1880, there were almost 12,000 horses hauling 1,500 omnibuses and streetcars. That brought another hazard: manure. Large draft animals deposited 30 to 50 pounds of fecal material a day. A small industry was devoted just to scooping it up for fertilizer.

Everyone agreed that some form of "rapid transit" was needed, some alternative to the gridlock at street level. The options were elevated lines over the streets or underground lines beneath them. Both posed technical challenges, but vested interests and the city's monumental corruption were the biggest impediments.

The main engineering challenge was propulsion, particularly for underground lines. Electric motors weren't powerful enough to pull long trains until the very end of the 19th century, and the steam and smoke from conventional locomotives would build up in long tunnels, making the air unfit to breathe.

The political barrier was Tammany Hall, the club that controlled the local Democratic Party machine and, through it, city government. William "Boss" Tweed, who dominated Tammany Hall from the late 1850s through the early 1870s, was an investor in horse-drawn street railways—forerunners of electric trolleys—and he spearheaded plans for a massive rail viaduct along the east side of Manhattan. Naturally, he opposed any project that could mean competition. Since Tweed was, at various times, a congressman,

In the late 1880s, New York's congested streets were perilous for both pedestrians and carriage passengers.

member of the city's Board of Supervisors, commissioner of public works, schools commissioner, and a state senator, he had many levers to use against rivals.

As early as 1863, Hugh B. Willson, a railway engineer from Michigan, proposed a subway line up Broadway, after visiting London, where a partly underground rail line had opened that year. Willson arranged $5 million in financing but was blocked by Tweed and his allies in the legislature. Similarly, when Charles Harvey built a cable-drawn elevated line from the Battery to 30th Street in the late 1860s, Tweed sponsored a bill in the legislature to dismantle it. Tweed even laid plans to have a mob attack Harvey's structure. (Harvey's line was eventually extended up Ninth Avenue.)

One visionary, Alfred Ely Beach, succeeded in building a short underground line in 1869, but he had to resort to trickery to get around Tammany. Beach told the city his pneumatic tunnel under Broadway would transport only mail. When it opened in 1870, he revealed that it was actually built to carry people (see Other Means of Transport, page 13).

When Tweed was jailed in 1873 for embezzling tens of millions of public dollars, Tammany Hall was put on the defensive and things looked up for new forms of transit. An 1875 state law allowed cities to grant franchises for elevated rail lines. That set off a construction boom and, by 1880, els, as they were known, ran up Second, Third, Sixth, and Ninth Avenues from the southern tip of Manhattan to Harlem and into the Bronx, all hauled by small steam engines. Across the East River in Brooklyn, in the late 1880s, el tracks began radiating out from the Brooklyn Bridge and the ferry landings.

The els were far faster than the horse-drawn streetcars, but it still took close to an hour and a half to cover the 10 miles from Wall Street to 155th Street on the Ninth Avenue line.

Moreover, the elevated lines were deeply unpopular. Their locomotives belched smoke and cinders, startled horses, and dripped lubricants on pedestrians. The trains rumbled, clattered, and hissed outside apartment windows, and the streets below were kept in perpetual shadow. One visitor called them "a permanent disfigurement" and "aerial nuisances."

The els didn't solve the congestion, either, because the city grew faster than the capacity of the trains (see chapter 10). By the 1880s, business leaders

William "Boss" Tweed had stakes in streetcar lines and opposed new forms of transit.

BRIBERY & CORRUPTION

NEW YORK

RIGHT UNDER HER NOSE; EVERY DAY IN THE WEEK

The epic corruption of Tweed and the so-called Tammany Ring was fodder for the political caricaturist Thomas Nast.

worried that New York would choke on its traffic, and commerce would be diverted to rival ports such as Boston and Philadelphia.

Social reformers, too, were persistent advocates for better transit. They saw it as the solution to Manhattan's crowded, unsanitary slums. For them, the subway marked "the emancipation of the larger part of the city's population from excessively cramped and uncomfortable manner of living," allowing them "to reach comparatively cheap land in half an hour."

Dreams of a subway thus persisted. Sixteen companies obtained charters to build underground lines between 1864 and 1902. The turning point came in 1888 when Abram Hewitt, a Democratic mayor, put forward a detailed proposal. He envisioned underground trains traveling at a nearly unthinkable 45 miles an hour from City Hall to Grand Central Terminal, across 42nd Street, and then up Broadway—essentially the route chosen a decade later. While the street railroads and els had been built entirely with private money, under Hewitt's plan, the city would pay part of the cost of a subway.

It was a bold plan, but Hewitt couldn't get it adopted. Though he had been elected with support from Tammany Hall, he was a Protestant, anti-immigrant businessman who was soon on the outs with the predominantly Catholic, heavily Irish, Tammany wing of the party, which relied on immigrant support. It didn't help that Hewitt skipped a St. Patrick's Day parade, refused to indulge in patronage politics, strictly enforced tavern closing hours, and shut down brothels. Meanwhile, businessmen who generally supported Hewitt feared that, if the city constructed the subway, it would be an open invitation to graft. Hewitt's proposal died in the city council, and he lost his bid for reelection the same year.

Hewitt's vision lived on, however. A reconstituted Board of Rapid Transit Commissioners, formed in 1891, drew up a plan for a privately financed subway and put it out for bids from contractors. It received just one offer, a $1,000 bid that was not deemed serious. It wasn't until 1894 that the pieces began to fall into place. That year the city's Chamber of Commerce allied with Republicans in Albany to form a new board independent of city politicians. Six of the eight commissioners would come from the Chamber itself—the law specified five members by name—and the commissioners were appointed for life with the power to name their successors. They were, in effect, accountable to no one. The bill's proponents "thought responsibility for a subway should be entrusted to a special breed of honest, upright, farsighted men—namely, themselves," in the words of historian Clifton Hood.

Mayor Abram Hewitt's 1888 proposal for a publicly funded subway that could run at up to 45 mph went nowhere while he was in office, but it was the basis for the first line when it was built in 1900–1904.

The Chamber succeeded in its end run around the city's politicians, and electric motors had advanced enough by 1894 that it was now viable to use electricity instead of steam power, so the Board moved forward. Various routes were contemplated, including Hewitt's and an alternative scheme where two lines would branch north of Union Square, one continuing up Broadway to the West Side and another heading up Madison Avenue, Park Avenue (then Fourth Avenue), or Lexington Avenue to the East Side.

Chatham Square showing
Doubledeck Elevated,
New York City.

An antique post-card shows the maze of criss-crossing and double-decked el lines that blanketed Chatham Square. There hasn't been any rapid transit here since the Second and Third Avenue elevated lines were demolished. The Second Avenue subway is slated to run through the intersection eventually.

The financiers behind the street railway and elevated line companies, which were threatened by a subway, didn't give up without a fight, however. They delayed matters by making vague offers to extend their lines, forcing the Board to postpone a final decision about the subway route. The "fine, high-minded, soft-hearted old gentlemen" on the Board were no match for "the impossibly alert young fellows of Wall Street, with their unlimited money, with their control of the political machines, with the best legal brains at their disposal," journalist Ray Stannard Baker wrote in 1905, explaining the years of delay.

In addition, property owners sued to block the project. State law required the Board to obtain the consent of at least half of the adjacent property owners. If it couldn't, it had to go to court for approval. Those with buildings along the proposed route feared the digging would undermine foundations and disrupt business. (The "not in my backyard" concept is not new.) Uptown, where speculators had snapped up large swaths of undeveloped land along the route, owners objected to plans to run the trains on elevated tracks along Broadway north of 92nd Street to save money. The speculators pleaded (successfully) for it to be submerged.

Finally, in 1898, the last suits were settled, and the Board got down to the nitty-gritty financial and engineering details. A protracted financial crisis in the mid-1890s had persuaded even the business community that public money would be needed, and a scheme was devised to use a combination of public and private capital and a private contractor and operator. The city would borrow money to pay for the construction, and it would put the job out for bids. To entice offers, the winner would get to operate the subway and collect the profits under a 50-year lease, with the option for a 25-year renewal. It would pay for the cars and other equipment and pay a yearly sum to the city to cover what the city paid in interest on the construction bonds.

This approach reflected the long shadow that Boss Tweed cast more than 20 years after he died in the Ludlow Street Jail. By employing a private company to do the work at a fixed price, the reformers and the Board hoped to prevent municipal officials from skimming money and doling out contracts to political supporters. And since the company would operate the line for decades, it would have an incentive to see that the job was done right.

In January 1900, John B. McDonald was awarded the contract after making the low bid, $35 million. The Irish immigrant had compiled an impressive track record building difficult train tunnels. He was a subcontractor on the 4.75-mile Hoosac Tunnel in western Massachusetts, the second longest in the world when it opened in 1875, and he had constructed a technically challenging electrified rail tunnel under Downtown Baltimore in the 1890s.

But the city required the winning bidder to post $7 million in deposits and surety bonds—money McDonald did not have. So he teamed up with August Belmont Jr., a powerful Wall Street banker, who provided the capital. In exchange, McDonald handed over to Belmont the right to operate the subway when it was completed. Conveniently, McDonald had ties to Tammany Hall, and Belmont was a major player in the establishment wing of the Democratic Party.

It had been 37 years since Hugh Willson first proposed a subway for New York. By the time work began in New York, London had been operating a fully underground electric line for 10 years, and Paris was poised to debut its Metro. When New York's subway finally opened in October 1904, electric underground railroads were also running in Boston, Berlin, and Budapest.

OTHER MEANS OF TRANSPORT

The need for a better form of propulsion inspired a generation of visionaries.

Before steam power was adopted for elevated rail lines in the 1870s and electric trains became feasible in the 1890s, inventors hatched a variety of alternative propulsion systems for elevated and underground transit. Some look downright zany today.

Charles Harvey built a cable-drawn elevated rail line from the southern tip of Manhattan to Cortlandt Street in 1867, and by 1870 it reached 30th Street along Greenwich Street and Ninth Avenue. The cable, which was powered by stationary steam engines, was prone to snap, however, and could pull only a limited number of cars. In the 1870s, a heavier track structure was installed, and the line was converted to steam locomotives.

ABOVE: The Arcade Railway plan called for a new street for pedestrians and horse vehicles built over train tracks on the original street level.

CLOCKWISE FROM TOP LEFT: An 1853 elevated train proposal envisioned passengers riding in cars hung below a track, connected to a steam engine running overhead. • Rufus Gilbert proposed a pneumatically powered elevated line with tubes supported by Gothic arches. • Anders Anderson patented designs for a propeller-driven, underhung monorail elevated line.

Others put their faith in pneumatic power, or forced air. In 1870, Alfred Ely Beach, the owner of *Scientific American* magazine and an outspoken advocate of technology in all forms, opened a two-block demonstration line under Broadway next to City Hall that used enormous fans to push a pod-shaped car on rails at up to 10 miles an hour. Then the fans were reversed and the car was sucked back to the starting point. Beach was a gifted promoter, and his system had what we might call bling. The interior of the car resembled a Victorian parlor with plush, upholstered seats for 22 passengers and lamps. The waiting area featured oil paintings, a grandfather clock, settees, and a goldfish tank.

More than 400,000 people paid to take the short ride on his line in its first year. Beach eventually won permission to extend the line, but forced air wasn't practical over longer distances, and he couldn't move enough people to make a dent in congestion. A financial downturn in 1873 forced him to shut the line before he could extend it, and the tube was

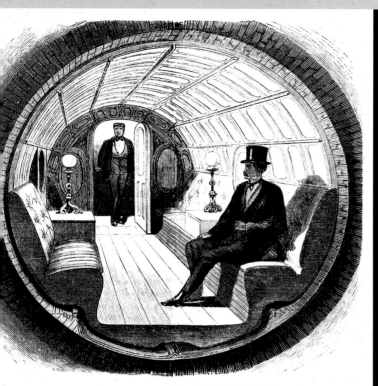

INTERIOR OF THE PNEUMATIC PASSENGER-CAR.

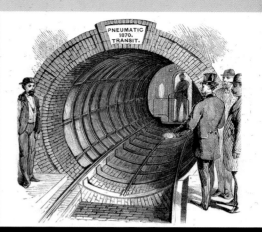

THE ELEVATED RAILWAY.

CLOCKWISE FROM LEFT: A short pneumatic subway that Alfred Ely Beach built near City Hall featured plush upholstery in pod-like cars. • The Beach train cars were pushed by fans through round tunnels. • Charles Harvey's pioneering, cable-driven elevated line on the West Side was begun in 1867 and by 1870 reached from the Battery to 30th Street.

sealed up. When a subway line was built in the same area in 1915, workers discovered Beach's tunnel, complete with the original car and a grand piano in the waiting area.

Dr. Rufus Gilbert, a physician who crusaded for better public health and transit, sketched seven different proposals, including an elevated line with pneumatic tubes suspended from lacy gothic arches. Others drew up plans for moving sidewalks and elevated lines with horses pulling cars suspended from overhead rails. Propellers figured in other proposals. Another option: a roller coaster—like elevated line where trains were hauled up inclines by cable, then coasted downhill by gravity.

By the late 1880s, electric motors were powerful enough to be used on street trolleys, and in 1890, London opened a rail line under the Thames River, with electric locomotives hauling three cars (see chapter 4). That was the dawn of the subway as we know it.

Men, Mules, and Dynamite: Building the IRT

2

A thousand police were on duty to hold back the 25,000 onlookers who converged on City Hall on March 24, 1900, to witness the official beginning of construction. John Philip Sousa's brass band played as Mayor Robert Van Wyck employed a silver shovel from Tiffany's. The throngs were so dense that August Belmont Jr., the banker behind the subway, and John B. McDonald, the lead contractor, struggled to make their way from the building to join Van Wyck.

That was the photo op. The real work began two days later at the corner of Bleecker and Greene Streets, where the Rapid Transit Commissioner's chief engineer, William Barclay Parsons, used a pickax to dislodge the first paving stone as a crowd of men hovered around, tools in hand, hoping to be hired on. The site, a full four blocks west of the subway's future path up Lafayette Street, was telling. A sewer line ran east along Bleecker and would have to be lowered seven feet to pass beneath the subway. It was an omen of the upheaval the subway would unleash on the city for the next four years. The project would require a wholesale makeover of the city's underground infrastructure, and not just directly along the line.

On Parson's recommendation, the Board opted for the "cut and cover" approach, laying tracks just below the surface of the street. This was much cheaper than boring deep through bedrock and would make it much easier for passengers to access stations than it would have been with elevators. The bedrock is schist, which is famously hard, but also uneven and prone to fractures, so tunneling would be treacherous.

But building near the surface had its own perils. Beneath the streets in built-up neighborhoods—particularly south of 42nd Street—lay a thick tangle of water mains, sewers, gas lines, and electrical conduits, much of which had to be torn up. The subway was bisecting the island with a trench, which posed a problem for sewers, which flow by gravity. Some that emptied into the

The Rapid Transit Board's chief engineer, William Barclay Parsons, commences the digging at Greene and Bleecker Streets, March 26, 1900.

Hudson River had to be diverted to the East River. So, in addition to seven miles of new sewer lines along the subway's path, another five miles had to be replaced under other streets.

Complicating the work, the city required that important streets remain open as much as possible. Thick timber decking was therefore laid over the trenches, allowing pedestrians, carriages, and even trolleys to pass overhead while digging continued.

South of what was then Lafayette Place, buildings were demolished to clear a path for the subway and a wide new thoroughfare, Lafayette Street, was created over the line (see Scars Left Behind, page 144).

There were many other obstacles. At Sixth Avenue and 42nd Street and again at Broadway and 64th Street, the subway had to pass beneath the footings of elevated tracks. At 59th Street, a thick new concrete foundation had to be laid under the 724-ton granite pillar for Christopher Columbus's statue so the monument wouldn't be undermined by the underground tracks skirting it. In front of Grand Central Terminal and at Times Square, the steel and concrete subway tunnel was threaded through the basements of new buildings going up.

Sometimes things didn't go as planned. A half-built subway tunnel caved in along Park Avenue (then Fourth Avenue) between 37th and 38th Streets in March 1902, undermining the front walls of a row of grand town houses.

It's almost inconceivable today, but most of this work was carried out by hand with pickaxes and shovels because steam-powered excavators were just coming into use. The men had only a few powered aids such as hydraulic jacks. Horses and mules

Few mechanized tools were available when work began in 1900. Here men break up the pavement at 50th Street and Broadway with pickaxes.

Dozens of people, horses, cars, and bicycles fell into the pits created during construction.

hauled away rock and earth in carts, or steam-powered hoists lifted them to the surface. At three points along the route, there was no getting around the schist and the builders had to resort to dynamite instead of shovels: on Murray Hill just south of Grand Central Terminal; under Central Park between Broadway and Lenox Avenue; and in Washington Heights on upper Broadway.

Eight mules were kept underground during the tunneling under Washington Heights, between 157th Street and Dyckman Street. One, which some workers called Jim, stayed in the tunnel for two years and kept his eyes shut at all times. Jim and the other mules reportedly were unfazed by the blasting. Other mules were not so compliant. One that was about to be lowered into a pit at a site downtown put up a struggle after hearing the hee-haw of his predecessor being hauled out of the hole. It required five workmen, a passing horse cab driver, and two cops to shove the recalcitrant animal backward into a crate so it could be sent below.

The "solid, grim" but "masterful" chief contractor John B. McDonald oversaw more than 10,000 workers and finished the first line, from City Hall to Washington Heights, in four and a half years.

Remarkably, McDonald, the chief contractor, kept his subcontractors and a work force of up to 12,000 on schedule despite the complexity of the undertaking, accidents, and labor strife. Warm and cuddly, McDonald was not, but he proved to be an outstanding manager. "A solid, grim man with a thick chest, brawny arms, and an iron jaw; masterful, self-controlled, capable," one journalist described him. A man "of powerful frame and much shrewd ability," wrote another chronicler of the work.

The scale of the disruption across the city was epic, four years of "utter wearisomeness." If the dust and temporary streets weren't nuisance enough, there was the steady drum of explosions. "Many Harlemites . . . assert that . . . because of the frequent explosions of dynamite beneath their homes their legs have a tendency to double up," the *New-York Tribune* reported wryly. "No matter what one's ideas on religious matters, he was likely at any time to get down on his knees as if in prayer."

There were real dangers, too. Nineteen people and 32 horses tumbled over the sides into the subway pits or fell through the temporary decking in the first three and a half years of work. One man rode his bicycle 30 feet down into the construction site and survived.

The nearly completed station at 14th Street–Union Square shows the four-track layout that was unique to New York.

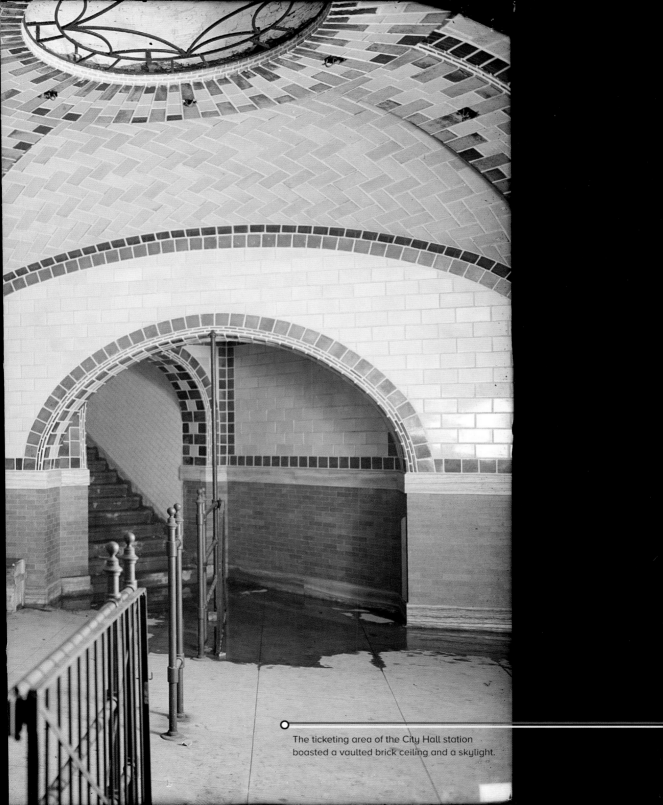

The ticketing area of the City Hall station boasted a vaulted brick ceiling and a skylight.

Others weren't so lucky. In January 1902, a dynamite shed caught fire at Park Avenue and 41st Street, setting off an explosion so powerful that it shattered windows for blocks around and scarred the façade of Grand Central Terminal. Six people died, including construction workers and employees of the posh Murray Hill Hotel, which faced onto the site. Another 125 were injured, many by shattering glass. There were several other dynamite accidents along that stretch later.

The most deadly incident was under 195th Street in Washington Heights the following year, where workers were boring a tunnel 180 feet below the surface. When a crew returned to remove rock and rubble after a set of dynamite blasts, enormous slabs of rock broke loose from the ceiling. Ten men were crushed and a dozen more injured. Irregularities in the schist were blamed there. Five had been killed in a similar cave-in under 164th Street in 1901.

In June 1902, Parsons, the mastermind of the subway, was nearly crushed while inspecting the seemingly jinxed Park Avenue section, where the dynamite shed had exploded. He and the subcontractor, Ira Shaler, a longtime friend, were discussing some dangerous, fragile rock on the ceiling near 39th Street. When Shaler stepped out from under a timber beam bracing the rock to take a closer look, a 1,000-pound slab fell on him, just feet away from Parsons. Shaler, who had been indicted over the earlier deadly explosion, died of his injuries eleven days later.

By the time the work was complete, at least 54 workmen, foremen, and bystanders had been killed and more than 300 injured. Given the size of the

In 1904, there were 133 kiosks, modeled on those in Budapest, that protected the subway stairs. Different cupola styles were used for entrances and exits.

labor force, the difficulty of the task, and the lax workplace safety standards of the day, the toll could easily have been higher. In any event, labor was plentiful and casualties were accepted as the price of such an undertaking.

In 1900, when work began, immigrants were flooding to America, and the men who swung the picks, hauled the rock, and risked their lives were mostly newcomers—Irish and Italian in the main, but also Swedes and Germans. There were also many black Americans. Unskilled positions paid $2 for an eight-hour day. The $3.75-a-day wage for deep, hard-rock tunneling attracted experienced miners from as far away as Europe and Appalachia.

The subway was first and foremost a feat of engineering, but as early as 1891, the transit commissioners had called for station decorations that would "bring brightness and cheerfulness." That was addressed with glass bricks in the ceiling, allowing daylight to stream into the stations from sidewalks above. (Most of the glass bricks have long been paved over.)

The stations aimed to be aesthetic models as well as functional. Some design features trace to a tour of European transit systems that Parsons and others made in 1894. The Berlin and Paris stations were attractive, he noted, while London's were drab. Parsons drew some ideas from the Paris stations

CLOCKWISE FROM TOP LEFT: At Columbus Circle, the walls were decorated with ceramic images of Christopher Columbus's ship, the *Santa Maria*. • The Wall Street station features images of the city's early wooden wall for which the street was named. • Beavers—source of the Astor family fortune—decorate the Astor Place stop.

he admired, and 133 ornate kiosks that covered the stairs at entries and exits were closely modeled on similar structures in Budapest. (Only one replica kiosk remains, at Astor Place. They were removed, in part, because of complaints that they blocked the view of drivers.)

While Parsons and his engineers designed the structures, Heins and LaFarge, an architecture firm best known for its churches—including the mammoth Cathedral of St. John the Divine near Columbia University—was retained in 1901 to design the station interiors. They specified marble, Roman brick, and glazed tile for facings, and they designed the colorful ceramic plaques that still draw praise today—beavers at the station named for fur magnate John Jacob Astor, for instance, and Christopher Columbus's ship, the *Santa Maria*, at Columbus Circle. The jewel of the system was the curved, loop station at City Hall, with a vaulted ceiling by the Spanish architect Rafael Guastavino, a master of complex brick arches. A great arc of skylights crowned the platform. Passengers accustomed to the utilitarian stations of the elevated lines were awestruck by the gleaming subway stops.

FROM LEFT: Mayor Seth Low (holding mallet, looking to the left) drove a silver spike at Columbus Circle on March 14, 1903, to commemorate the start of track laying. As Low struck the spike repeatedly, "his face grew red from the exertion of bending back and forward so as not to drop his tall silk hat," the *New York Times* reported. "The Mayor did not seem to realize that no force was needed to hammer down the spike into the cavity already scooped out for it in a soft pine [tie]." • On opening day, the crowds at City Hall cheered at every mention of August Belmont Jr., William Barclay Parsons, and John B. McDonald.

To the credit of McDonald and Parsons, the line was completed to 145th Street in just four and a half years, on schedule and on budget, and by all accounts it was executed without corruption. A month later, that line (today's 1) was extended to 157th, the branch that ran east and under Lenox Avenue in East Harlem (2, 3) opened to 145th, and a line in the Bronx was inaugurated from the intersection of Third Avenue and 149th Street to 180th Street (2, 5). Sixteen months later, a bridge extended the Broadway line to the west Bronx and tunnels carried the eastern branch to the central Bronx. By then the Interborough Rapid Transit (IRT) was also building the original line south from City Hall to Brooklyn—what is now the 4 and 5.

Opening day for the original line, October 27, 1904, brought tens of thousands out to ride the new wonder. From City Hall to 145th Street and Broadway, the interim terminus, gawkers stood, waiting to hear the first trains in the tunnel, "getting that half-shocking sense of the unfamiliar as the heads and shoulders came up from underground," the *New York Times* reported. That evening, "it was carnival night in New York. Every noise-making instrument known to election night was in operation." Police reserves had to be called out at 145th Street to control an overflow crowd pressing at the entrance. At a City Hall ceremony, the crowd broke out into cheers each time Belmont's, Parsons's, and McDonald's names were mentioned.

Observers gushed at the achievement. "The Ptolemies and the third Rameses built monuments in their day, but they did nothing so vast as this," the Richmond, Virginia, *Times-Dispatch* commented, comparing the combined floor space in New York's stations to "the caves of Elephanta and the temples of Karnak and of Aboosimbel on the Nile bank."

Even Ray Stannard Baker, a crusading journalist who criticized the city's reliance on private companies, had to tip his hat in respect:

A hole twenty-two miles long through rocks and bogs and sand, here just concealed under a corner swarming with humanity, there burrowing deep in a tunnel; crooking through the very basement of an enormous steel building, with human occupation both above and below, darting out across a splendid bridge, with glimpse of water and distant hills. . . . Sunlight coming through from the streets above, outside entrances of some architectural pretense, inside waiting-rooms lined with costly tiling, arranged in forms of beauty!

New York was late to get its subway, but it had outengineered and outconstructed even the capitals of Europe, and New Yorkers were proud that it was theirs. This "most stupendous scheme of municipal improvement and expenditure ever undertaken," a judge wrote in 1906, signaled "the destiny of people of what we have reason for thinking will be the greatest city in the world."

UNDER THE EAST RIVER TO BROOKLYN

←——— →———

The IRT's mile-long tunnel to Brooklyn forever altered commuting patterns.

By October 1904, when the first line debuted, work on an extension south from City Hall and Brooklyn Bridge to Brooklyn was already underway.

When the original route was mapped out in the 1890s, New York City consisted of just Manhattan and the southwestern parts of Bronx County. With the 1898 merger of Brooklyn, Queens, and Staten Island into New York, a rail link was needed between Manhattan and Brooklyn, the most populous of the boroughs. In 1902, the IRT was awarded the contract.

This so-called Contract 2 project included a 1.2-mile tunnel as much as 100 feet beneath the East River. The twin tubes had to pass through soft, shifting silt, making them vulnerable to cave-ins from the enormous weight of the water overhead. To protect against that, pressurized chambers were used to hold out the water until steel rings could be inserted as permanent tunnel walls. The air in the front chamber immediately behind the boring machinery was pressurized up to 40 pounds per square inch, nearly three times normal sea-level pressure. Work shifts there were limited to four hours, and sandhogs were paid according to the level of pressure they were subjected to.

While the compressed air protected against tunnel collapses, it had a tendency to force its way out where the harbor floor was thin, so workers kept bags of hair, hay, sawdust, or clay at the ready to plug leaks. This primitive patching didn't always work. In March 1905, 24-year-old Richard Creeden was jamming bags in a leak just off the Brooklyn shore when a gaping hole opened above him, and he was propelled upward in a geyser through the silt and muddy harbor water. Miraculously, he survived with just a few scrapes. He was plucked out of the water shivering, bandaged up, and given some whiskey. A few hours later, he was in good spirits, "suffering more from the libations administered to ward off pneumonia" than from the accident itself, according to a newspaper account.

"Pooh! Pooh! It didn't amount to such a lot," Creeden said, brushing off the incident. "I was drawed into the flow and shot out at the other end. Then all of a sudden I strikes

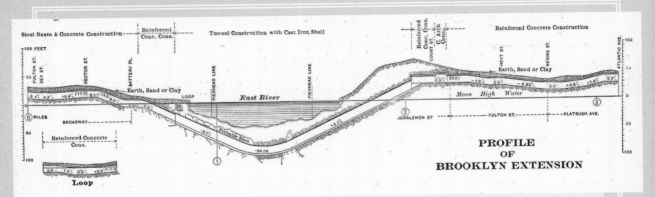

Steel Beam & Concrete Construction   Reinforced   Tunnel Construction with Cast Iron Shell   Reinforced Concrete Construction
                                        Conc. Cons.

100 FEET   100

50   PIERHEAD LINE   PIERHEAD LINE   Earth, Sand or Clay   50

                              Earth, Sand or Clay   LOOP   East River   Mean High Water
0   MILES   0
                                                                                                                          JORALEMON ST.   FULTON ST.   FLATBUSH AVE.
50   BROADWAY   50
        Reinforced Concrete   Probable Rock
        Cons.
100   100

        Loop

PROFILE
OF
BROOKLYN EXTENSION

water and opens my eyes. I was flying through the air, and before I comes down I had a fine view of the city." (In 1916, a worker digging the N and R tunnel in the same area suffered the same fate and survived, but two colleagues drowned.)

When the IRT tunnel entered service in January 1908, the trains "were packed to the doors from morning till night." A few months later, the line was completed to the Atlantic Terminal on Flatbush Avenue, where riders could catch trains to Long Island.

The new line dramatically altered commuting patterns. The Brooklyn Rapid Transit Company (BRT) ran shuttle trains over the Brooklyn Bridge to Manhattan, and some of its elevated trains ran over the Williamsburg Bridge to a depot on Delancey Street, barely in Manhattan. But riders had to change to streetcars and pay another fare, or two, to reach most places in Manhattan. On the IRT, passengers could ride from 180th Street in the Bronx through Manhattan to Brooklyn without changing trains, all for a nickel. It siphoned traffic away from the BRT's bridge lines and marked the beginning of the end for the ferries that shuttled across the East River.

COPYRIGHT BY ILLUSTRATED POSTAL CARD & NOVELTY CO. N.
East River Tunnel, New York. 96-48

ABOVE: The IRT's first line under the East River and New York Harbor in 1908, commemorated in this postcard, was a much faster alternative to the ferries or the Brooklyn or Williamsburg bridges. **OPPOSITE FROM TOP:** The Joralemon Street tunnel to Brooklyn, used by today's 4 and 5 trains, passed through both hard bedrock and the loose, silty bottom of the East River, as this cross-section shows. The portions under water were bored out and then lined with cast-iron rings. • The workers who dug the tunnels under the East River worked in clammy conditions with air at pressures much higher than on land. That sometimes caused the half-built tunnels to blow out.

UNIQUE FEATURES OF THE SUBWAY

New York lagged other cities in opening underground lines,
but its system was cutting-edge.

New York learned from the new underground transit systems in Boston and Europe, but it boasted significant innovations:

- New York employed a four-track design with two inside tracks for express trains up to 96th Street. That allowed IRT trains to speed from City Hall uptown to 135th Street in about 20 minutes. That didn't quite live up to the rallying cry of subway proponents ("Fifteen minutes to Harlem"), but it was pretty close, and not bad considering that the final route jogged across 42nd Street from East Side to West Side.

- Reinforced concrete, a new and somewhat controversial construction technology, was used extensively. During construction, the bricklayers and masons union threatened to strike over the technique, and won some minor changes to limit its use.

- Fittingly for a city of immigrants, the transit system built by immigrants commanded by the immigrant contractor John B. McDonald had no separate first-class cars. Riders could not avoid the hoi polloi by paying extra, as they could in London and Paris. Everyone was equal on New York's subway. The Paris Metro operated higher-fare, first-class cars until 1991.

- Innovation continued, particularly in the 1920s, when the IRT sought to cut costs. As a labor-saving move, new cars were equipped so that a single conductor could open and close the doors of an entire train. Until then, a guard was required on each car for that purpose. For safety, sensors were installed in the edges of the doors so they would reopen if they had closed on a passenger. When questions were raised about the reliability of the sensors, Frank Hedley, the general manager of the IRT, demonstrated by putting his nose in the path of closing doors. His proboscis survived unharmed.

Frank Hedley, an IRT executive, risked his nose to make a point about safety. • **OPPOSITE:** The New York subway's four tracks allowed for express service on most of the original line.

The Forgotten Mogul

3

August Belmont Jr. had invested in elevated and mainline railroads before he bankrolled the first subway.

As the American representative of the Rothschild banking family, Belmont was sometimes the target of anti-Semitic attacks. This 1904 cartoon in the *New York American* asked why Belmont couldn't pay subway workers more, given that Nathaniel Charles Rothschild had just paid a large sum for two rare Arctic fleas. Rothschild purchased the specimens for a vast entomological collection he amassed for research. He was just 27 at the time, nothing like the elderly Jew portrayed.

Building the subway required throngs of immigrant

workers, pickaxes, dynamite, and tens of millions of dollars.

The man with the money was August Belmont Jr., one of the most powerful bankers in America's Gilded Age. When the United States government's gold reserves were drained by a financial panic and President Grover Cleveland turned to J. Pierpont Morgan for a bailout in 1895, Belmont joined Morgan in the White House talks and helped orchestrate the plan as the American representative of the Rothschild banking family of Europe.

FOR TWO FLEAS ROTHSCHILD PAID $5,000.

Too bad he will not allow his agent Belmont to pay decent wages to workmen on the underground railroad. Are fleas so much more precious than engineers?

Belmont's legend has faded, unlike those of contemporaries such as Morgan, but he was a boldfaced name in his day. His every move was chronicled in the press—his role in corporate takeover battles, his string-pulling in the Democratic Party, his travels, his race horses, his America's Cup yachts, even the infractions of his scores of servants.

Belmont's father, August Sr., made a fortune as a young man representing the Frankfurt, Germany, wing of the Rothschild banking family. Arriving in New York in 1837 at age 23 amid a severe financial crisis, he used the Rothschilds' credit to buy assets on the cheap and soon became one of New York's richest men and gained entrée to its best social circles. Though born Jewish, he married into a prominent Protestant family, cementing his social position.

By the time the elder Belmont died in 1890, August Jr. (1853–1924) had largely assumed the reins at their bank, August Belmont & Co., and he was well versed in railroads and transit lines. He had invested in Brooklyn elevated lines, he controlled streetcar lines in Queens, and he was for many years chairman of the Louisville & Nashville Railroad.

August Jr.'s biggest foray into transportation came in 1900, when he provided backing to John B. McDonald, the contractor who had placed the winning bid to build the first subway. Belmont supplied capital and McDonald assigned to him the right to operate the completed system.

When the subway opened in 1904, Belmont was lauded for making it possible. But he quickly developed an image problem. It was the era when great industrial monopolies were being formed and railroads were merging left and right, and Belmont pursued his own monopolist strategy locally, gaining control of all the elevated lines in Manhattan and the Bronx and a major Manhattan streetcar company. By 1905, he had a lock on "rapid transit" in the two boroughs (see chapter 6).

In addition, the subway proved so popular that it was frequently overcrowded, a source of constant complaint. Belmont was seen as "behaving like a tyrant and an oppressor, extorting from the patrons of his roads the very last penny of obtainable tribute, and giving in return the meanest accommodations." Activists and politicians were pushing back on the power of industrialists and financiers, and Belmont became a lightning rod for anyone with a beef about crowded trains, or with capitalism generally. At the Democratic convention in 1912, William Jennings Bryan, the populist who ran for president several times, mentioned Belmont by name among a list of Wall Street evildoers.

Belmont at the races, 1913.

Nothing in Belmont's nature made him a sympathetic figure to the common man. His statements to the press often had a haughty ring. After one of Belmont's polo ponies escaped and injured a local boy on Long Island, the boy's father confronted the financier on a train platform, demanding reimbursement for his doctors' bills. When the father wouldn't take no for an answer, Belmont whacked him on the head with his cane.

Today we would call Belmont a control freak. He scrutinized minor bills for the subway and dictated the terms of the free subway passes for employees. He was so compulsive about picking up pins around the office that "his office boys had strict instructions to see there were none about when important conferences were pending." (Pins were used to attach papers before staplers and paper clips became common.)

"August would be a genius if he did not submerge himself so much in detail," said one good friend.

At times, however, he displayed a kinder face to those beneath him—noblesse oblige, perhaps. When an IRT ticket taker who had been ill wrote Belmont asking to switch from the night to the day shift, Belmont intervened on the man's behalf.

Among those he considered equals, August Jr. was a bon vivant with a playful and theatrical streak. The "little, dapper man . . . with a flower in his buttonhole" threw dinner parties for 48 at the family mansion in Newport, Rhode Island. When he "felt particularly expansive, he would drop in at Walter T. Smith's turtle shop in Front Street near Fulton Market, pick out a few hundred terrapin from the tanks, and send them to friends," the *New Yorker* magazine reported.

Man o' War, perhaps the greatest American stud of all time, was bred at Belmont's stables.

The term "conspicuous consumption," coined by the sociologist Thorstein Veblen in 1899, was ready-made for Belmont. He entertained on his 85-foot, 20-knot steam yacht *Scout,* and in 1900, he commissioned the 70-foot racing sloop *Mineola* to defend the America's Cup, the second entry he backed.

Even more than boats, Belmont loved racehorses, a passion he inherited from his father, who established the Belmont Stakes prize. Under August Jr., the family stables produced Man o' War, perhaps the most famous American stud ever. When the future King Edward VIII of Britain attended a polo match on Long Island in 1913 and inquired how many horses Belmont owned, the banker replied, "Sire, I never count them for fear my conscience would trouble me." He built the grand Belmont Park racetrack on Long Island and named it for his father—and conveniently also for himself.

His 1,100-acre Babylon, Long Island, estate included a nine-acre trout lake, forests stocked with game for hunting, a mile-long racetrack, barns, and staff for breeding fox terriers, cattle, and hogs. It boasted a heated garage for 40 cars. Grand oil portraits of Belmont horses lined the walls of the main house.

Belmont also had the mogul's sine qua non: a private rail car. Two, actually. One was unique, for it was built to run on the subway. Christened Mineola—named for his sailboat—the mahogany-paneled car had hot and cold running water, leaded glass, a kitchen with an electric grill and oven, a toilet, and a rolltop office desk. A second private car for long-distance rail trips, also named *Mineola*, was staffed with a French chef and a porter.

"A private railroad car is not an acquired taste. One takes to it immediately," his adoring second wife, Eleanor, wrote, fondly recalling a trip to Canada so her husband could hunt moose.

These pleasures were easy to afford when the subway was paying rich dividends to shareholders, as it did through the First World War. But, by the time of Belmont's death in 1924 at 71, his finances were a shambles. Fares were frozen at the original five cents despite steep inflation set off by the war. On top of that, Belmont had overpaid for the elevated lines and streetcar lines, and the rental fees and interest were now too much for the IRT to shoulder. The company swung from $8 million in profits in 1917 to a $3.8 million loss in 1919. It didn't have the money to pay off bonds that were coming due that year and was forced to borrow for six months at much higher rates to pay off the old bonds. When that debt came due, the company was in no better position, and it had to ask creditors for repeated extensions. One unpaid supplier sued to put the IRT in receivership. Friends who had bought IRT bonds began writing Belmont seeking personal reassurances.

Eventually terms for the elevated and streetcar takeovers were renegotiated and Belmont kept the IRT out of bankruptcy during his lifetime, but transit was no longer making him money and he had largely abandoned banking.

He faced a second crisis with the Cape Cod Canal, a problem-plagued eight-mile trench across the isthmus of the Cape, the second great infrastructure project that he financed. By 1920, at the same time the IRT's creditors were breathing down his neck, Belmont was struggling to keep the canal company out of bankruptcy. At one point, he went hat in hand to the widow of railroad baron E. H. Harriman, who anted up $500,000.

On Belmont's death, estimates of the value of his estate ranged up to $50 million, about $750 million in current dollars. But that was probably overstated, or else omitted his debts. "Owing to the heavy burden of the Cape Cod Canal, . . . the future of our family fortunes seemed highly precarious," his widow recalled in her memoirs. She was forced to auction all her husband's

beloved horses. The Babylon estate, which he had specified in his will would be Eleanor's for her life, also had to go. The state bought the main house and the lake for a park, but the bulk of the property went to developers, who ringed the mansion grounds with middle-class homes. Today a six-lane highway abuts the site where his mansion once stood.

His private subway car, later used by track workers, now sits at the Shore Line Trolley Museum in Connecticut, awaiting restoration by volunteers.

There are no libraries, universities, or hospitals bearing the Belmont name, as there are for contemporaries like the Morgans, Vanderbilts, and Rockefellers. Just the racetrack and the prize money (both named for his father), the state park, and a modest plaque alongside the canal. In his crowning achievement, the subway, his name appears only in the decommissioned City Hall station. There Belmont is just one among dozens of names on two plaques—mayors, commissioners, engineers, and contractors. Few subway riders have any idea who August Belmont Jr. was.

Mineola, Belmont's private subway car, was outfitted with a rolltop desk, a kitchen, and a toilet.

BETTER SKIN, FEWER COCKROACHES

For advertisers, riders were a captive audience looking for distraction.

New Yorkers adored the subway's ornate tile work and ceramic station crests when they were unveiled. They were shocked when, just days after opening, workmen began drilling into the tile and installing frames to hold advertisements. Soon passengers were bombarded with pitches for soft drinks, cocoa, and cures for dandruff and constipation.

An early photo of City Hall station, after its walls were covered with ads.

The poster advertisers were . . . educating our sense of form and color, till we could thrill with the subtle beauties of a carmine corset upon a purple background, could palpitate with joy at the chiaroscuro of an ultramarine whiskey bottle against a gamboge sunset, could almost faint with ecstasy at the composition of lilac lingerie amid a sea-green cloud effect.

—*Evening World*, November 4, 1904

WATCH YOUR STEP
Wide Gap Between Car
And Platform Edge

THE WALKING DEAD FINALE

SURVIVAL SUNDAY

SUBWAY ADVERTISING IN 1907

As Foreseen Through THE SPECTROPHONE

Guardians of the city's aesthetics, such as the Architecture League of New York and the Municipal Art Society, were aghast. The city sued to have the ads removed, but it lost because its contract with the IRT did not ban ads; it simply said they couldn't interfere with passengers' ability to tell what station they were in, implying that ads were permitted. The company expected to rake in an estimated $100,000 a year from station ads, so it wasn't going to let public opinion get in the way.

Ads on platforms have been a fixture ever since. They and the ads inside the cars are a clue to the subway's demographics, or at least to the audience that advertisers believe rides the trains. For most of its history, most ads were lowbrow. In the early years, pitches for cheap liquor and patent medicines were common. Cockroach cures were touted later, and decade after decade, trade schools have promised to give riders a brighter future.

Perhaps the most famous ads in recent decades were those for Dr. Jonathan Zizmor, who promised riders solutions to all their skin problems. His ads disappeared when he retired in 2016, at the age of 71, to devote himself to the study of the Talmud.

Today the Transit Authority's ad department sells the rights to outfit entire trains with ads entirely covering the walls inside and out.

ABOVE: Amid an outcry over ads on station walls in 1904, cartoonist Winsor McCay imagined what the subway might look like a few years hence. **OPPOSITE FROM TOP:** Whole trains can be wrapped in an ad, like this one for the TV series *The Walking Dead*. • Dermatologist Dr. Jonathan Zizmor was so well known through his subway ads that New York newspapers covered his retirement in 2016.

LIGHTS, CAMERA, ACTION

The subway quickly took on starring and supporting roles in movies.

- *2 A.M. in the Subway*, a short but suggestive silent movie released the year after the subway opened, highlighted the shenanigans one might come upon in the wee hours. Two drunken women stumble off a train on the arms of a tipsy man. A cop scolds them, and a subway employee shoves the three onto the next train going in the opposite direction. A moment later, two stockinged legs are seen kicking out of the car window, suggesting that the partying has continued at a new, racier level on that train. It's then revealed that they were just mannequin legs belonging to another passenger, who evidently thought it would be fun to provoke the police.

- In Buster Keaton's 1922 *The Frozen North*, a parody of westerns, the filmmaker takes the train to the end of the line and emerges from an IRT kiosk to find himself in an icy, Alaskan landscape.

- In the popular 1927 film *Subway Sadie*, now lost, a fur saleswoman and a subway door guard fall in love and become engaged, but their future is threatened when she is promoted and will be sent to Europe. In the end, she forsakes her career for love and is rewarded when it turns out the groom is not just another working stiff but actually the son of the president of the subway.

- The jam-packed train in the 1928 silent comedy *Speedy* is remarkably similar to today's rush-hour scenes, but the star, Harold Lloyd, has a strategy. He drags a dollar bill along the floor on a string. As other passengers get up to grab it, Lloyd and his girlfriend take their seats.

A fur saleswoman and a subway guard met and fell in love underground in the popular romantic story *Subway Sadie*. • **OPPOSITE:** Buster Keaton rode the subway to Alaska in *The Frozen North*.

Harold Lloyd, center, squeezes on a train with his girlfriend, played by Ann Christy, in the comedy *Speedy*.

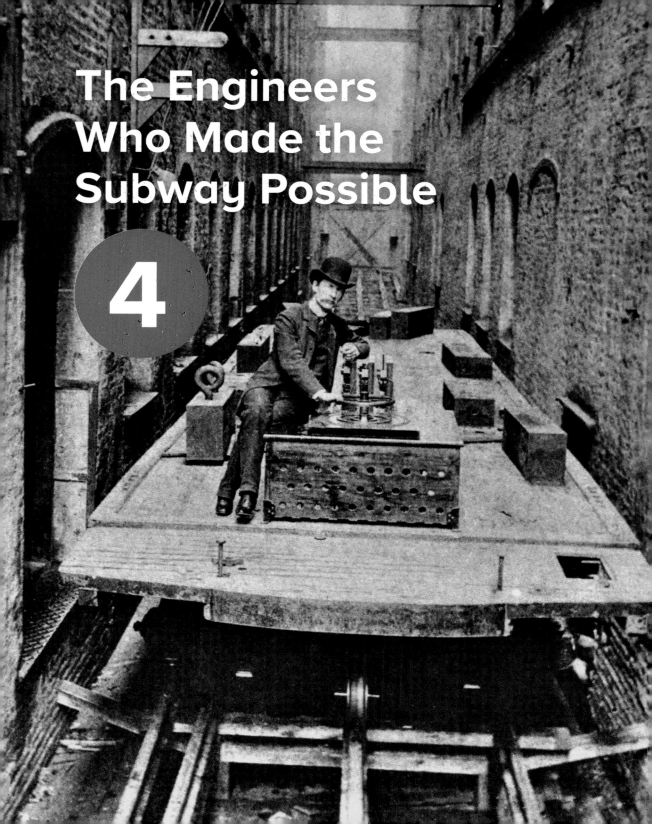

The Engineers Who Made the Subway Possible

4

The first subway was a testament to the remarkable talents of the two young engineers who laid its groundwork.

From the opening of London's first underground line in 1863, subways were dogged by a problem: how to power long trains in tunnels. Steam locomotives were the standard means of propulsion at the time, but they belched smoke and steam, and electric motors weren't yet powerful enough to haul heavy trains. London's first lines were steam powered and therefore only partly underground. Tunnels alternated with stretches of open track, and engines carried tanks to capture steam and smoke along the covered portions.

A series of inventions by the American electrical engineer Frank Sprague (1857–1934) at the end of the 1800s solved the problem.

Sprague worked briefly with Thomas Edison, the famous inventor and pioneer of electric light. But Edison was focused on light bulbs and showed little interest in electric motors, Sprague's passion, so Sprague struck out on his own. In 1885, a year after founding his own firm, the 28-year-old built a prototype electric locomotive for New York's elevated lines. Unfortunately, when he demonstrated it for the el's controlling shareholder, the financier Jay Gould, a fuse blew with a loud explosion and a flash of light, scaring the daylights out of Gould, who attempted to jump off the car. "My explanation that this young volcano [the fuse] was only a safety device was not convincing and he did not return," Sprague wrote later. So much for selling equipment to Gould's company.

Sprague's first big success came in 1888 when he installed one of his new motors and an improved throttle mechanism in a trolley that ran on a

Frank Sprague was a prolific inventor and successful entrepreneur who sold several motor and controls businesses to bigger companies.

OPPOSITE: Frank Sprague on a test car with a set of his motor controls.

steep hill in Richmond, Virginia. The experiment was a huge success and set off a boom in trolley railroads. The cause of electric railroads got a further boost in 1890 when a three-mile, fully underground, electrified line opened in London, running under the Thames River. The locomotives could haul only three small, cramped cars slowly through the tunnel, however, so the passenger capacity was limited.

For a while in the early 1890s, Sprague turned his attention to the nascent technology of electric elevators, which had only just begun to compete with hydraulic and steam-powered lifts. Among his innovations was a call button that could summon a single elevator from a bank of them. This was not merely a convenience for passengers. His mechanism utilized the elevators much more efficiently, which in turn reduced the number needed. That was a critical advance because the taller a building is, the more elevators it requires, and their shafts take up floor space. Elevators thus are a limiting factor in building heights. Sprague's efficient controls made taller towers possible.

The motors, throttle controls, and overhead poles that Sprague invented led to a boom in trolley lines in the 1890s.

Sprague soon realized that the same principles behind his elevator relay mechanism could be put to use on trains. He could eliminate locomotives by installing motors on each car, linked to a single throttle in the lead car. With this system, known as multiple-unit control, long trains could be powered by the motors of the day, and the available power increased as cars were added. In 1891, with his concept still untested, he confidently assured the chairman of New York's Board of Rapid Transit Commissioners that he could outfit its proposed subway completely with electric power if given the contract. It was typical of Sprague, who made similar guarantees to Richmond about his trolleys and to building owners about untested elevator systems. In each case, he delivered. Eventually, Chicago bought one of his multiple-unit trains in 1897. It was a success, and he was soon selling to Boston and other cities.

Sprague's inventions were not the only link between office towers and subways. As steel-framed construction became more widespread, taller and taller buildings were built, cramming more workers into Manhattan's business zones. That exacerbated congestion gave new impetus to demands for better transit.

"The true parent of the subway is the elevator, or better yet, the grand-parent," journalist Ray Stannard Baker observed in 1905. "The elevator made possible the skyscraper, the skyscraper led to underground transportation." He might have added that Sprague was the great-grandparent of both.

When Sprague died in 1935, he was ranked with Edison and Alexander Graham Bell, "the third of a remarkable trio of American inventors" who changed lives in the late 1800s with their ingenuity.

Sprague was also a shrewd businessman. Today he would be called a serial entrepreneur, founding a succession of technology-based companies and then selling each to bigger companies. He sold his trolley motor and controls business to Edison General Electric, his former boss's company. Otis Elevator bought Sprague's first elevator company. In 1902, he sold his multiple-unit train control business to General Electric, as well. Years later, Westinghouse bought a second company that developed additional elevator inventions.

Sprague was a master of motors and controls. It's impossible to describe William Barclay Parsons's genius so succinctly because it was so varied.

Parsons (1859–1932) was just 35 when he was named chief engineer of the city's Board of Rapid Transit Commissioners in 1894. Though his master's degree was in mine engineering, he began his career working for a railroad and worked for several private investor groups developing subway plans, and then as the board's number two engineer. The subway would call on both his rail and mining expertise.

In the early 1890s, Parsons conducted a meticulous geological survey of the subway's proposed route and discovered that Manhattan's schist bedrock was surprisingly close to the surface at many points, while at other spots soft soils ran deep. The survey convinced Parsons that the tunnels should be dug near the surface to avoid tunneling through the rock.

Soon after his appointment as chief engineer—even before Sprague devised his multiple-unit controls—Parsons told the commissioners that electric power would be the best option, based on a tour of European transit systems. Parsons's report was dense with statistics on the air consumed by steam locomotives and the volume of noxious fumes and moisture they emitted, and compared the energy lost using steam engines with the inefficiencies of power plants, transmission lines, and electric motors.

The monumental task of designing a new transit system from scratch fell to Parsons, who eventually supervised more than 300 engineers, who revered him. Tunnels were mapped through crowded streets, and draftsmen plotted tracks, switches, and signal systems; station entrances had to be designed around existing buildings; and a graceful 13-block viaduct was engineered to bridge a deep valley at 125th Street. To remove the water that inevitably seeps into tunnels, pumping systems were devised. The subway required its own hulking power plant on the Hudson River and its own power grid. Parsons oversaw it all, studying the minute details, and then seeing that the plans were executed when construction began in 1900. His mind could bridge engineering theory and practicality, right down to how tiling could be most visible to passengers inside a train so they would know at which station they had arrived.

Parsons was "the real author of the underground system, the man from whose brain and executive genius . . . the finished subway has sprung," said August Belmont Jr.

William Barclay Parsons, dubbed "a militant genius of the city age," oversaw more than 300 engineers designing the first subway. Later, he commanded a corps of army engineers on the Western Front in World War I and wrote histories of the submarine and Renaissance engineering.

Parsons, at right in cap, took leave from his subway work in 1898 to survey a rail line into sometimes dangerous regions in the interior of China.

Parsons was a blue-blooded, cultured product of America's old Protestant elite, bred to lead. On both sides of his family he was descended from British loyalists in the American Revolution, and his mother's ancestors were large colonial landowners. When he was a child, the family moved to Europe and he attended English boarding school. That was followed by several years studying with tutors touring France, Germany, and Italy. When he returned home, he asked to be called Barclay rather than William.

Even as a young man, he had a powerful bearing and exuded rectitude; his tall, erect figure stands out in group photos. Conspicuously smart, he had "a baffling front of well-bred composure," as the *New York World* put it in 1904. He appeared to be "a born general and diplomat," whether as president of his college class, masterminding the engineering of the subway, or on the front lines in France in World War I. While he cultivated relationships with powerful men such as Belmont and Mayor Seth Low, he wasn't afraid to fend off complaints from Belmont or to brush off politicians who sought jobs for their friends and relatives.

Like Sprague, he had an unshakable self-confidence. When the Transit Commission's work on the subway stalled in 1898, American investors hired Parsons to survey the route for a 750-mile railroad line in China from Canton on the coast inland to Hankou. It was a time of political unrest, and the 500-odd force of soldiers and laborers provided to Parsons was skittish about

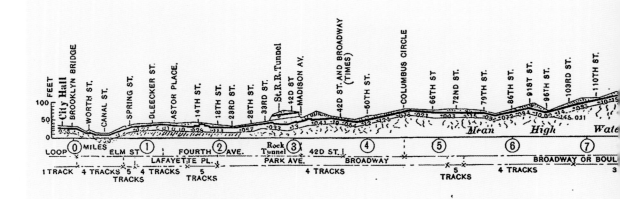

PROFILE
OF
RAPID TRANSIT RAILROAD
MANHATTAN AND BRONX LINES.

trekking through the hinterlands, where the locals were notoriously hostile to outsiders, but Parsons cajoled them into going. In one town, he was pummeled with clods of dirt by locals, but he refused to retreat.

"It undoubtedly took someone with his kind of whiz-kid hauteur to dig an underground train tunnel . . . through the world's second most populous city—and finish the whole thing in little more than four years," the *New York Times* said on the subway's centennial in 2004.

When the first stage of subway construction was complete in late 1904, Parsons resigned. Belmont, who had backed the Chinese railway project as well as the subway, then hired Parsons to engineer the Cape Cod Canal in Massachusetts, a nine-year, problem-plagued undertaking. Parsons also found time to advise President Theodore Roosevelt on the Panama Canal, serve on a commission studying London traffic problems, and chair Chicago's rapid transit board. When the United States entered World War I in 1917, Parsons enlisted

A profile map of the original line shows the geological challenges Parsons faced. At Canal Street and again at 116th Street in Harlem, the line was at or just below the water table in soft soils. At other points, tunnels had to be dynamited through bedrock.

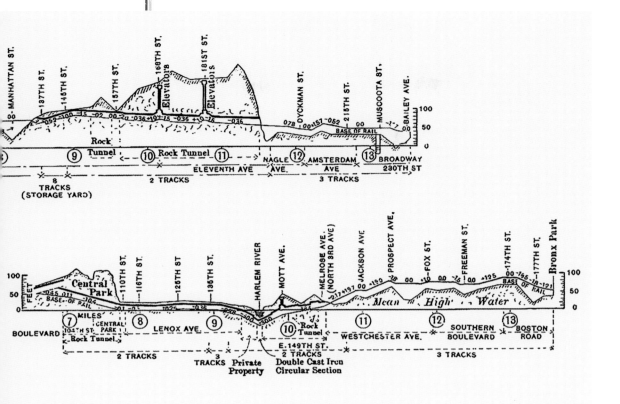

in the army, at age 58, and was put in charge of a company of engineers building trenches and railway tracks at the front, sometimes under artillery fire.

The engineering firm he founded, Parsons Brinckerhoff, became one of the world's largest, but Parsons never limited himself to tunnels, railways, trenches, or canals. A prolific author, he wrote closely observed accounts of his exploits in China and France, as well as a book on the history of the submarine. At the time of his death in 1932, he was hard at work on a monumental illustrated history of engineering in the Renaissance. It encompassed famous cathedral domes, bridges, and, of course, tunnels and canals, but also metallurgy, sewers, road building, and street-cleaning techniques. Engineers hadn't received enough credit for their contributions to that golden age, he wrote. The work was published posthumously and was so thorough that it was republished in 1968.

"A militant genius of the city age," his obituary called him.

SIGNALING AND CAPACITY

Technology from 1900 has kept trains safe, but it limits capacity.

To understand how the subway works, and what ails it, you have to understand the century-old, electromechanical signals and the digital technology slated to replace it.

The legacy system, known as automatic block signaling, is built around track sections called blocks. If two trains are separated by enough track blocks, a combination of signals and automated braking mechanisms will keep them from colliding. When a train passes into a block, signals turn red behind it. In addition, a hammer-like arm known as an automatic stop or trip stop rises from the track bed. If a train behind runs a red signal, a metal arm on the underside of the car (a trip cock) will strike the trip stop on the tracks and activate the train's brakes. Subway lines are configured so that the two blocks behind a train show red signals, with trip cocks up. Behind those, a third block will have a yellow signal, telling the motorman on the train behind to go slow.

It's old-fashioned technology, but it's proved extremely reliable. The block system has one big drawback, though: It limits the number of trains on a line because it requires at least two empty blocks between trains, regardless of speed. Blocks can be as long as 1,000 feet. When the line is at capacity, any delay causes all trains behind to slow or stop. The equipment, which relies on primitive switches and motors along the tracks, also requires a lot of maintenance and is vulnerable if water builds up on the track bed.

Block signaling is slowly being replaced in New York by a system known as CBTC, for Communications-Based Train Control. It uses electronic sensors that monitor train positions and speeds, continuously adjusting the minimum safe spacing between trains and their maximum safe speeds. It allows trains to follow each other more closely, particularly at slower speeds, when the block system imposes unnecessarily long gaps. Capacity on one line in London increased 22 percent when CBTC was installed, and travel time was cut 22 percent on another. Delays fell 40 percent.

New York is late to adopt the technology, which has been installed in Europe for decades. The L line was the first to get CBTC in New York. That was switched on in 2007, based on technology in service in the Paris Metro since 1998. The 7 line

How Traditional Block Signaling Works

Signal lights reflect the status of the block ahead, informing drivers how to proceed.

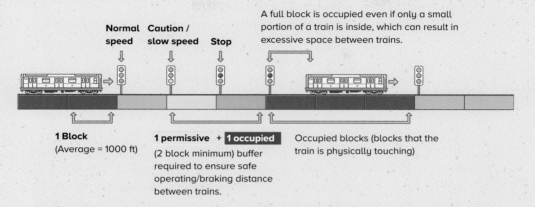

Normal speed **Caution / slow speed** **Stop**

A full block is occupied even if only a small portion of a train is inside, which can result in excessive space between trains.

1 Block
(Average = 1000 ft)

1 permissive + **1 occupied**
(2 block minimum) buffer required to ensure safe operating/braking distance between trains.

Occupied blocks (blocks that the train is physically touching)

Most subway lines use a variant of technology that dates back to the early 1900s in which train axles complete circuits, turning signals red and yellow behind the train.

How Electronic CBTC Signals Work

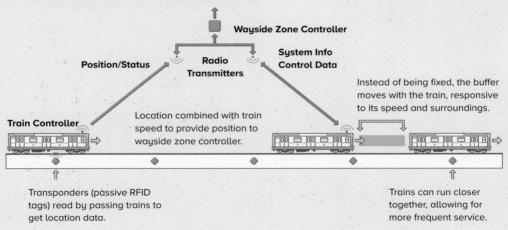

Wayside Zone Controller

Position/Status

Radio Transmitters

System Info Control Data

Instead of being fixed, the buffer moves with the train, responsive to its speed and surroundings.

Train Controller

Location combined with train speed to provide position to wayside zone controller.

Transponders (passive RFID tags) read by passing trains to get location data.

Trains can run closer together, allowing for more frequent service.

Communications-Based Train Control (CBTC) relies on data transmissions between cars and trackside monitors.

switched over to CBTC in 2019. Those lines were chosen because they are isolated—they do not merge with other lines—so the entire route could be converted more easily. Electronic signaling for other lines is still many years away.

There's another way the old signals can slow down trains unnecessarily: timing signals. They regulate speed, regardless of whether there's a train ahead, stopping a train if it passes too quickly through a block. Traditionally these were placed on down-hill grades, at sharp turns, and ahead of some stations, but scores of new ones were installed after a fatal collision on the Williamsburg Bridge in 1995. That crash revealed that many blocks that worked for partly wooden cars in the early 1900s were too short to allow heavier, modern, all-metal cars to stop in time if they pass a red signal.

Over time, the timing signals went out of adjustment, so they triggered emergency brakes even when trains observed the speed limits. Train operators then overcompensated, running extra slowly at some points—say, 15 miles per hour when the speed limit was 20. In 2018, the Transit Authority began inspecting and resetting or removing timing signals. In some cases, allowable speeds were doubled. That not only speeds up passengers' rides but increases capacity because more trains can pass the same point every hour.

Ever notice how a conductor

waves his or her finger out the window when the train comes to a stop? They're pointing at the striped centering board, which they're required to do at every station as a check to make sure the train is positioned properly before the doors are opened. If the train has stopped at the right spot on the platform, the conductor will be next to the board. If the conductor isn't in front of the zebra stripes, one end of the train could be in the tunnel and it would be unsafe to open the doors.

Entertain yourself by observing different conductors' styles. Some snap their wrists, as if firing a pistol. Others do little more than wave a finger or flop their hand limply.

Midcentury turnstiles were made in a streamlined style.

COLLECTING FARES

Chip technology is supplanting swipe cards,
and tokens are just a memory.

Technology, fare increases, and labor costs have altered the way riders pay.

The original method now seems quaint. Riders purchased paper tickets at a booth and presented them to a "ticket chopper" at the gate, who cut the tickets and admitted the passenger. As a labor-saving measure, turnstiles were installed in the 1920s. Riders simply inserted a nickel in a slot.

The first subway turnstiles were like those at this IRT station, with wide wooden arms.

FROM LEFT: As fares rose, new tokens were minted so older, cheaper ones could not be used. • New turnstiles installed beginning in 2019 allow riders to pay by tapping a credit card or swiping their mobile phone.

That worked as long as the fare could be paid with a single coin, which it could until 1953, when the price rose from 10 to 15 cents. The increase gave rise to the token, a specially minted coin for the subway. As fares increased over the years, new tokens of different sizes, sometimes with cutouts and inserts, were created so older, cheaper tokens wouldn't work.

In 1994, the Transit Authority began implementing an electronic fare system, using the MetroCard swipe card—technology that had been used for years in other cities. As card vending machines were installed, fewer clerks were needed and many token booths were closed. Tokens were finally phased out in 2003, after a long period in which passengers could use either a card or a token to enter.

The MetroCard was finicky. It took practice to swipe it through the turnstile slot correctly—not too fast, not too slow, and perfectly level. The swipe has to be between 10 and 40 inches per second, to be exact, equivalent to 0.57 to 2.27 miles per hour. Natives soon polished their technique, but visitors struggled, swiping and reswiping when error messages displayed.

In 2019, installation began of a tap-card system called OMNY, allowing riders to pay using credit cards with embedded chips or with their smart phones. That should speed up entry. OMNY is slated to completely replace the MetroCard by 2023, and it will be used on the MTA's commuter rail lines, as well.

Once again, New York was behind other cities. The credit card technology had been in use in London since 2014, and both London and the San Francisco Bay Area introduced transit tap cards in the 2000s.

One casualty of the switch to electronic fare collection was the money trains, which had become part of subway lore. Until 2006, special armored, two-car "revenue trains," staffed with armed guards in body armor, picked up cash from stations and brought it to 370 Jay Street, an MTA office building in Downtown Brooklyn. Beneath the structure were two special platforms for the revenue trains: one on the 2 and 3 line near Borough Hall station and another on the R near Lawrence Street station, serving the old IRT and the BMT-IND lines, respectively. Elevators carried the coins and bills to a second-floor counting room, where they were sorted and tallied by workers, who stripped and changed into pocketless overalls before entering the room.

With the MetroCard, many fares were paid with credit cards, so there was less cash at stations. Since 2006, cash has been collected by armored trucks and taken to a counting facility in Queens.

The Transit Authority never said much about the money trains, which looked like beat-up old work trains. Their moment in the spotlight came in 1995 in the heist flick *Money Train*, starring Wesley Snipes, Woody Harrelson, and Jennifer Lopez, about a plot to hijack a train and steal the day's proceeds.

The deepest station in the system, the 191st Street station on the 1 line, is 180 feet, or about 17 stories, below ground. Passengers can take elevators from St. Nicholas Avenue, or enter on foot through a 1,000-foot passageway to the platforms from Broadway, which is far below St. Nicholas Avenue. The nearby 190th Street station on the A line, 160 feet below street level, was used by a Fordham University physics professor in 1947 to take radiation measurements when he needed an environment that was protected from cosmic rays.

Stone removed for Brooklyn subway tunnels was used as landfill to expand Ellis Island in 1905 and 1906, and schist tunneled for the Second Avenue subway provides the contours at Ferry Point Park and the golf course there.

Defects in the New Marvel

5

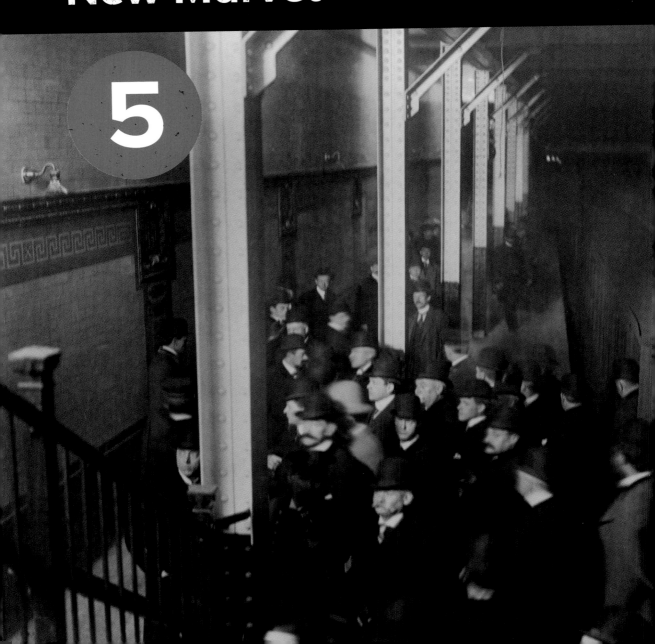

Experts struggled to address overcrowding and steamy, stinky stations.

The subway proved more popular than anyone imagined, and platforms were too small at busy times.

The original subway was a wonder, but engineers had to scramble to fix unforeseen defects after it opened. Many of the problems are familiar, and unsolved, more than a century later.

From day one, the subway was plagued by overcrowding, particularly express trains, which proved more popular than expected.

The original IRT was designed for seven-car express trains and five-car locals, with stations of corresponding size. The first, makeshift response was to add an eighth car on express trains and leave the ends of the train in the tunnels beyond the platform ends. The front doors on the first car and the back doors on the last car were simply left shut. That was just a temporary answer, however, and in 1910 and 1911, streets were torn up again to lengthen all express stations to fit 10 cars. In the 1940s, some local stations were extended for 10 cars, but it wasn't until the 1960s that all local stations were lengthened.

The idea of running longer trains with some doors left in the tunnels at stations resurfaced in a modified form in 2018 when transit officials solicited suggestions for system improvements. One of the winners was a Manhattan attorney named Craig Avedisian, who proposed operating double-length trains, with only one half opening its doors at each station. The other half would open at the next station.

Loading and unloading took too long. Early on, end doors were enlarged and new doors were added in the center of the cars to speed up loading and unloading, which increased capacity by reducing station delays.

The problem has never gone away. Doors are wider on cars delivered since the 2000s than on earlier models, and newer trains on the lettered lines have more doors per train because they have more cars (see Rolling Stock, page 132).

Out of safety concerns, the original signal system kept long distances between trains, sharply limiting the number of trains that could fit in the tunnels. In 1909, the signals were modified to allow a train to creep

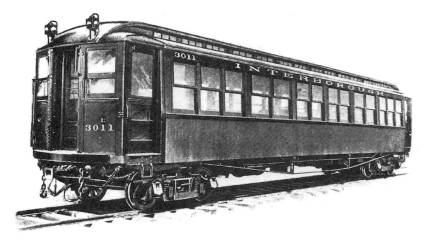

closer to the next one ahead as it approached a station, increasing capacity by two or three trains per hour.

Train spacing and speed controls continue to limit capacity (see Signaling and Capacity, page 62).

Then, as now, stations are steam baths in the summer. A heat wave in July 1905, the first summer of operation, brought outside temperatures to more 100 degrees Fahrenheit. At first, IRT management brushed off complaints, saying it was still cooler underground than on the street. In a public relations move, the company held a board meeting on a private subway car so directors could experience temperatures along the route. "Board Met in Subway and Found It Cool; Temperature Really Low," a headline proclaimed.

No one was buying the company's contention, however, and the transit commission's engineers set out to find solutions. A dozen office-sized fans were installed at the busiest station, Brooklyn Bridge, in 1905, but passengers noticed little improvement. Moreover, for each fan installed, a light bulb had to be removed, and that made the station dingy. The next year, a primitive form of environmentally friendly air-conditioning was installed there, using chilled water from an artesian well. But the experimental equipment was expensive, and it reduced the temperature only slightly.

The glass ceiling bricks that let light flood into the stations were part of the problem. They turned stations into greenhouses in the summer, and many were replaced with open grates to let heat escape. Others were covered over. On the advice of an engineer, large new ventilation grates were added at many places along the route in 1906 and 1907.

The first IRT cars had only narrow doors at the ends, which slowed loading and unloading as passengers tried to squeeze by in both directions. Later, center doors were added, and subsequent cars came from the factory with three sets of doors and wider end doors. Modern cars have much wider double doorways.

The IRT began installing fans inside cars in 1910. "It isn't really any cooler," IRT general manager Frank Hedley told reporters on a test train. "We're just stirring up the air. But you notice how much more comfortable it is." Standing passengers and bald men would benefit most, he observed.

The heat buildup was aggravated again with the introduction of longer express trains after 1911. That meant more motors and more brakes throwing off more heat in the tunnels.

Things got much worse when air-conditioned cars were introduced in the 1970s. While it was comfortable inside the new trains, their cooling equipment expelled heat to the tunnels and stations. In 2018, the Regional Plan Association measured the temperature at 104 degrees Fahrenheit on the platform for the 4, 5, and 6 trains at Union Square when it was only 86 degrees outside.

Unfortunately, air-conditioning isn't feasible at most stations because the cool air would simply be pushed into the tunnels by each passing train.

Costly glass walls at the platform edge would be required. The temperatures were so oppressive on the Lexington Avenue platform at Grand Central–42nd Street (4, 5, 6) that a cooling system was added in the 2000s to mitigate the heat. But anyone who has been in that station on a hot summer day can testify that it is a far cry from being air-conditioned. The deep new stations on Second Avenue, at Hudson Yards, and Cortlandt Street also have air-cooling systems.

Stations smelled. Experts hired by the transit commission in 1905 and 1906 concluded that subway air was healthier than air at street level—not a crazy conclusion at a time when the streets were packed with horses, the city was heated by coal, and industrial fumes were unregulated. The off-putting odors underground came from the gravel track bed, lubricants that dripped from the trains, and new cement and plaster, the experts said.

One doctor even proclaimed that the underground atmosphere was beneficial. "I have positively and scientifically demonstrated that the air of the subway is pregnant with ozone," declared Dr. S. Wesley-Smith, a regular rider who claimed to have researched the air, the odors, and ventilation. "Ozone is good for victims of malaria. I have suffered from malaria, and the ozone of the subway does me good."

The smells never went away. In the 1940s and 1950s, the Transit Authority had an employee, James P. "Smelly" Kelly, whose job it was to track down the source of off odors. In one case, after some sleuthing, he determined that the unpleasant smell came from elephant dung that had washed into the subway years earlier from a circus after a water main broke.

Many found the subway an assault on the visual senses as well. Riders and motormen were "dazzled"—in a bad way—by the flash of the tunnels' white structural columns as lights from the train struck them. They fretted about damaging their eyes. "A well-known occulist says that looking at the rows of white columns is very straining. Therefore, don't look at them," the *New York Times* advised on opening week.

The IRT responded by painting the columns dark brown, but the debate continued over possible harm from watching other objects pass by so quickly. Nonsense, one doctor opined in 1906. If you don't read too much by the dim car lights or keep your eyes focused out the windows continuously, "the eyes will experience an exhilaration from the exercise." Likewise, the din of the trains will strengthen the ear muscles, he said.

COMPLAINING

Sardine-packed trains? Nasty smells? They're nothing new. Unpleasant aspects of the subway experience inspired some colorful complaints in the early 20th century:

- "In the Bronx subway I have sat next to pipes [that] . . . give forth such a rancid, noisome odor as to make one think an asafoetida bomb had been exploded someplace in the train."—Quoted in the *New York Times*, 1912

- "Had I treated German prisoners during the war as passengers on the transit lines are here being treated, I would have been court-martialed."—Major General John F. O'Ryan, member of the Transit Commission, 1924

- "We do not get a civilized ride for a nickel today. We get instead a chance to hang on, like a chimpanzee, to a flying ring suspended from the roof while we are crushed to a point of indecency by our fellow sufferers. . . . The trains are like cattle cars."—Open letter from the City Club to the city Board of Estimation and Apportionment, 1927

ABOVE: A 1905 cartoon in the *New York Herald* showed a train with "Interborough Rattled Transit" emblazoned on its front with the motto "Trains Run at the [Company's] Convenience." On the crowded platform, a sign boasted, "Three Hours to Harlem," a far cry from the 20-odd minutes express trains were scheduled to take.

SEX AND THE SUBWAY

←⊷ ⊶→

The new underground world fueled dreams of love and less noble urges.

The subway revolutionized transportation for New Yorkers. It also awakened new fantasies about love and sex beneath the streets. For decades, strangers of different classes and races, men and women, had been thrust together on crowded trolleys and omnibuses, but now they were in an enclosed space below ground, hurtling at 45 miles an hour in the semidark amid a deafening racket. There was something electrifying about the experience, and it wasn't just the 625 volts of the third rail.

At its worst, the subway opened up new opportunities for groping. A 1912 magazine article lamented male passengers who were "not too chivalrous, and sometimes coarse grained, vulgar or licentious." When trains filled with young women office workers, it often resulted in "a violation of the laws of decency."

The prospect of accidental physical contact with the opposite sex—or contact that could plausibly be portrayed as accidental—was exciting, at least to lyricists. That was the focus of the 1912 vaudeville hit "The Subway Glide," a new dance and song:

> *Rush in, crush in, reach for a handle strap*
> *Then turn right around and flop in a lady's lap. . . .*
> *Ev'ry body you rub, When you're doing the Sub.*
> *When you're doing the Subway Glide.*

Though we think of the early 1900s as a time of uptight Victorian propriety, songwriters were quite comfortable describing casual and even illicit encounters in the new underground world. Take "Down in the Subway," written the year the IRT opened:

> *There's a new place at last to go spooning,*
> *Where lovers can love with delight, . . .*
> *The show girls and even her chappie,*
> *Will now lead a subcellar life,*
> *If married and home is unhappy,*
> *You can now hide away from your wife.*

FROM TOP: The rocking and swaying of trains, and accidental contact with the opposite sex, was the inspiration for the 1912 dance tune "The Subway Glide." • In the postcard below—a sort of Gilded Age soft porn—a young woman lifts her skirt and petticoat for a white-haired man as two passengers and a ticket agent look on. On the card, her skirt is a flap of fabric that can be lifted. Uncle Reuben's hat has flown off in excitement of "seeing the subway."

Other lyricists had more noble thoughts. True love discovered on the subway was a recurring theme. In "The Subway Express," a 1907 duet, a man offers a lady a supporting arm after she jabbed him in the back when the train sped around a turn. She declines his offer, only to have a subway employee tell her to move closer together in the crowded car. "Clearly there was nothing else to do," she sings in mock regret at this command.

Love takes off from there:

> GIRL: I felt I'd known you all my life
> When we reached Twenty-Third.
> BOY: You won my heart in Harlem.
> GIRL: At the Bronx, I murmured yes.
> BOY: We lost no time in that hour sublime
> On the Subway Express.

The 1964 play *Dutchman* by LeRoi Jones (later known as Amiri Baraka) layered racial politics and black identity on top of a potent sexual theme. In the ominous opening scene of the stage production and the 1967 movie adaptation, which sets the tone for the rest of the work, a blonde comes on to a young black man in a suit on the subway.

Today love on the subway is chronicled in the "Missed Connections" section of Craigslist, where people seek out fellow riders they were attracted to:

> Riding the G to Court Sq. You had an adorably floppy dog,
> sweetly scooped half on your lap. We caught eyes, smiled at
> each other, you said hi and I replied in kind. No one ever says hi
> in NY. . . . I thought of asking about your dog, or if you needed
> help when we got to the last stop. I wanted to; I just got shy.

Soul mates, perhaps. Other posts appear to aim at more fleeting connections:

> You left your rose lipstick behind. I could give those lips the
> attention they deserve.

OPPOSITE: Long before he gained fame as a film director, Stanley Kubrick photographed life in the subway for a 1947 *Look* magazine feature. This jarring image was posed. The woman was Toba Metz, Kubrick's first wife.

The Lost Decade and the Dual Contracts

6

1922)M-A-2-259
AVE. 2-20-1912

Commissioning new lines proved as hard as launching the first one.

Despite the fanfare over the subway's debut in 1904
and its enormous popularity, expansion plans quickly bogged down. Neighborhoods across the city clamored for subways, and year after year ambitious schemes were floated for new lines, but no comprehensive plan for a citywide subway system was settled until the "Dual Contracts" expansion was agreed to in 1913.

The delay stemmed from the same issues that stalled a first subway for decades. Which routes should get priority? How could the city pay for new lines? Could it attract private capital for construction while still retaining significant control? As before, property owners filed suit. In addition, top city officials were often at odds with the state-appointed commissions that controlled the subway.

Only two other short new lines were approved in the nine years after 1904. One, a partly underground "Bridge Loop" was approved to carry BRT Brooklyn trains from the Williamsburg Bridge through a tunnel to City Hall, near the west end of the Brooklyn Bridge (part of today's J and Z). That would allow trains from Brooklyn to run well into Manhattan and relieve pressure on the overcrowded shuttle trains on the Brooklyn Bridge. The second was a subway along Brooklyn's Fourth Avenue, eventually extending to Bay Ridge (D, N, R). The loop opened from the Williamsburg Bridge to Chambers Street on the Manhattan side in 1913, and the Fourth Avenue line opened to passengers to Bay Ridge Avenue in 1915.

The slow buildout wasn't for lack of ideas. New schemes issued forth regularly from commissions and rival transit companies. In March 1905, the rapid transit board released what amounted to a wish list. It included 19 new

While the Dual Contracts were being negotiated to extend the IRT and BRT lines, the city went forward with construction of a new subway tunnel along Fourth Avenue in Brooklyn, which was later used by the BRT (D, N, R). By 1912 the area between Union and Ninth Street at the edge of Park Slope was a massive construction zone.

proposed routes, more than the city could possibly afford. Some were intended as extensions of the IRT, but others were designed without links to an existing line. The commissioners expressed confidence that other transit companies and even mainline railroads would bid for the latter.

Belmont protested, saying his company had a "moral right" to build all future subways because it took the risk of building the first one, and he threatened not to bid on new lines in Brooklyn unless the IRT was given exclusive rights to rapid transit in Manhattan. It was a transparently hollow threat. "I don't suppose Mr. Belmont will cut off his nose to spite his face, will he?" a city official retorted.

The commission's ambitious plan went nowhere, however, and the commission was soon disbanded as complaints mounted that it hadn't done enough to build more lines. Belmont contributed to the demise of the sympathetic commission by overplaying his hand in 1905.

From the start, critics charged that the 50-year lease (with a renewal option) that the IRT obtained in 1900 was a giveaway. Concerns only multiplied when Belmont engineered a takeover of all the Manhattan elevated lines in 1903. But it was a second merger, announced in December 1905, that solidified opposition to the IRT. Belmont's company struck a deal to absorb the Metropolitan Street Railway Company, which operated streetcars in Manhattan. Together with the els, it gave Belmont a monopoly over rapid transit in Manhattan and the Bronx.

Lexington Avenue was too narrow to run four tracks abreast, so the express tracks were placed below the local ones.

Belmont's hand was forced when Thomas Fortune Ryan of the Metropolitan made a brash offer in 1903 to build a subway from Wall Street to Grand Central and then up Lexington Avenue to the Bronx—a route Belmont believed was rightfully the IRT's. Though Ryan's company would have struggled to come up with the money for construction, Ryan hired John B. McDonald, the master contractor for the first subway, giving the Metropolitan proposal credibility.

In fact, Ryan's Lexington Avenue plan was a savvy ploy to provoke a buyout by Belmont, who obliged.

In 1910, when the Public Service Commission was searching for competitors to take on the IRT and BRT, the Hudson and Manhattan Railroad (today's PATH system) proposed to operate subway lines in Manhattan, Brooklyn, and the Bronx that would connect with its subways to New Jersey.

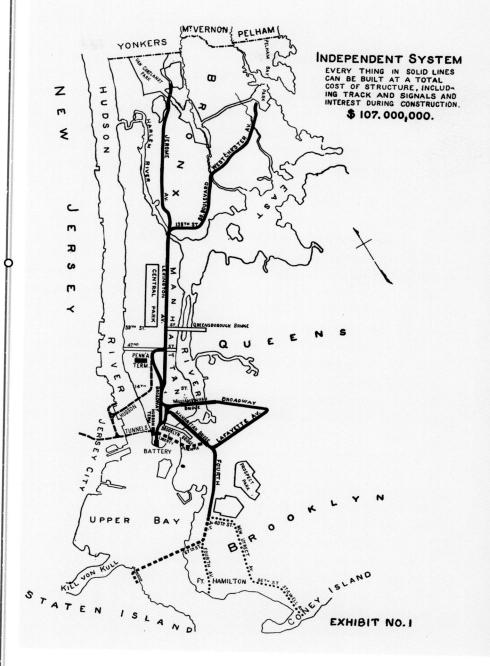

INDEPENDENT SYSTEM

EVERY THING IN SOLID LINES CAN BE BUILT AT A TOTAL COST OF STRUCTURE, INCLUDING TRACK AND SIGNALS AND INTEREST DURING CONSTRUCTION.

$ 107,000,000.

EXHIBIT NO. 1

"Well, we couldn't stand that kind of competition, and so we combined with them," Belmont confided years later.

The commission, which had been working to entice other companies to build new lines, "saw in the merger the collapse of competition," and the political blowback was intense. The merger "leaves the city practically helpless to compel the construction of projected subways," the *World* declared.

The 1906 gubernatorial election only intensified scrutiny of the IRT. The city controller said the IRT should be compelled to run more trains so no one had to stand. The populist press baron William Randolph Hearst, a persistent IRT critic, won the Democratic nomination for governor, ensuring that transit was a major campaign issue.

Hearst lost, but it was a close election. The next year the Republican reformer who beat him, Charles Evans Hughes, agreed that the pace of new construction had to be accelerated, and he signed a law replacing the Board of Rapid Transit Commissioners with a new Public Service Commission. On July 1, 1907, five reform-minded commissioners who wanted competition for the IRT and better transit for the working class were installed in place of the business-friendly figures of the previous commission.

Six months after they were sworn in, the new board issued a fresh blueprint for future subway lines known as the Triborough Plan. It called for a doubling of IRT mileage as well as new lines not connected to the existing subway. Henceforth, the city would also have the right to take back any new franchise after 10 years if it reimbursed the operator for its outlays plus a modest profit.

More delays followed. The IRT repeatedly offered to build extensions as a way to head off competition, and each offer had terms very advantageous to the company. Finally, in September 1910, the commission solicited bids for its proposed routes. To its surprise, not a single company offered to pay up for the right to operate a line. No one wanted to invest in a franchise the city could take away at will.

Still, the IRT had demonstrated how lucrative transit investments could be, and in November 1910, another successful subway entrepreneur, William Gibbs McAdoo, came forward, offering to build lines that were a variant on the Triborough scheme. One would run up Broadway, one up the East Side to the Bronx, and a third through a tunnel to Brooklyn.

As the driving force behind the Hudson and Manhattan Railroad Company, which built two subways under the Hudson River from New Jersey

A mule hauls a cart of debris as a tunnel is carved through Central Park in 1915 to carry the BRT Dual Contracts tracks from Seventh Avenue to East 60th Street and on to Queens (N, R).

(today's Port Authority Trans-Hudson, or PATH, subways; see chapter 7), McAdoo was a credible bidder. But his offer was conditioned on the city paying for construction. Moreover, he and Belmont relied on some of the same financial backers, most important among them J. P. Morgan, Sr. and Jr. The H&M lines were built without public subsidies, and McAdoo's company had $100 million of debt in 1906, so the New York project would be a financial stretch. Belmont seized on that, quickly countering with an offer to extend IRT lines and add extra tracks, mostly in Manhattan. Belmont correctly calculated that

if investors had to choose between two competing subway ventures, they would lay their bets on the financially robust IRT. The H&M was unable to get financing, and McAdoo withdrew the offer.

A new rival soon emerged, however. In January 1911, Brooklyn Rapid Transit Company submitted a plan for a web of underground lines in Manhattan, plus new elevated lines in Brooklyn and Queens, all connecting to the BRT's existing els in Brooklyn. The BRT held a lock on els and street railroads in Brooklyn just as tightly as the IRT did on its Manhattan lines, but it couldn't transport passengers beyond the fringe of Manhattan.

This was the negotiating lever the commission had been waiting for. Ten days after the BRT offer, the city formed a three-man panel to investigate the companies' offers, led by George McAneny, the 41-year-old Manhattan borough president, a former reporter and civic reformer who had conducted detailed research on population density and transit policy. Today he would be called a policy wonk. He proved to be a patient and canny bargainer, and he built a consensus among the fractious city officials and commissioners. After several months of talks with the companies and the commission, in June 1911, McAneny released what was called the "Dual Contracts" solution. It would extend the IRT's lines in Manhattan and Brooklyn and award the IRT a new route in Queens, while offering the BRT most of what it wanted. The city would cover roughly half the construction costs.

Once again, the IRT said it would not participate, but Belmont soon came back to the table. McAneny spent more than a year haggling over the details with the two companies. For real estate developers poised to capitalize on new

The temporary wooden street surfaces built over subway construction sometimes collapsed under the weight of traffic. On Nostrand Avenue in Brooklyn, in 1916, a trolley fell into the pit created for the new IRT line (2, 5).

lines, the wait was unbearable, and they complained that people were moving to New Jersey for want of more subways in New York.

Finally, in March 1913, McAneny nailed down a deal with the companies. The BRT was awarded what today are the J, M, N, Q, R, W, and Z routes in Manhattan, including a trunk line from Whitehall near the Battery to Times Square, mostly along Broadway. At the south end, that line linked to Brooklyn and, at the north, it ran into Queens. The company was also given a contract to operate a tunnel across 14th Street in Manhattan extending to Williamsburg and Bushwick in Brooklyn (L). In 1915, the BRT began service in the city-built Fourth Avenue line (D, N, R), with connections to two existing BRT lines to Coney Island (D, N).

The IRT lost its subway monopoly in Manhattan, but it remained the exclusive operator north of 60th Street, including a new Lexington Avenue route north of Grand Central (4, 5, 6) that Belmont had long hoped to build, plus a line down Seventh Avenue from Times Square past the soon-to-open Pennsylvania Station to Wall Street and Brooklyn (1, 2, 3). When the Manhattan work was complete in 1918, the IRT routes resembled an H. The 42nd Street tracks were converted for use as a crosstown shuttle, with north–south routes on either side of the island.

In Brooklyn, the IRT's 1908 line to Atlantic Terminal would stretch eastward under Flatbush Avenue to Eastern Parkway (4, 5) and Nostrand Avenue (2, 5). In Queens, the IRT was commissioned to build an elevated line to Corona—and later Flushing—across what was then mostly farmland (7). That was connected to Manhattan via a never-used trolley tunnel under the East River at East 42nd Street that Belmont had purchased years earlier. The IRT kept its monopoly in the rapidly developing Bronx and added elevated lines on Jerome Avenue (4) and to Pelham Bay Park (6).

When the bulk of the Dual Contracts work was complete in 1920, there were five East River tunnels tying Manhattan to Brooklyn and Queens and two bridge routes over the East River, and Queens had its first two elevated lines. In all, New York had 202 route miles of rapid transit, surpassing London's 157. Every borough except Staten Island had at least two lines, and there was even talk of a branch to Staten Island from the new Bay Ridge line.

SONGS OF THE SUBWAY

Lyricists and composers found their muse
in the transit system.

The subway spawned a wave of popular songwriting, much of it about onboard encounters between the sexes (see Sex and the Subway, page 76). But musicians and lyricists have addressed many other facets of the system in the century since it opened.

Perhaps the best known song about the subway is Billy Strayhorn's 1939 jazz standard "Take the A Train," which celebrated the new IND express that shot riders nonstop from Columbus Circle to 125th Street. Strayhorn worked for Duke Ellington, who lived in Sugar Hill in Harlem and made the piece famous.

> *You must take the "A" train*
> *To go to Sugar Hill way up in Harlem.*
> *If you miss the "A" train*
> *You'll find you've missed the quickest way to Harlem.*

Paul Simon and Art Garfunkel posed for the cover of their 1964 debut album, *Wednesday Morning, 3 A.M.*, in the Fifth Avenue–53rd Street station (E, M) and, in the hit track from the album, "The Sounds of Silence," they proclaimed that "the words of the prophets are written on the subway walls." Bob Dylan also alluded to the seamier side of the subway in "Visions of Johanna" (1966), singing that "the all-night girls they whisper of escapades out on the D train."

Despite what it might sound like at first, the title of Petula Clark's 1967 hit "Don't Sleep in the Subway" wasn't a warning about crime. It was a plea to a lover who walked out after a fight:

> *Take off your coat, my love, and close the door*
> *Don't sleep in the subway, darlin'*
> *Don't stand in the pouring rain*
> *Don't sleep in the subway, darlin'*
> *The night is long.*

By 1985, when Tom Waits recorded "Downtown Train," later a hit for Rod Stewart, the underground world was anything but romantic:

The downtown trains are full
With all those Brooklyn girls
They try so hard to break out of their little worlds.
Well, you wave your hand and they scatter like crows
They have nothing that will ever capture your heart
They're just thorns without the rose
Be careful of them in the dark.

By then, others were riffing on the subway in different ways, such as the 1983 mesmerizing electronic hip-hop hit by I.R.T. (Interboro Rhythm Team), "Watch the Closing Doors." Michael Jackson set his 1987 music video "Bad" in the Hoyt–Schermerhorn station in Downtown Brooklyn (A, C, F, G). It was directed by Martin Scorsese, who made a career of portraying New York on the big screen, from *Taxi Driver* and *Mean Streets* to *Gangs of New York*.

More recently, the lowly G train—the only line that does not pass through Manhattan and is known for its short and infrequent trains—has inspired at least four music videos on YouTube. Alan James Markley of the Plastic Cannons describes his "The G Train, A Reluctant Love Song" as "a song about my complex relationship with the G train, featuring jungle drumming and sweet synthesizers."

"I could kiss you when I see your headlights glowing / 'Cause I know in my heart 20 minutes is hard to wait," Ross Brunetti's swoons in his performance of "I'll Wait for You (G Train Song)."

Comedian and musician Rob Paravonian, too, proclaimed his loyalty in the YouTube video "G Train":

People laugh and say it should try to go somewhere
But the G train does its own thing
It doesn't really care. . . .
If the G train doesn't go there, it's no place that I want to be.

OPPOSITE, CLOCKWISE FROM TOP LEFT: Billy Strayhorn took his inspiration from the new IND line to Harlem, where Duke Ellington lived. • The Ramones posed for album covers in the subway in 1983, as Simon and Garfunkel had in 1964.

Musicians performed on trains from an early point, asking for donations. The passengers do not appear impressed by the accordion player in this 1938 photo by Walker Evans.

Q: What should I do if I fall onto the tracks?

A: The Transit Authority refuses to give advice on this topic, but various online chats suggest that your best bet is to run ahead to the front end of the platform. That will give the motorman more time to see you and stop the train before it reaches you. The train will stop before the end of the platform, so you're safe if you make it beyond there. There are stairs at the ends of the platforms.

Don't try to climb back onto the platform in the middle of the station—it's high and much harder to clamber up than you think. Many people who have tried to do this have been hit by trains.

Don't assume that you can lie flat and not be hit by the train. In some stations, there isn't enough clearance under the trains.

Don't try to squeeze between two sets of tracks, either, because the electrified third rail is there.

DOS AND DON'TS ON THE TRAIN

Prohibitions reveal a lot about how the world has changed.

The subway is the city writ small, cramped and subterranean, and it is a window onto antisocial behavior over time.

Judging by signage, the most pressing problems in the early years were spitting and smoking—including pipes and cigars. The Health Department and the police arrested 200 men for spitting or smoking in a February 1909 station sweep. Since tuberculosis was common then, spitting was a major health issue.

Even unlit cigars and cigarettes were a problem. An editorial in the *New York Times* chided "the men and boys who are willing to discommode their fellow-beings for the sake of saving the butts of cheap cigars. . . . No effort should be spared . . . to prevent the carrying of ill-smelling, vulgar fractions of cigars in the trains."

ABOVE: Some issues are perennial.

In the early decades of the subway, smoking and spitting were both common in stations, and men often carried smelly, snuffed-out cigarettes and cigars onto trains.

During the Great Depression, begging and busking became a problem, and the BMT banned both on its trains. "Mendicants of all kinds, as well as vendors of pencils, chewing gum and shoe laces" had become a plague, the *New York Times* lamented in 1933. Moreover, "beggars carried musical instruments and were accompanied by announcers, who took a stand at one end of the car and made known the next tune to be played."

Skip ahead to the 1970s and 1980s, and deafening music from boom boxes was the problem. That gave rise to **NO RADIO PLAYING** signs. Now that listening devices have shrunk, the Transit Authority pleads with riders to keep the volume down on their earbuds and headphones. It also asks passengers to take their knapsacks off their backs at crowded times.

Some behavioral problems have defied the rule makers for a century, such as passengers blocking car doors and what is now called manspreading.

It may come as a surprise to riders, but the Transit Authority's Rules of Conduct prohibit "commercial activity," including selling "food, goods, services or entertainment" or "the solicitation of money for them." Panhandling is also prohibited, at least on paper.

Also prohibited are the making of any noise over 85 decibels at five feet and the use of amplifiers on station platforms. And in case you are tempted to crawl out a window, beware that "no person shall enter or leave a subway car, bus or other conveyance operated by the Authority except through the entrances and exits provided for that purpose."

Keep The Doors Clear
So Others Can Board

Bottom line:
Blocking doors blocks traffic,
and slows service for everyone.
You get the picture.

Dude...
Stop The Spread,
Please

It's a space issue.

Newer etiquette guides from the Transit Authority address both long-standing problems as well as some that are distinctly modern, such as backpacks worn at crowded times, makeup sessions on the train, and acrobatic dance acts.

Those are the official rules. Other, informal ones are learned the hard way by riders. "Beware the empty train car," advises the online city etiquette guide Wise Bread. "It's empty for a reason." Common reasons: no air-conditioning, a bad smell, or bad people.

The most crucial unspoken rule of all: Avoid eye contact. The sociologist Erving Goffman coined the term "civil inattention" for the studied disregard of others in various city situations. Delving deeper into the subject, later researchers found less eye contact in central city areas than on commuter trains. The best rule of thumb on the subway: Avert your glance.

A Very Different Subway

7

COPYRIGHT 1909
PIERRE P. PULLIS

HUDSON & MANHATTAN SUBWAY
TERMINAL NEW YORK.

Dreams of a subway tunnel tying New Jersey to New

York date back almost as far as the first plans for underground trains in Manhattan. Tunneling for what we now know as the PATH tubes got underway in 1873, 27 years before work commenced on the New York subway. And, when the lines under the Hudson River were completed in 1908 and 1909, they offered creature comforts undreamed of on the New York subway.

The project was jinxed for its first 25 years. Work began in Hoboken, New Jersey, in 1873 but was soon halted when a railroad that feared competition for its ferries obtained an injunction. Digging recommenced in 1879, and by the following summer, the tunnel extended 280 feet under the river. Then a blowout, due to the pressurized air in the tunnel, drowned 20 workers. Work was relaunched the next year, and more than 1,500 feet of one tube and 570 feet of the second were built. Then the money ran out. Work began again several times in the 1880s, but then there was another blowout. A financial crisis in 1891 halted work again when the tunnel was at 3,700 feet, after which it sat dormant for nine years.

It took William Gibbs McAdoo (1863–1941) to get the project underway again. A lawyer and transit investor who had moved to New York from Chattanooga, Tennessee, McAdoo was frustrated at having to take a ferry across the Hudson to catch a train to Philadelphia or Baltimore. He

OPPOSITE FROM TOP: The architecture of H&M's stations, including its terminus at Herald Square, was quite different from the IRT's. • Stock certificates for the H&M showed one of its trains running beneath warships on the Hudson.

RIGHT: William Gibbs McAdoo raised the money to complete two abandoned, half-built tunnels under the Hudson River to New Jersey—what are now the PATH tubes. He went on to serve as US Treasury Secretary during World War I.

imagined a subway connecting the three main train stations on the New Jersey shorefront to Manhattan. In 1901, the 38-year-old arranged for a tour of the abandoned tunnel and had an epiphany:

> The Fates had marked a day when I was to go under the riverbed and encounter this piece of dripping darkness, and it would rise from its grave and walk by my side. I was destined to give it color and movement and warmth, but it would change the course of my life and lead me into a new career.

The half-built tunnel exercised a kind of mystical power over him:

> As I entered the tunnel, I had a powerful feeling of visiting a place I had known well many years ago. . . I was like a man who walks through a wrecked and dismantled house that he had lived in when he was a boy.

He formed a company in 1902 and began knocking on doors to raise the money he needed to buy and complete the tunnel, which was then owned by creditors.

It took six years to finish the 1.1-mile-long trans-Hudson tunnels and a subway to Sixth Avenue and 19th Street in Manhattan. By 1910, his Hudson and Manhattan Railroad Company was running trains to 34th Street. A second tunnel from Jersey City, New Jersey, to the future site of the World Trade Center in Lower Manhattan was begun in 1904 and opened in 1909. McAdoo also planned a branch across Ninth Street to Astor Place and an extension to Grand Central Terminal that were never built (see chapter 11).

Like August Belmont Jr., who controlled the IRT, McAdoo was a rail enthusiast with a knack for showmanship. McAdoo relished leading reporters on tours of the tunnels and, one day, during construction of a massive, two-square-block office building over his downtown station, he hopped on a steel beam that was about to be hoisted to the top of the building. He rode it 275 feet into the air, where he and the beam were deposited on the rising frame. "Good morning, gentlemen," he called out to surprised ironworkers.

Unlike the short, thin-skinned, and frequently haughty Belmont, McAdoo was tall and lanky, solicitous toward his employees, and modest. He wrote the

Hudson and Manhattan Tube.
New York City.

The underground intersection of the Hudson and Manhattan's lines beneath Hoboken, New Jersey, is as complex as anything in the New York subway.

local newspapers imploring them not to use the term "the McAdoo tunnels" because many people shared credit. In his subway, he stressed what today we would call the user experience. Searching for a motto, he took the railroad baron William H. Vanderbilt's infamous remark, "The public be damned," and inverted it. His company's motto, McAdoo declared, would be, "The public be pleased."

He studied New York's subway and learned from its shortcomings. H&M's terminuses had platforms on both sides of the tracks so exiting passengers didn't collide with those entering. Instead of the wood-sided cars of the New York trains, McAdoo ordered strong, fireproof, all-steel cars with features adopted only later on New York City cars, such as batteries for the lights in

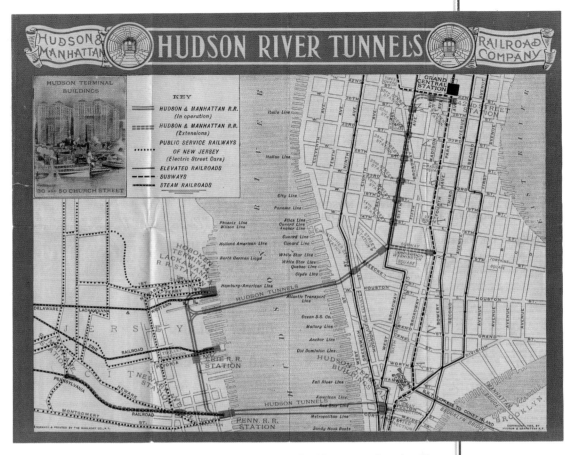

case power was lost and three sets of doors on each side to speed up loading and unloading.

H&M offered service more like that of long-distance luxury trains. There were redcaps to help with bags and parcels and, for a while, separate baggage cars. He employed women exclusively as ticket agents after a manager told him that they were more courteous and efficient and would work for lower wages. McAdoo accepted the part about courtesy, but ordered that women be paid the same as men—unusual at the time.

McAdoo was solicitous of female customers, too. Baggage room clerks doubled as concierges: After shopping trips to Manhattan, wives could check their parcels for their husbands to lug home on their evening commutes. Responding to complaints from a women's group about groping on trains, H&M set aside the last car on each train exclusively for women during rush hours. (The experiment ended after a few months when usage dropped off.

H&M won permission to construct a branch across Ninth Street to intersect with the IRT subway at Astor Place and an extension of its Sixth Avenue line up 42nd Street and then east to Grand Central Terminal, but neither line was built.

THE McADOO POLICY.

CARTOON IN THE JERSEY CITY EVENING JOURNAL

McAdoo consciously catered to his passengers, offering redcaps to carry bags, concierge-like services, and cars reserved for women.

"There's no one in there under twenty-five," a conductor told a reporter. The atmosphere in the cars was somewhat tense, the story hinted, as each passenger "kept her eyes fixed upon her neighbors' clothes.")

In 1910, McAdoo applied without success for the right to build three additional lines in New York City (see chapter 6). Three years later, he resigned from the H&M and embarked on a third career, serving as secretary of the treasury under President Woodrow Wilson from 1913 to 1918. There he was instrumental in establishing the Federal Reserve Bank. In both 1920 and 1924, he was a leading contender to win the Democratic presidential nomination. In 1932, at age 69, he was elected United States senator from California and served until 1938.

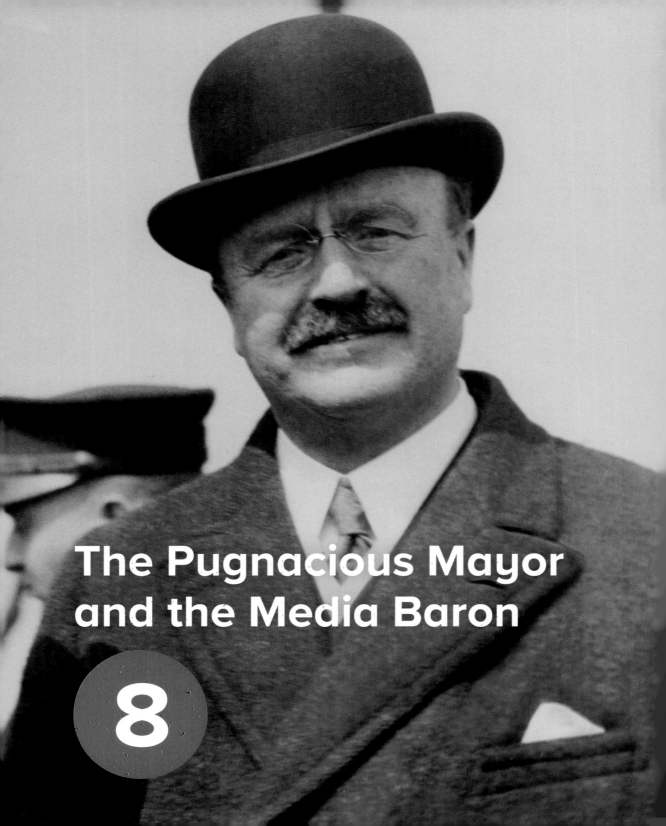

The Pugnacious Mayor and the Media Baron

8

John Hylan got the IND built, seemingly out of spite.

In the 1920s, the progressives who had clamored for a municipally owned and operated subway triumphed, and the city began work on the third and last great expansion of its rapid transit network, the Independent Subway System, or IND.

The man most responsible for making a city-owned subway a reality was John Francis Hylan, the city's bullheaded mayor from 1918 to 1925. Hylan had a visceral hatred of the transit companies and pressed relentlessly to "recapture" the private lines and build a system of the city's own. His biggest backer was the publishing magnate William Randolph Hearst, whose newspapers had crusaded for city ownership even before the first line opened in 1904.

Unlike most of the mayors, businessmen, and financiers who shaped the subway in its early years, Hylan (1868–1936) had a hardscrabble upbringing. He dropped out of school at an early age to help his family on their struggling Hudson Valley farm. In 1887, at 19, he made his way to Brooklyn and hired on to lay tracks on an elevated line that was later absorbed into the BRT. Eventually he rose to become a motorman, driving trains. In his spare time he completed his basic schooling and went on to study law in the mornings before heading to work on the el.

His transit career came to an abrupt end in 1897 when he nearly ran over a senior supervisor with his train. The supervisor, named Barton, emerged from a signal tower and crossed the elevated tracks just as Hylan was rounding a bend. Barton leapt safely out of the way, but he summoned Hylan the next day and fired him. The company said Hylan had been going too fast. Hylan retorted that Barton was getting on in years and was careless. Whatever the truth, it is hard not to think Hylan's animus toward the private companies didn't trace at least partly to this incident.

Hylan had nearly earned his law degree when he was fired, and later that year he set up his own law office. He joined the Brooklyn Democratic Party, where he quickly made valuable contacts, which won him a spot on the bench in 1906. His vocal criticism of the Dual Contracts deal with the IRT and BMT and his role as a leader in a group devoted to putting the IRT and BRT in public hands brought him to Hearst's attention.

Like Hylan, Hearst (1863–1951) was an outsider among New York's elites. He was the heir to a great fortune, but his father was a rough-edged mining engineer who struck it rich. The son used his inheritance to buy the *New York American* and the *New York Evening Journal* and moved from California to New York in 1894 to oversee them. In an era when economic power was rapidly being concentrated in the hands of powerful industrial and railroad monopolists, Hearst staked out a position on the left wing of the Democratic Party and used his growing nationwide newspaper chain to attack the new moguls. Armed with skilled cartoonists, and unburdened by any great concern for fairness or balance, Hearst's New York papers pummeled the subway companies year after year, accusing them of victimizing the city and passengers.

Hearst served two terms in Congress and ran for mayor (twice), governor, and president (twice). When he wasn't running himself, he was pulling strings in the Democratic Party in support of other progressives. That repeatedly

THE TRUST THAT TREATS
THE PEOPLE LIKE SWINE

Transit company executives were demonized by the cartoonists at Hearst's newspapers.

pitted him against August Belmont Jr., who was an influential player in the business-friendly wing of the party. In 1904, Belmont donated $250,000— equivalent to more than $7 million today—to Hearst's opponent for the presidential nomination. So it wasn't just transit where the men clashed. They had fundamentally different visions for the nation.

Hearst engineered Hylan's nomination as the Democratic candidate for mayor in 1917, after party bosses split over two other candidates. Hylan won the election on a platform of protecting the little guy against the "traction interests" (i.e., the IRT and the BRT), taking control of the subways for the city, and preserving the five-cent fare. Hylan freely acknowledged his political debt to the publisher. He named a city ferry for him in 1923 and appointed the father of Hearst's mistress, Marion Davies, as a magistrate.

Hearst was instrumental in winning the Democratic mayoral nomination for Hylan in 1917 and ensuring his reelection in 1921. In this cartoon by Winsor McCay in one of Hearst's papers, Hylan is giving the "Traction Ring" nightmares. McCay created the highly successful Little Nemo comic strip.

In November 1918, early in Hylan's first term, a horrific train accident in Brooklyn provided him ammunition against the private companies. During a strike, a substitute motorman with little training rounded a corner too fast at Malbone Street near the Prospect Park Station (B, Q) and derailed his train. At least 93 passengers were killed and 200 more were injured as the cars' wooden sides splintered and the rear cars ran up over those in front.

Hylan rushed to the scene. The next day, utilizing an obscure city law, he named himself an investigative magistrate and began summoning witnesses to testify. Six weeks later, he ordered the arrest of five top BRT executives on manslaughter charges. In Hearst's papers, the mayor was heralded as the advocate of the victims against the wealthy corporate powers.

All five men and the motorman, who was charged separately, were ultimately acquitted or had their charges dropped, but Hylan's bullying tactics set the tone for all his dealings with the transit companies.

He blocked the completion of parts of the BRT's Dual Contracts lines, which disrupted its operations and reduced its revenue. He threatened to throw IRT President Frank Hedley in jail, alleging that Hedley colluded with union leaders to raise wages so the IRT could seek a fare increase. In 1922, he even launched an investigation of working conditions in the Pennsylvania coal mines that supplied the IRT.

Like other progressives, Hylan regularly took aim at "international bankers" and "America's secret dynastic rulers," but he also had his more personal grievances, grousing, for instance, that the newspapers didn't print his notoriously soporific speeches in full.

Perhaps inevitably, Hylan alienated other Democrats. In 1924, Governor Al Smith, a fellow progressive, appointed a judge to investigate the incessant squabbles between Hylan and the state-controlled Transit Commission created in 1920—a calculated move to undercut Hylan going into the 1925 mayoral election. The judge delivered the desired conclusions, finding that Hylan was the chief reason no new lines had been commenced since 1913. It was the beginning of the end of Hylan's political career.

Though Hylan always portrayed the IRT and BRT as profiteers, by the time he took office in 1918, their profits had largely evaporated, victims of a fierce round of inflation set off by the American entry into World War I in 1917. The coal that fueled their power plants doubled in price between 1917 and 1920, and steel prices tripled, driving up the cost of the new lines they had agreed to build for a fixed price.

Liabilities from the Malbone Street wreck pushed the BRT into bankruptcy at the end of 1918. The IRT started losing money in 1919 and soon stopped paying some creditors. In 1921 and 1922, it struck a deal with its bondholders to reduce its payments, and it staved off bankruptcy until 1932. Still, as the companies struggled to get out of the red in the early 1920s, Hylan was adamant that fares could not be increased, calling "the permanency of a five-cent fare" a "property right" and "the corner stone of the edifice which we call New York City."

Governor Al Smith was returned to office in 1920 promising to give the city control over rapid transit, but he was often at odds with Mayor Hylan.

Construction of the IND brought another round of disruptive construction for New Yorkers in the 1920s and 1930s. Church Street in Lower Manhattan had been excavated to the base of building foundations in this 1927 photo. Trucks and power equipment had replaced the mules and pickaxes used in the first decade of the century.

Tormenting the IRT and BRT was easy. Arranging for the city to build new lines was not. It wasn't until 1924, six years after Hylan was sworn in, that a compromise was reached in Albany that gave the city power to build new lines through a new Board of Transportation, appointed by the mayor. The state-controlled Transit Commission retained jurisdiction over the IRT and the BRT's successor, the Brooklyn–Manhattan Transit Corporation, or BMT. But the change was a great victory for Hylan and Hearst (see City Versus State, page 113).

It came with one large string attached, however. Any city-owned lines had to charge a "sustaining fare"—they had to break even—in three years. As a practical matter, that forced the city to build its lines in built-up areas where there would be lots of riders. In other words, mainly where the IRT and BMT already had lines. For Hylan, that wasn't a problem because "the IND was built by the city for the express purpose of siphoning riders away from the two other systems in order to ruin them and take them over," as the *New York Times* put it decades later. Besides, Hylan had opposed the idea of building lines to spur development in outlying areas. Over time, however, the routes dictated by the "sustaining fare" requirement would have a profound impact on the city's development.

In December 1924, the Hylan board set out plans for a new, third subway system. Unlike proposals from the state-controlled commissions, these lines would not be extensions of the IRT and BMT networks. To the contrary, the city's IND would be a system unto itself, and only a line along Queens Boulevard would pass through thinly settled areas. The rest of the new routes lay in Manhattan or parts of Brooklyn, Queens, and the Bronx that were already urbanized.

Three months later, Hylan broke ground for the first leg of the IND on March 25, 1925, at 123rd Street and St. Nicholas Avenue in Harlem, on what is now the A, B, C, and D lines. With typical flourish, he told that crowd that the work represented "the beginning of the emancipation of the people of the City of New York from the serfdom inflicted upon them by the most powerful financial and traction dictatorship ever encountered."

Over the next 15 years, the IND was built out almost exactly as originally planned. It consisted of the lines today designated by the letters A through G, from the Bronx through Midtown Manhattan along Sixth and Eighth Avenues, with a crosstown line under 53rd Street to Forest Hills, Queens, plus a line to the eastern edge of Brooklyn. In addition, there was a crosstown line from Queens to Brooklyn (G). But Hylan never had the opportunity to dedicate any of the lines. Shortly after the ceremonial shovel was planted at 123rd Street, Governor Smith and the Democratic Party dumped him in favor of another candidate for mayor.

The IND was as remarkable in its own way as the original IRT line had been. No expense was spared to make it by far the best of the three systems. All the new lines were entirely below ground. (In Brooklyn, the A and F lines came aboveground to connect with existing elevated lines.) Its platforms were longer and much wider to prevent overcrowding. Express lines ran nonstop for 66 blocks on the West Side, from 59th Street to 125th Street (A, D), and for 2.5 miles under Queens Boulevard (E, F). The improvements allowed the IND to move 50 percent more passengers per hour per track than the IRT.

Still, the IND never inspired the affection that the IRT and BMT did. There was not even a ceremony when the first leg opened in September 1932 along Eighth Avenue from Washington Heights to Lower Manhattan. By then the subway's novelty had worn off; aesthetics had taken a backseat to functionality. Instead of ornate wall tiling and terra-cotta plaques, IND stations had plain colored tiles that never inspired oohs and aahs.

Moreover, the city still suffers from Hylan's war on the private companies. The IND was deliberately built with no transfers to the IRT or BMT. Changing between lines of the three legacy systems remains awkward even now because they were built as competitors to one another.

Just as bad, the routes Hylan's board chose effectively ceded the outer edges of the city to the automobile,

The wide platforms of the IND can be seen in this photo taken in the new 207th Street station.

which by the 1920s was affordable for the common man. Gone was the vision of transit as an instrument for city development. Real estate developers, who were strong supporters of earlier subway expansions, lost their enthusiasm, fearing that property taxes would be raised if the city built more lines.

By enshrining the five-cent fare as a political right, Hylan ensured that there would be little investment in the IRT and BMT systems, or in new lines in the decades to follow. By the time fares were finally raised in 1948, the system had been starved of needed investment for years. The seeds of the subway's long downhill slide were sewn by Hylan and Hearst.

Q: How noisy is the subway?

A: On some subway platforms, noise levels can exceed 100 decibels, roughly the level of a jet 1,000 feet away, health researchers found in 2006. At that level, just a few minutes of exposure can cause hearing loss.

There are several sources of the loudest noises. Those deafening screeches in curves come from the flanges of the car wheels brushing against the edge of the rail. Another culprit is worn joints in the rail, where track sections are bolted together. Over time, the ends of each section of rail wear down, creating a dip in the rail where the sections meet. When trains hit those at speed, bam! Welded rail, with longer ribbons of rail welded rather than bolted together, reduces this form of noise. A third common noise is the thumping of a wheel that has worn flat on one surface from braking. At higher speeds, the thumping can be quite loud.

Transit Authority rules prohibit passengers from making noises louder than 85 decibels, the level of a kitchen blender.

CITY VERSUS STATE

◄━━━ ◄ ━━━►

City leaders have battled with Albany over control of transit since the 1800s.

Mutual suspicions between city and state leaders plagued the subway even in the 19th century. They account for the ever-changing succession of commissions, boards, and authorities in charge of city transit.

Often it was just partisan politics. The city historically has been dominated by Democrats, while Republicans often hold power in Albany. But some of the bitterest turf wars were between governors and mayors of the same party. Governor Al Smith and Mayor John Hylan, both progressive Democrats in the 1920s, loathed each other and fought over the subway. And there was no love lost between Governor Nelson Rockefeller

ABOVE: Relations between Mayor Bill de Blasio (left) and Governor Andrew Cuomo, both Democrats, were not always so cordial.

Governor Nelson Rockefeller (above) didn't get along well with his fellow liberal Republican, Mayor John Lindsay (opposite).

and Mayor John Lindsay, two liberal Republicans with national ambitions in the late 1960s and early 1970s. (Lindsay eventually became a Democrat.) More recently, the rivalry and animosity between Governor Andrew Cuomo and Mayor Bill de Blasio, both Democrats, has played out in part over the subway.

In the 19th century, state officials feared the rampant corruption of the city's Tammany Hall political machine. There was also concern the city would run up too much debt, so the state set caps on the city's debt, which curbed subway construction.

Starting in 1907, control became a political football. That year, the newly elected Republican governor Charles Evans Hughes created a state-controlled Public Service Commission (PSC) to replace the 1894 Board of Rapid Transit Commissioners, which had built the first line, because the board had been unable to build additional lines

and it was viewed as a pushover for the private operators. The PSC was in place when the Dual Contracts extensions were agreed to in 1913, an arrangement derided by many Democrats because it awarded the new lines to the private operators.

When Democratic governor Al Smith took office in 1919, he replaced Hughes's PSC with an Office of the Transit Construction Commissioner, and transferred to it some of the powers of the city's Board of Estimate, which had clashed repeatedly with the transit commissions. Although Smith named John Delaney, a Tammany Hall loyalist, to head the TCC, the effect was to shift some power to the state-appointed commissioner and away from Mayor Hylan, a Democrat.

The TCC was short-lived. After Republican Nathan Miller defeated Smith in 1920, Miller shut down the TCC and created a new, state-appointed Transit Commission, giving it the politically sensitive power to set fares. The city retained a veto over routes and any borrowing, but that was all. In another slap to Mayor Hylan, the governor appointed George McAneny, who negotiated the 1913 Dual Contracts as chairman—a man Hylan accused of being in the pocket of the private companies. Score another one for the state.

In 1922, Smith defeated Miller and returned as governor the next year, after promising to give the city control of transit. The Republican-controlled State Assembly refused to go along, however, and Smith and Hylan had to settle for a compromise. The city would form a Board of Transportation, appointed by the mayor, to oversee new routes, while the state-appointed Transit Commission retained control over the IRT and BMT lines, insulating them somewhat from Hylan, who had waged a campaign to take them over.

That was a net gain for the city, allowing Hylan to push forward with construction of the city-owned IND system. And, when the city bought the bankrupt IRT and BMT in 1940, under Republican mayor Fiorello La Guardia, the entire subway system came under the Board of Transportation.

In 1953, with the subways hemorrhaging money, the pendulum swung back. The Republican-controlled legislature and Republican governor Thomas Dewey created the New York City Transit Authority (Transit Authority, or TA) to take over the subway and city buses, and the city's Board of Transportation went out of business. The TA's mandate was to break even and, as a state authority, it had the power to borrow by issuing bonds, changes the Republicans hoped would make the TA more efficient and business-like. Control was 50-50: The five-person board was made up of two gubernatorial appointees and two from the mayor, with the fifth chosen by the first four.

But the losses continued and, in 1968, under Republican governor Nelson Rockefeller, a new entity was created: the Metropolitan Transportation Authority (MTA). It became the parent for the TA, the Long Island Railroad, the commuter rail lines to the north of the city (now known as Metro-North Railroad), and the Triborough Bridge and Tunnel Authority. The idea was that profits from bridge and tunnel tolls on the East River crossings would help offset losses on the rail operations.

The political result was to dilute the city's power over the subway because the surrounding counties were also represented on the MTA board. The city got to "recommend" only two of the MTA's nine directors, and the governor made the actual nominations, which then went to the state senate for approval. Today, with an expanded board, the city has four of 14 votes, the counties have four, while the governor gets six. Six is short of a majority, but enough to give the governor effective control.

BIGGER, BETTER, FASTER

The IND was loaded with engineering bells and whistles, and, because it was built with the expectation of many future extensions, it has extra capacity that isn't used.

- Queens Boulevard express trains (E, F) take a short cut via Northern Boulevard from Queensboro Plaza to Jackson Heights, while local trains take a longer path through Astoria on Steinway Street and Broadway. There is also a shortcut for express trains under Prospect Park between the Seventh Avenue and 15th Street stations (F, G).

- IND tunnels accommodate cars up to 75 feet, longer than the longest BMT cars, and turns had large radiuses so trains don't need to slow down as much.

- On Eighth Avenue in Manhattan (A, C, E) and at two places along the F and G lines in Brooklyn (at Bergen Street and between Seventh Avenue and Church Avenue), tracks run on two levels. The lower level on Eighth Avenue is abandoned south of 50th Street, but the TA announced in 2019 that it would reinstitute some express service on the F line using the lower level east of Seventh Avenue.

- The West Fourth Street station (A, B, C, D, E, F, M) boasts eight tracks on two levels with a mezzanine in between, and the grand junction at Hoyt-Schermerhorn in Downtown Brooklyn (A, C, G) had six tracks abreast, though two are no longer in service.

- Along Central Park West (A, B, C, D) and between Rockefeller Center and 42nd Street on Sixth Avenue (B, D, F, M), express and local tracks change places, from inside to out, twisting over each other between stations. Ride south from Rockefeller Center or north from 59th Street at the same time another train across the platform is leaving in the same direction, and you'll find that train and yours are in opposite positions by the next stop.

ABOVE: The IND's tunnels are wide enough to accomodate extra-long, 75-foot cars such as this R-46.

BENEATH THE STREETS

By the time the IND routes were completed in 1940, Downtown and Midtown Manhattan and Downtown Brooklyn were crisscrossed with lines threading over and under each other, and sometimes zigging and zagging where the path straight ahead was already taken by an earlier line—twists that you can't see on the official map.

Five trunk lines traverse Downtown Manhattan. The green loop is the original City Hall station, now used only by the 6 train reversing direction.

In Downtown Brooklyn, the red, green, and yellow IRT and BMT (2, 3, 4, 5, R) lines from Manhattan, built in the 1900s and 1910s, converge from the left edge of the diagram at the Court Street–Borough Hall station. The IRT and BMT routes then diverge before meeting up again at Atlantic Avenue–Barclays Center.

The blue and orange IND tracks that enter from the upper left (A, C, F) came later and had to be built beneath the earlier lines.

The yellow and orange lines running diagonally from upper left are the B, D, N, and Q lines, using the old BMT tracks from the Manhattan Bridge. Some unused tracks are not shown.

Between 42nd Street and Central Park, five trunk lines with 20 tracks are squeezed between Lexington and Eighth avenues, all invisible to passersby on the street. The junctions on 53rd Street at Sixth and Eighth avenues are particularly complex, with trains branching in three directions at Sixth Avenue.

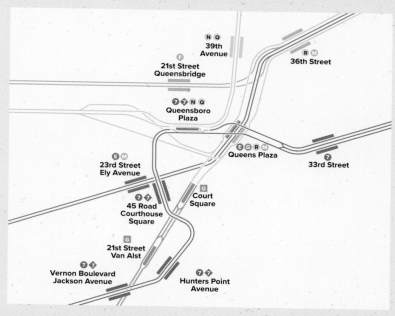

Long Island City is host to a complex tangle of overlapping lines, transfer points, and junctions. Three underground lines from Manhattan—the 53rd Street tunnel (E, M), a branch of the 60th Street tunnel (R), and the 63rd Street tunnel (F)—plus the crosstown IND line (G) all feed into the Queens Boulevard trunk line within a few blocks of one another. Overhead, the elevated Flushing (7) and Astoria (N, Q) lines meet across the platform high above the street at the Queensboro Plaza station.

Unification and Demolition

9

After the city took control of the private lines, it tore down elevated lines, and new construction largely ceased.

OPPOSITE: The Second Avenue elevated line was demolished between 1940 and 1942, with no replacement. This 1942 photo shows the view south from 13th Street on Second Avenue. Scrap steel was in high demand in World War II.

The IRT's bankruptcy receiver hands over the subway company to Mayor La Guardia.

In 1940, under Mayor Fiorello La Guardia, the city finally achieved complete control of the subway, the goal of progressives for four decades. That year also marked the last major expansion of the city's underground transit system. Since then, "the system has been largely frozen in time."

La Guardia, a feisty, five-foot-two-inch fireplug of a man, shared many of the populist views of his predecessor, John Hylan, including a desire to unite all three subway systems under city control. But unlike the dour Hylan, who droned on in his speeches and alienated allies, La Guardia was a stirring speaker who pounded lecterns, shouting until his voice broke and his hair was mussed. He could also turn on the charm, in person and on the radio. He famously read comics over the air during a newspaper strike in 1945.

A six-term Republican congressman before he ran for mayor, he chose the party as a young man because he despised the corruption of the Democratic Tammany Hall machine, and as an Italian-American, he figured he didn't have much of a future in Irish-dominated Tammany circles.

When La Guardia took office in January 1934, the Eighth Avenue IND line (A, C, E) had opened, and the rest of the IND was under construction, but the city was so strapped financially from the Depression that La Guardia tapped the federal government to help pay for the IND. Moreover, the city system faced a state-imposed deadline to break even or raise fares, and it was losing money.

The private companies were faring no better. The BMT had been in receivership since 1918 and the IRT since 1932. They had rarely generated any profits to share with the city under the Dual Contracts, and IRT ridership fell 19 percent during the Depression. The drop was 12 percent on the BMT. Even before he was sworn in, La Guardia had begun negotiations to acquire the IRT and BMT, and he reached a deal with them in 1935. By combining the three operations, La Guardia hoped to cut overhead and break even.

Mayor La Guardia cuts the ceremonial tape to open the Sixth Avenue IND line at 34th Street–Herald Square (B, D, F, M) in December 1940.

The Sixth Avenue elevated line is dismantled at 30th Street while subway construction continues next to it, circa 1939.

In 1937, an election year, the Transit Commission nixed the agreement La Guardia had reached in late 1935 to buy the IRT and BMT for a combined $431 million, saying the price was too high. The state-controlled commission by then was stocked with Democrats, who didn't want to ratify a major achievement for La Guardia in an election year. La Guardia came out the winner anyway. Not only was he reelected in a landslide, but the companies' financial situation deteriorated, so when new terms were hammered out in 1939, the price was just $346 million, and this time the companies' streetcar and bus assets were thrown in, in the bargain.

The city took possession of the IRT and BMT in June 1940. For the first time, it was in control of virtually all the transit within its borders. La Guardia, who never missed a chance to dedicate a monument or cut a ribbon, posed at the controls of the last BMT train to run through Times Square on the eve of unification.

His next order of business was to demolish the elevated lines made redundant by the new IND underground lines. That reduced operating costs and opened up el-blighted streets to sunlight.

The Sixth Avenue el had already come down in 1939 to make way for the Sixth Avenue IND subway (B, D, F, M), which opened in early 1940. Later in 1940, Manhattan's Ninth Avenue el was disassembled, since the IND Eighth Avenue subway (A, B, C, D, E) was running a block away.

In Brooklyn, the elevated structure along Fulton Street was removed from downtown all the way to Rockaway Boulevard because the new IND (A, C) traversed the same route. Likewise, the el from Park Slope to Bay Ridge on Fifth and Third Avenues came down, since the Fourth Avenue subway (D, N, R) was just a block away.

The Second Avenue el in Manhattan was demolished, too, beginning in 1940, despite the fact that there was no money to build a replacement. When the nearby Third Avenue el was eliminated in 1955, the East Side, which had three lines in 1940, was left with just one: the overtaxed IRT subway along Lexington and Park Avenues (see chapter 16).

More els came down over the following three decades, but most were lightly used and were replaced by buses or nearby subways.

In 1948, the city finally made the unpopular decision to raise the subway fare to 10 cents, but that didn't even cover the cost of deferred repairs, let alone new lines. Hence, only a few, relatively modest additions have been made to the system in the 80 years since unification, two of them existing rail lines that were repurposed:

1941 ↘
Dyre Avenue line.
The city bought the defunct New York, Westchester & Boston railroad in the Bronx and made it the Dyre Avenue line (5) of the IRT north from 180th Street.

1946–1956 ↘
Fulton Street extension.
Brooklyn's Fulton Street IND line (A, C) was extended to Euclid Avenue and then to Lefferts Boulevard in Queens, construction that had been deferred due to World War II.

1955 ↘
60th Street Connection.

A connection was built from the 60th Street BMT tunnel (N, R, W) that allowed trains to run to the Queens Boulevard IND line instead of to Astoria (R).

1956 ↘
Far Rockaway line.

The city acquired an abandoned Long Island Railroad line across Jamaica Bay to Far Rockaway and incorporated it into the IND (A).

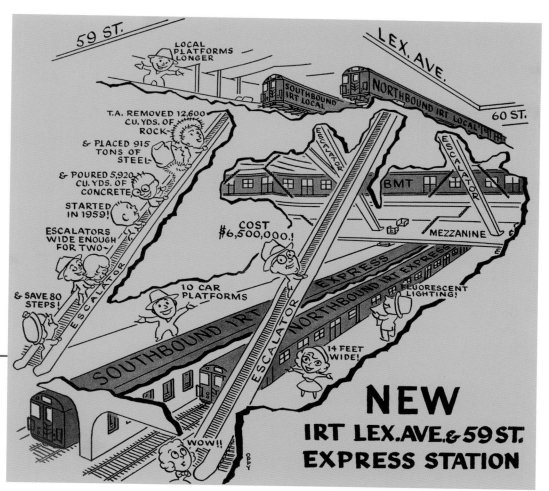

A new express stop at 59th Street and Lexington Avenue (4, 5), opened in 1962, was carved out of rock. The express tracks were already there, but they ran far below the local station (6) because they had to pass beneath the BMT line under 60th Street (N, R, W). Long stairs and escalators connect the express and local platforms for the IRT station.

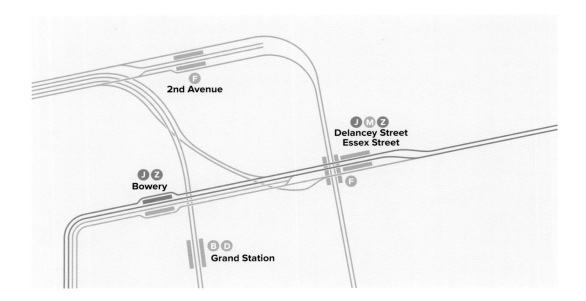

1967 ↘

Sixth Avenue express tracks.

The original 1940 Sixth Avenue subway
had express tracks only as far south as 34th
Street. Below that, the Hudson & Manhattan (now PATH) tracks ran up the center of
Sixth Avenue, blocking the IND's path. (The
uptown and downtown local IND tracks
run in separate tunnels on either side of the
H&M trackway.) It took six years of work
in the 1960s, and a great deal of dynamite,
tunneling at depths up to 80 feet, to take
the express tracks (B, D) south to West
Fourth Street. The roof of the express tunnel is 28 feet below the H&M at points. The
new tracks were essential once the Chrystie
Street Connection opened the same year,
sending more trains up Sixth Avenue.

1967 ↘

Chrystie Street Connection.

A few short links on the Lower East Side
had an enormous impact on the subway
system, expanding capacity and providing
much better service from Brooklyn to Midtown Manhattan. New tunnels and switches
allowed trains from the Manhattan and
Williamsburg Bridges, which previously ran
south to City Hall and Wall Street or across
Canal Street, to flow across East Houston
Street and then up Sixth Avenue. The links
merged the BMT and IND systems, allowing
lines that begin on former BMT tracks in
one borough to end on IND rails in another.

The new connection also shaved more
than two hours off the record for traveling
the entire subway system, to less than 22
hours, Transit Authority officials later said.

1988 ↘

Archer Avenue (Queens) extension.

The Queens Boulevard line sprouted a three-station branch at its eastern end, bringing the E to a new terminus at Jamaica Center–Archer Avenue. In addition, the Jamaica line (J, Z) was extended to the same end point.

1989 ↘

63rd Street tunnel.

Construction on this branch under the East River began in 1969 but was halted during the city's financial crisis in 1975. When it opened, the line dead-ended in Long Island City, Queens, and carried few passengers.

Extra trackways were included under 63rd Street for the Second Avenue line (Q), which began using them in 2017. Eventually, Long Island Railroad trains will run through a lower deck in the East River portion of the tunnel that has been sitting unused. That line, known as East Side Access, will carry Long Island commuters to Grand Central.

2001 ↘

Queens Plaza Connection.

The 63rd Street line (F) was extended a few blocks from its dead end in Long Island City to a junction with the other Queens Boulevard lines. That created a fourth through line from Queens to Midtown and significantly increased capacity on the Queens Boulevard line.

2015 ↘

Flushing Line extension to Hudson Yards.

The Flushing line (7) was stretched from Times Square to 10th Avenue and 34th Street, providing subway service to the Javits Convention Center and the Hudson Yards office and residential development. This was a short but technically challenging project. West of Times Square, the line dives down a steep grade so it can pass under the unused lower level of the Eighth Avenue subway and then under the mouth of the Lincoln Tunnel. As a result, the new station is 125 feet below ground.

2017 ↘

Second Avenue subway.

The first three stations of the long-promised Second Avenue subway opened on New Year's Day 2017, adding badly needed service for Manhattan's Upper East Side (see chapter 16).

MEET MISS SUBWAYS

For 35 years, women competed to get their faces before weary straphangers.

It began as a plan to advertise ads. It quickly became part of New York lore.

The company that sold ads on trains came up with the idea in 1941. Each month, a pretty young woman would be named Miss Subways. The idea was to draw attention to the fact that millions of passengers read ads on their commutes every week, and it would "increase eye traffic for adjoining ads," in the words of one of the men who ran the contest for years.

It worked. The contest was a hit and lasted into the 1970s, adapting along the way to changing cultural expectations.

Girls had to be pretty and models of feminine virtue, as it was understood at the time. The ad company worked with John Robert Powers, who ran a modeling agency and picked the girls for the first two decades. He and his scouts spotted candidates

ABOVE: While many winners listed career ambitions, in the 1940s and 1950s, a number of Miss Subways preferred marriage instead. • **OPPOSITE:** A bench full of Miss Subways turned out for a 1968 onboard party to celebrate the opening of the 57th Street station on Sixth Avenue, a terminus for the F train.

around the city and picked others from submissions. One was a manicurist who did Powers's nails at the Waldorf Astoria Hotel.

A few salient facts were included on the placards for the winners, highlighting their talents, hobbies, and ambitions—which often included finding a man. Enid Berkowitz, a Hunter College art student who won in July 1946, was billed as "plugging for a B.A. but would settle for M.R.S." Riders learned that Terry Flannigan's "dream dish" was stuffed cabbage. As the contest gained popularity, brothers, boyfriends, and coworkers submitted nominations, as did some women themselves.

Meet *Miss Subways* Judith Burgess

She's pretty as a picture...and even more personable in person.

While acquiring an accounting degree at N.Y.C. Community College, Judith became a section head at Morgan Guaranty Trust Company. She has a reputation for expertise in the figuration of commissions in stocks and bonds.

Her own figure merited modeling in two fashion shows. Other interests: Judith plays piano; likes tennis, skiing and bowling.

Miss Subways was "supposed to look like the girl next door." Powers wanted "no 'glamor gal types or handpainted masterpieces.'"

After 1963, the public had a role, voting on six finalists chosen by the ad agency. With the chance to swing the vote, one candidate, Marcia Kilpatrick, pulled out all the stops, handing out postcard ballots to fellow union members and canvassing along her policeman father's beat.

The contest was such a hit by 1944 that it was the basis for a hit Broadway musical, *On the Town*, with music by Leonard Bernstein. There a sailor on shore leave falls for that month's Miss Turnstiles after seeing her picture on the subway. The musical made fun of the clean-cut image the Miss Subways campaign cultivated. In the play, Miss Turnstiles was a sideshow dancer at Coney Island, who was described as "a home-loving type who loves to go out night-clubbing; her heart belongs to the Navy, but she loves the Army." Gene Kelly, who played the sailor-protagonist in the 1949 film version, coos when he reads the part about the Navy.

Real-life men fell for real-life contest winners, too. An admirer sent Ruth Ericsson, a manicurist, "an orchid every day for six months." A bakery truck driver, besotted with another winner, delivered to her an enormous lemon meringue pie.

Miss Subways was a telling barometer of social attitudes. A year into the contest, in 1942, black New Yorkers began lobbying for a black woman to be chosen. Powers made no concessions. It would be another six years before there was a black Miss Subways, and then only after black leaders buttonholed the new mayor, William O'Dwyer, and the Board of Transportation. In April 1948, Thelma Porter, a Brooklyn College student, was picked. Her placard didn't mention that she was active in the National Association for the Advancement of Colored People. Civil rights leaders William Hastie and

Thurgood Marshall, the future Supreme Court justice, showed up at a reception to celebrate her selection.

It was a sign of change. A year earlier, Jackie Robinson broke the color barrier in baseball, and three months after Porter's selection, President Harry Truman ordered the racial integration of the armed forces, which had been segregated. Miss Subways actually was ahead of the curve in beauty contests. There was no black contestant in the Miss America Pageant until 1970, and the first black Miss America wasn't crowned until 1983.

By the late 1960s, Miss Subways was an anachronism. The award, which had gone bimonthly in 1952, was switched to semiannual in 1974. The organizers tried to stay abreast of the times, featuring more women with substantial achievements. Copywriters even tried to sound hip, calling Josephine Lazzaro, one of the last Miss Subways, a "Now Yorker" and an "altogether person."

But the times, and the subway, had changed, and the whole idea seemed incongruous as the city decayed, cars were covered with graffiti, and Miss Subways posters were frequently defaced. In a 1976 piece headlined "Token Women," *New York Magazine* suggested it was time to call it quits: "Miss Subways beams down on eight purse-snatchings a day. Obscenities bloom from her lips, sex organs from her ears."

In the hit Broadway musical and later movie *On the Town*, a sailor on shore leave falls for the Miss Turnstiles he sees in the subway. • **OPPOSITE:** The first black Miss Subways, Thelma Porter, won the title in 1948 after black community leaders pressed for the Board of Transportation to break the color barrier, but most of the winners for the remaining 26 years of the contest were white. Judith Burgess was named in 1972.

ROLLING STOCK

One legacy of the three original, competing transit systems is that subway cars come in two basic sizes: short and narrow (A Division, formerly the IRT) and long and wide (B Division, the former BMT and IND lines). Or, depending on how you categorize them, short, medium, and long. Division A cars are 51 feet long and eight feet, nine inches wide. They have three pairs of doors to a side. Division B cars range from 60 to 75 feet long and are 10 feet wide, with four sets of doors on each side.

The BMT's cars were 60 to 67 feet long. The IRT's were shorter and narrower so they could pass through tight turns and loops. By the time the IND was begun in the 1920s, the emphasis was on capacity and higher speeds, so its tunnels were built for cars longer than any that existed at the time. Beginning in the 1970s, 75-foot cars were ordered for those lines on the theory that fewer cars for a given passenger capacity would lower maintenance costs. Since 2000, the Transit Authority has ordered only 60-foot cars for the lettered lines. One reason: A 600-foot train of ten 60-foot cars has about the same capacity as a 600-foot train made up of eight 75-foot cars, but there are 40 doorways on each side of the 10-car train versus 32 on an eight-car train. More doors means faster loading and unloading at busy hours. In addition, the 60-foot cars can be used on any B division line. Sharp curves prevent 75-foot trains from running on some former BMT lines.

CLOCKWISE FROM TOP: In the 2000s, 2,800 retired car shells were dumped, or "reefed," along the Atlantic seaboard from New Jersey to South Carolina. • On the ocean floor, they protect against shoreline erosion and attract sea life. Black bass, flounder, and blue mussels are particularly fond of them. • The oldest cars running in 2020 are model R-32s built by the Budd Company in 1964–1965, easily identified by their corrugated sides. They outlasted many models built later. • **OPPOSITE:** Neatly stacked shells of retired R-32 cars on a barge pass through the Harlem Ship Canal in 2008, headed for the bottom of the Atlantic.

Since 2000, cars for both divisions have featured wider doorways. Benches are set back a few inches from the door so passengers standing in the doorways won't block (as much of) the path.

The newer cars incorporate computer-controlled airbag suspension in place of springs, and more efficient alternating current (AC) motors instead of direct current (DC) motors, which were standard since the earliest trolleys. The AC motors allow regenerative braking. When the brakes are applied, the motors become generators, creating additional drag and producing power that is returned to the third rail.

KNOW YOUR SUBWAY CARS

Subway rolling stock has evolved with technology and changing aesthetics. The cars for Division A (the numbered lines), a sampling of which are shown on this page, have always been 50 feet long. Cars for Division B (the lettered lines), opposite, have ranged from 60 to 75 feet, and longer in the case of some articulated trainsets. The dates indicate each model's years in subway service.

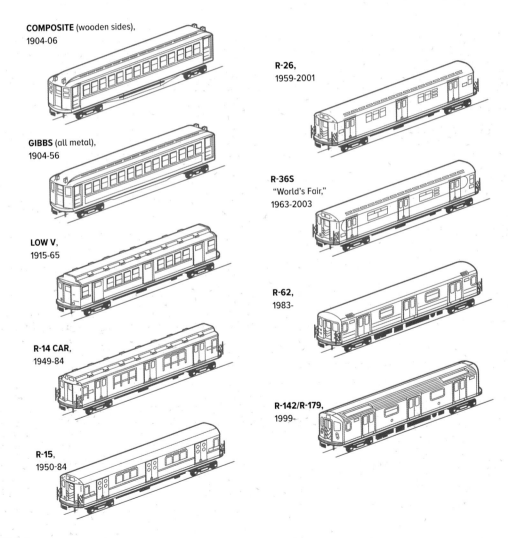

COMPOSITE (wooden sides), 1904-06

GIBBS (all metal), 1904-56

LOW V, 1915-65

R-14 CAR, 1949-84

R-15, 1950-84

R-26, 1959-2001

R-36S "World's Fair," 1963-2003

R-62, 1983-

R-142/R-179, 1999-

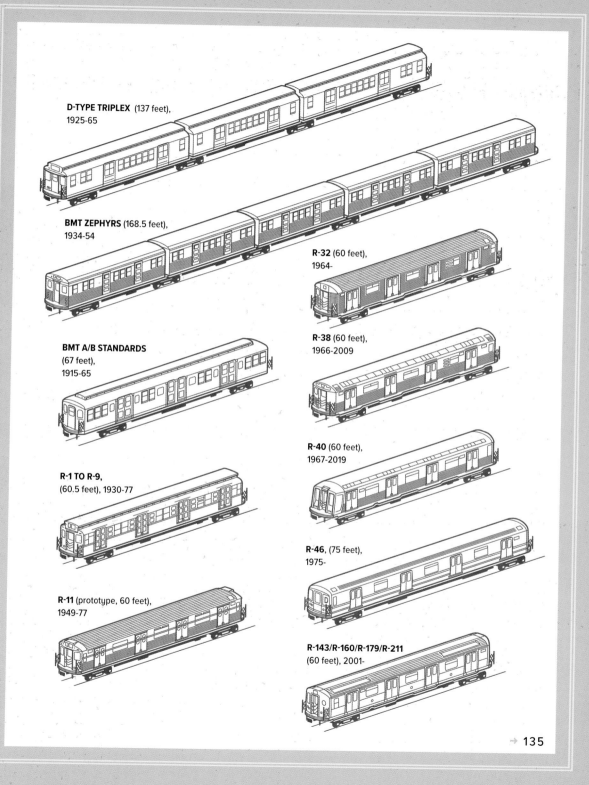

D-TYPE TRIPLEX (137 feet), 1925-65

BMT ZEPHYRS (168.5 feet), 1934-54

R-32 (60 feet), 1964-

BMT A/B STANDARDS (67 feet), 1915-65

R-38 (60 feet), 1966-2009

R-1 TO R-9, (60.5 feet), 1930-77

R-40 (60 feet), 1967-2019

R-46, (75 feet), 1975-

R-11 (prototype, 60 feet), 1949-77

R-143/R-160/R-179/R-211 (60 feet), 2001-

How New Lines Shaped the City

10

WESTCHESTER CONN

YONKERS

STAMFORD

MOUNT VERNON

GREENWICH

PORT CHESTER

RYE

MAMARONECK

LARCHMONT

NEW ROCHELLE

THE BRONX

PELHAM MANOR

FT. SLOCUM
DAVIDS ID.

EXECUTION ROCKS
LIGHT HOUSE

CITY ISLAND

HART ID.

SANDS POINT LIGHT

GLEN

MANHASSET NECK

HEMPSTEAD

THROGG'S NECK

STEPPING STONE LIGHT

PORT WASHINGTON

PORT MORRIS

N. BROTHER I.

S. BROTHER I.

RIKER'S ISLAND

LONG ISLAND

FT. TOTTEN

MANHASSET BAY

RANDALL'S ISLAND

SUNKEN MEADOW

GREAT NECK

WARD'S ISLAND

COLLEGE POINT

LITTLE NECK BAY

BLACKWELL'S

WHITESTONE

DOUGLASTON

FLUSHING

BAYSIDE

CORONA

ELMHURST

NEWTOWN

QUEENS

GLENDALE

RICHMOND HILL

JAMAICA

WILLIAMSBURG BRIDGE

WOODHAVEN

NAVY YARD

BROOKLYN

BEDLOES ID.
STATUE OF LIBERTY

CASTLE WILLIAM
COLUMBUS
GOVERNORS

BIRDS EYE VIEW

New transit routes helped develop outlying areas, but things didn't always turn out as expected.

The subways were intended to reshape the city— to break up the slums and make it easier to commute from outer neighborhoods to the industrial and business centers of Manhattan and Brooklyn. And they did. But market forces produced a cityscape quite unlike what reformers hoped for, and real estate speculators were sometimes caught by surprise when lines they had counted on didn't materialize. It was all part of the symbiotic relationship between transit and real estate in New York.

Manhattan's population peaked in 1910 at more than 2.3 million, nearly half again as many people as there are today. Nearly 600,000 immigrants, mostly Eastern and Southern European, were packed into the Lower East Side, the most densely populated area on earth at the time. Across the island and uptown, San Juan Hill, west of Columbus Circle, had emerged as a dense, largely black and Puerto Rican slum.

Successively tighter building codes improved the ventilation and sanitary facilities in the tenement apartments where the poor lived, but the laws did nothing to reduce density. As the population rose, landlords simply built six-floor walk-up apartment houses to the new standards instead of four-floor ones. As one advocate for the poor wrote:

> Conditions are uncivilized in those sections. Cheap rapid transit is the solution to the problem of the slums. The City will become a civilized city just in proportion as it shall provide adequate transit.

Into the 1910s, much of Queens, southeast Brooklyn, and eastern areas of the Bronx remained rural, as this 1909 bird's-eye view shows. The Inwood section at the northern tip of Manhattan was also unexploited. The urbanized strands in central and eastern Queens lay along the Long Island Railroad's lines.

Reformers imagined workers commuting from their own houses with gardens, where the air was clean. The wealthy, meanwhile, felt that overcrowding had to be addressed in order to integrate the immigrants into American society—and to head off socialism and class warfare.

The elevated lines of the late 1800s were supposed to help, but they were simply too slow. As the population mushroomed and spread north in Manhattan, the newly developed areas also became densely settled. Development simply outran the transportation system. The new areas reached by transit were never enough to satisfy demand, so land prices rose sharply. In the Bronx, as transit improved from 1904 to 1916, the price of lots in developed neighborhoods rose tenfold.

For the real estate industry, this was a golden opportunity. When it comes to development, "subways are to New York what water is to the West."

Transit-driven development did not occur overnight. A decade after the Ninth Avenue el was built along what we now call Columbus Avenue in 1879, Columbus and Amsterdam Avenues were lined with apartment buildings and shops, but there were still many empty lots on the side streets and a backlog of unsold brownstone town houses. Henry Morgenthau, a real estate speculator, was convinced the market would pick up, and he snapped up 24 adjacent lots on West 74th and West 75th Streets at auction in 1888. Inspecting the land after his purchase, he was shouted at by two bird hunters. "Don't you see our traps?" one said to Morgenthau.

The bird hunters' days were numbered. Morgenthau soon sold the lots at a healthy profit, and developers filled those blocks with town houses, most of which remain to this day.

When planning for a subway progressed in the early 1890s, a line up Broadway to the northern parts of Manhattan was settled early on. Based on that, Morgenthau placed a huge bet on Washington Heights. In 1891, he paid $300,000 for 16 square blocks along 181st Street. At the time, it was the hinterlands, but he expected it would become a business corridor because it was linked by a bridge and trolley line to the Bronx. A few months later, he sold it all in parcels at auction, raking in $780,000, a 160 percent profit on the money he and his investors had put up.

Henry Morgenthau bought up land in northern Manhattan and the Bronx where subway lines were planned, then sold plots to developers. Morgenthau went on to serve as American ambassador to the Ottoman Empire during World War I.

Morgenthau was smart to sell when he did. John Reilly, a former city registrar who bought up all the lots on one side of St. Nicholas Avenue at 181st Street in the auction, gleefully reported to Morgenthau afterward that he had obtained inside information that the tracks would run under St. Nicholas and that a station would be built at 181st. He was right, but with all the squabbling over routes and financing, it was another 15 years before the station opened.

As the IRT neared completion in 1904, Morgenthau shifted his sights northward. He was "astonished to find that there had been no activity in anticipation" of the subway in some areas, so he bought 2,500 lots in the Bronx, the Dyckman-Inwood areas in Manhattan, and Washington Heights.

An even bigger land speculator was Charles T. Barney, who headed the Knickerbocker Trust Company, one of the city's biggest banks, and was an early investor in the IRT. Like Morgenthau, he saw opportunity in the subway. Before it was built, Broadway on the Upper West Side was littered with empty lots, and coal and lumber yards. Barney raised $7 million from investors, the equivalent of about $180 million today, to buy land ahead of the subway. He acquired the four then-vacant corners around the 86th Street station, as well as chunks of Washington Heights, Inwood, and the Kingsbridge section in the southwest Bronx.

In February 1904, as opening day neared, Barney offloaded 150 lots between 135th and 137th Streets. The week the subway opened, his group sold another $1.25 million of lots in Washington Heights acquired in 1902. The Belnord, the world's largest apartment building when it opened in 1908, occupies an entire city block on the northeast corner of West 86th Street and Broadway once owned by Barney.

Like many New Yorkers, Barney was in favor of the subway so long as it wasn't built right outside his front door. As it happened, Barney lived in a town house on Fourth Avenue (now Park Avenue) along the path of the first line, and he sued the IRT, seeking a court order to stop the work, arguing that the digging came too close to the foundation of his home. A judge denied his request, but Barney was right. The front of his house was undermined when the ground subsided along the tunnel in 1903. By then he had resigned from the IRT board.

Charles T. Barney made a fortune buying up land and parceling it out to builders as new subway lines were built.

(Barney came to a strange end three years later. In November 1907, a few weeks after a run on the Knickerbocker Bank led to Barney's ouster there, he shot himself in the abdomen at his home. He was still standing when his wife came running to his room. She called the doctor. Barney, fully alert, summoned his lawyers to draft a new will and gave instructions on business matters from bed. He died a few hours later as his doctors were patching him up, still at home. His wife said he had been depressed, and it was ruled a suicide.)

In economic terms, Morgenthau and Barney were capturing the value that the subway created. Those economics dramatically shaped the city that grew up around the new rail lines. As land prices shot up, builders couldn't afford to construct houses. Even apartment buildings with generous gardens were hard to justify. So, instead of the green, suburban areas reformers imagined, by 1910 Washington Heights, Inwood, and the Bronx areas near the line were covered with tenement apartments. Better tenements than on the Lower East Side, to be sure, but not the idyllic, leafy homes many had hoped for.

Real estate investors also shaped development in Brooklyn and Queens when the Dual Contracts and IND lines opened up the outer parts of those boroughs beginning in the mid-1910s, but development took different forms there.

Rather than a rush of small transactions and construction shortly before and after the lines opened, big developers such as the Queensboro Corporation and Wood, Harmon & Company bought great blocks of land, then built and marketed the homes themselves. Wood, Harmon shelled out $4 million for undeveloped property in Brooklyn through 1909 as plans were being laid for new lines, and it claimed to control 20 percent of Brooklyn's available land, much of which was still rural at the time. The companies aggressively advertised their offerings, stressing their public transit connections.

Under the Dual Contracts, the IRT and BMT were forced to invest in lines in some areas where there would be no riders at first in order to win lucrative routes through the core areas of Brooklyn and Manhattan. Photos of the new lines vividly show the Transit Commission's "build it and they will come" approach. The vast expanses tapped by those lines kept land prices low enough that developers could make a profit putting up single- and two-family homes in these neighborhoods. And where there was more concentrated apartment construction, it was a bit closer to the bucolic vision of the social reformers. The Queensboro Corporation's 350-acre Jackson Heights development was a model. After the Flushing line reached the area in 1917, the company began

BAY SIDE PARK

3D WARD, BOROUGH OF QUEENS, NEW YORK CITY.

PROPERTY OF THE

NORTH SHORE REALTY CO.

OFFICES ON 5TH AVE. AT 25TH ST.. ENTRANCE 1122 BROADWAY.
NEW YORK.

The North Shore Realty Company promoted its development in Bayside, Queens, in 1915, when it was still expected that the Flushing IRT line (7) would extend east from Downtown Flushing to this area.

building cooperative apartment blocks that formed walls around large, private gardens for residents. In ads, the company played up the 22-minute commute to Grand Central.

Things didn't always play out according to plan for the developers, however. Wood, Harmon invested heavily along Utica Avenue in Brooklyn in hopes of a line that never came (see chapter 11). Similarly, in Bayside, at the far northeast corner of Queens, the North Shore Realty Company built homes when the IRT's Flushing line (7) was expected to reach there. Instead, the line never went east of Downtown Flushing, well short of the homes.

In distant parts of the outer boroughs, land was cheap enough that developers could afford to construct single- and two-family homes such as these in Bensonhurst, rather than apartment blocks. • RIGHT: Sunnyside, Queens, was largely undeveloped when the Flushing line was constructed in 1914. Steel plates can be seen on the ground at the intersection of Gosman Street, later renamed 48th Street (foreground running left to right), and Queens Boulevard (at the right), with a portion of the new elevated structure already erected in the upper left on Roosevelt Avenue.

Even worse was the situation in Staten Island, where Wood, Harmon bought land and began touting its lots in 1912 based on the prospect of a subway line to Manhattan via Brooklyn. The route was first mooted the year before, and resurfaced repeatedly through the 1920s, but it was never built (see chapter 11).

By the time the main IND lines were completed in the Bronx, Queens, and Brooklyn in 1940, the subway had succeeded in mitigating the worst of the overcrowding in Manhattan. The city's total population rose 56 percent from 1910 to 1940, but Manhattan's fell 19 percent, and the most crowded neighborhoods, such as the Lower East Side and East Harlem, saw bigger drops. The population of Williamsburg, Brooklyn, jammed in 1910 with poor Jews and other immigrants who spilled across the East River from the Lower East Side, fell by a quarter.

Meanwhile, the areas around the new subway lines miles from the center of the city saw four-, five-, and six-fold population increases, and many of those areas had single- and two-family homes—as reformers had hoped.

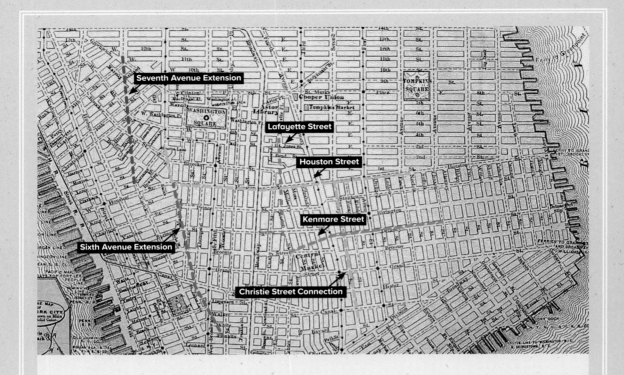

Seventh Avenue Extension

Lafayette Street

Houston Street

Kenmare Street

Sixth Avenue Extension

Christie Street Connection

SCARS LEFT BEHIND

*One can still see where whole blocks
were demolished for new lines.*

New rapid transit took a toll on the urban landscape, gouging great scars through Greenwich Village and the Lower East Side. Hundreds of buildings were demolished between 1900 and 1940 to make way for new underground lines. The hodgepodge of a street grid south of 14th Street was made even more chaotic by the subway's slices across it.

⤵ **Lafayette Street.** The Board of Rapid Transit Commissioners originally hoped to lay tracks under Broadway south of 14th Street, but the street was narrow and heavily trafficked, making construction difficult, and building owners fiercely opposed the route because of the disruption and the risk to their buildings. The solution was to sacrifice less valuable real estate to the east and impose a new street on the existing grid. At the time, the spacious Lafayette Place, site of some

The subway's brutal assault on Greenwich Village can be seen in this 1915 photo looking north from Morton Street as the IRT Seventh Avenue line (1, 2, 3) forces its way through the old streets. More than 250 buildings were demolished to make way for the tracks along the new Seventh Avenue South and Varick Street. • **OPPOSITE:** Lafayette Street, Kenmare Street, Sixth Avenue south of Third Street, and Seventh Avenue south of 12th Street were all created for the subway, and Houston and Essex Streets were widened beyond recognition. The Chrystie Street Connection brought more demolition to the Lower East Side in the 1950s.

of the grandest homes in the 19th century—and today of the Public Theater—ran only as far south across Houston Street as Great Jones Street. Buildings were demolished to carve a path south across Houston Street to what was then Elm Street for the trains (4, 5, 6). The work left an enduring scar: a strip of empty lots on the east side of the new Lafayette Street that remained undeveloped until recent years.

⬎ Kenmare Street was created at the west end of Delancey Street when the city constructed the Centre Street Loop, bringing the BRT's Williamsburg Bridge lines (J, Z) to City Hall in 1913. It was plowed through four solid city blocks.

⬎ Seventh Avenue originally ended at 12th Street. When the IRT was extended south from Times Square (1, 2, 3), a new, wide Seventh Avenue South was carved across the historic West Village street grid, and 35 extra feet were added to the west side of Varick. The cockeyed angles of many of the buildings along this

stretch tell the story of the demolition, which "cut the heart out of old Greenwich Village," as the *New York Times* said when the plan was unveiled in 1913. An old church, a seven-story apartment building, and a former brewery were among the 250-odd buildings that fell to the wrecker's ball. The many oddly shaped one- and two-story buildings that face onto Seventh Avenue along this stretch fill in the odd spaces left behind.

↘ **Sixth Avenue** originally ran only as far south as West Third Street and Carmine Street. The Sixth Avenue elevated tracks turned east on West Third before heading south again on West Broadway—two streets whose width is a clue to the fact that elevated tracks once ran overhead there.

When the IND Sixth Avenue subway was built, beginning in 1936, buildings were demolished on the east side of Sixth Avenue in Greenwich Village so the massive West Fourth Street station complex (A, B, C, D, E, F, M) could be excavated without interfering with the el structure. The basketball courts and small parks on the east side of Sixth in this area were created where the buildings came down. One tip-off to the history is the nearly windowless walls of the adjacent buildings, which were not built to face onto an avenue.

From West Third Street south to Franklin Street (A, C, E), Sixth Avenue had to be created from scratch, just as Seventh Avenue South was, making a hash of the

Before it was widened for the IND subway in the 1930s, Houston Street was like other narrow streets in the older parts of Manhattan. • **OPPOSITE:** The scale of the demolition for the IND line on East Houston Street can be seen in this 1931 photo, looking west to the Second Avenue elevated line.

old street grid. That left behind another path of oddly angled buildings and post–World War II apartment blocks built on the leftover pieces of land. If you squint, you can imagine the old neighborhood of narrow, colonial-era streets.

↘ Houston Street was once a narrow street like Bleecker and Prince Streets on either side of it. In the 1930s, the IND transformed Houston into a broad but charmless boulevard cutting across the island, carrying the Sixth Avenue tracks (B, D, F, M) to the Lower East Side and Brooklyn. Again, empty lots and the almost windowless walls of many buildings on the south side testify to the structures that had been there before. Since 2000, the lots between Lafayette Street and Sixth Avenue that sat empty for more than 60 years have slowly been filled with new buildings.

↘ Chrystie Street was radically altered in the 1930s when the city leveled dozens of tenement buildings along its east side to create Sara D. Roosevelt Park. Beginning in 1957, the park was torn up and more buildings were taken down for the Chrystie Street Connection, linking lines on the Manhattan Bridge (B, D) and the Williamsburg Bridge (M) to the IND tracks on East Houston leading to Sixth Avenue.

Dream On

11

The list of hoped-for lines never built is longer than the list of actual new routes.

The city's various transit commissions and boards made a hobby of drawing maps with ambitious new route systems. Commissioners and their staffs were never afraid to think big, and every several years up through the 1960s, a fresh plan issued forth.

Over the years, there were plans for subways on every major crosstown street from 23rd to 57th. There were schemes to blanket Queens and Brooklyn with a grid of lines. Tunnels to Staten Island kept popping up on maps. Engineers were so optimistic about future expansion that when the IND system was built, the shells of future stations were constructed at projected intersection points. New York was always dreaming (see chapter 16 for an account of the most famous dream: a Second Avenue subway).

Most of the schemes came to naught because the city couldn't afford them. Still, it's tantalizing to imagine what the city might look like if some of the wilder dreams had been realized.

HUDSON AND MANHATTAN NEW YORK LINES.

In 1910, when the city was trying to drum up competition for the IRT, William McAdoo's Hudson and Manhattan Railroad (now PATH) proposed to operate lines up and down Manhattan and to Brooklyn, linked to its subways to New Jersey. The H&M could not get financing for that, but it did win permission to construct a branch off its Hoboken–Sixth Avenue subway running east across Ninth Street to Third Avenue, with a connection to the IRT at Astor Place—a line connecting the East Village to New Jersey (see chapters 6 and 7). The H&M built 250 feet of that tunnel before work was halted, and the tube remains beneath the street, visible from the PATH Ninth Street station. In 1909, McAdoo obtained authorization to extend his Sixth Avenue line from 34th Street to 42nd, and then east to Grand Central Terminal, which he promised to complete by 1911. But the company repeatedly sought additional time to begin construction, and the extension was never built.

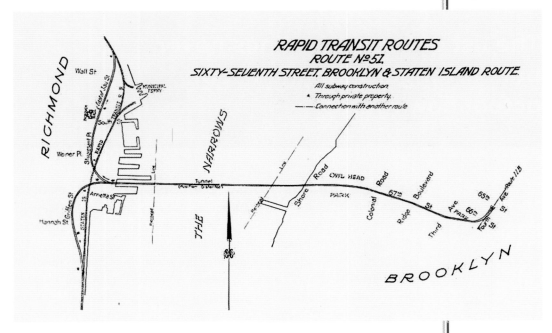

RAPID TRANSIT ROUTES
ROUTE Nº 51.
SIXTY-SEVENTH STREET, BROOKLYN & STATEN ISLAND ROUTE.

All subway construction.
▲ Through private property.
——— Connection with another route.

STATEN ISLAND TUNNEL.

As early as 1912, approval was granted for a line to Staten Island from Brooklyn, and new variations on the idea popped up every few years. In 1921, the chairman of the Transit Commission promised that it would be a top priority. Most proposals involved a branch from the Fourth Avenue–Bay Ridge subway line (R). There were debates over whether a tunnel should also carry freight trains at night from the Baltimore & Ohio Railroad (B&O), which owned the rail lines on Staten Island. Mayor John Hylan came to the view that the only way to pay for a Staten Island subway was to collect freight revenue. Moreover, a freight connection would spur development in Brooklyn.

The problem was that freight trains required larger tunnel bores, and because freight trains were much heavier, they could not run up steep grades the way light electric subway cars could. A shared tunnel would therefore have to have a larger diameter and be almost two miles long to avoid steep grades at either end, making it far more expensive. Since Staten Island had a population of only 127,000 in 1925, it was hard to see how the fare revenue could justify the cost of a passenger-only tunnel.

In 1912, the Public Service Commission, which oversaw the subway at the time, proposed a line to St. George on Staten Island from Bay Ridge, Brooklyn. It would have connected to the Fourth Avenue subway in Brooklyn, then under construction, branching off at 67th Street in Bay Ridge.

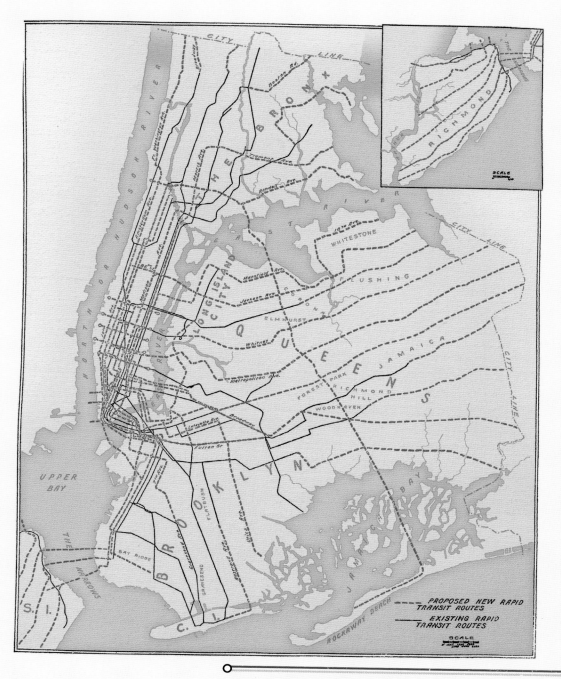

An ambitious 1920 plan from the Transit Commission projected stripes of new lines across Queens, Brooklyn, and Staten Island, indicated in red. The three lines to Staten Island were possible alternatives.

There were political twists, too. The B&O's rival, the Pennsylvania Rail-road, was lining up backers for a tunnel straight from New Jersey to Brooklyn, and other groups were pushing for a subway-only tunnel directly from Staten Island to Manhattan.

The state-controlled Transit Commission opposed a shared freight-subway line, and the Port Authority of New York preferred a New Jersey–Brooklyn tunnel, but Hylan went ahead and broke ground in April 1923 for a freight and subway tunnel near 67th Street in Brooklyn, and did the same on the Staten Island end not long after. The city dug shafts and constructed short tunnels on both sides, but opposition grew to the dual-use plan, and a state law was passed in 1925 requiring any tunnel to be used exclusively for transit. Before long, planners were focused on bridge options. The result, decades later, was the 4,260-foot long Verrazzano-Narrows Bridge, opened in 1964 without any provision for rail lines. Hylan's shafts remain unused.

IND SECOND SYSTEM.

By 1929, while the first round of IND construction was underway, plans were laid for the next stage, the so-called Second System, with more than 100 miles of new routes. Alongside a proposed Second Avenue subway, the other top priority was a route beginning in Tribeca, branching east from Church Street (A, C, E) under Worth Street to the courthouses on Foley Square, and then up East Broadway to the East River and Williamsburg. There it would meet up with another branch from Houston Street in a massive eight-track station on South Fourth Street between Havemeyer and Hewes Streets. From there, one branch would have run down Utica Avenue and another under Myrtle Avenue.

The Worth Street line got off the drawing board, but not far. Bids were taken, and tunnel mouths were built on the Eighth Avenue line (A, C, E) on Church Street so work on the line would not disrupt Eighth Avenue service. The peculiar layout of the Chambers Street IND station, with the terminus for the E train lying east of the through tracks (A, C), traces back to the Worth Street plan. What are now the E platforms were built to be the terminus for Worth Street trains, placed so the tracks from Worth Street would not have to cross over the tracks running down the West Side.

Evidence of the Worth Street plans can also be found in the East Broadway station (F), which has provisions for tracks and platforms overhead, and at

In 1929, the city's Board of Transportation proposed an ambitious expansion of the IND. It included two additional lines across the Lower East Side, leading to a mammoth junction in Williamsburg. Crosstown links were also sketched in Queens, and the Flushing line (7) would sprout branches to College Point and Bayside, Queens. The line across Jamaica Bay to Far Rockaway was the only part that was realized, by converting a Long Island Railroad line for subway use.

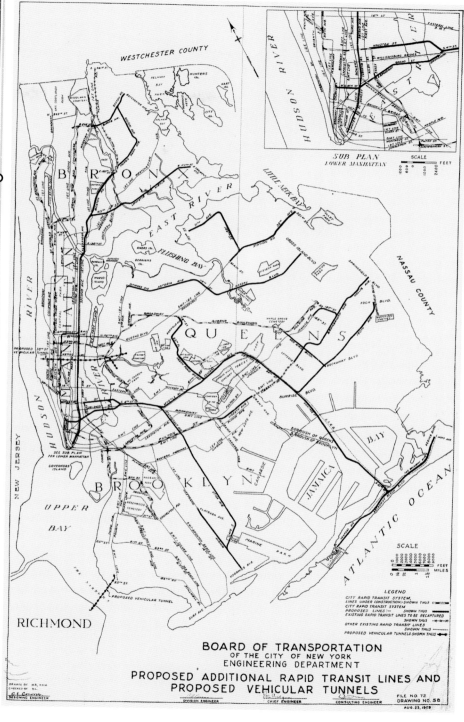

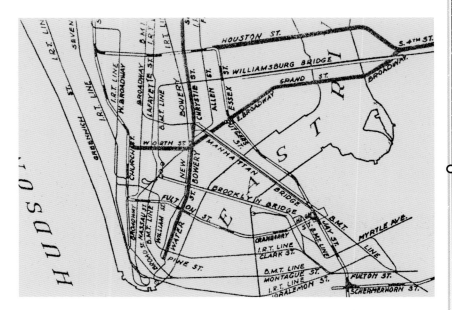

A detail from the 1929 plan shows a proposed line across Worth Street and East Broadway in Tribeca and another under East Houston Street. The plan called for the new lines to pass through two new East River tunnels before converging at a mammoth station in downtown Williamsburg in Brooklyn. There connections could be made to the planned Queens–Brooklyn line (G).

the Broadway station on the G line in Williamsburg. There, through openings in the platform ceilings, riders can gaze up at the shell for the planned eight-track station. East of the Second Avenue station on East Houston Street in Manhattan, where the F line turns south under Essex Street on the local tracks, the express tracks continue east—the beginnings of one of the two additional lines that would have led to Williamsburg.

The Worth Street line and many other IND extensions were still included in a 1938 Board of Transportation budget, but no tunnels were ever built. Had the Worth Street and East Houston lines been built, Downtown Williamsburg might once again have been a bustling hub, as it was when the Williamsburg Bridge opened in 1903. Instead, as the population dispersed from the Lower East Side and Williamsburg in the 1930s, and faster transit was available through Downtown Brooklyn, the neighborhood decayed. That part of Williamsburg was left with just an aging elevated line (J, M, Z) and the crosstown line (G), which never enters Manhattan. If the two tunnels had fed trains from Midtown and Lower Manhattan to a busy hub at South Fourth Street between Havemeyer and Hewes Streets on their way to the outer areas of Brooklyn, Downtown Williamsburg might now be filled with high-rise offices and apartments.

UTICA AVENUE LINE.

The IND Second System also included plans for a line down Utica Avenue, but that route has its own separate history stretching back to 1910, when local residents started pressing for rapid transit. Southeast Brooklyn had—and has—only two lines, the Nostrand Avenue branch of the IRT (2, 5) and the Canarsie line (L). In between is an unserved area more than three miles across. Utica Avenue was a logical place in the middle to put a route when locals began lobbying for a line in 1910. Early proposals called for this to be a branch of the Eastern Parkway IRT (3, 4) or the 14th Street–Canarsie line (L). Later plans called for it to link to new IND lines in Williamsburg. Despite heavy lobbying by the real estate company Wood, Harmon & Company, which had bought 500 acres of land in the area, plans were blocked by objections from residents of Stuyvesant Avenue, who objected to having their street dug up.

A Utica Avenue line appeared again in an ambitious 1968 proposal put forward by Governor Nelson Rockefeller and Mayor John Lindsay to expand the city's rapid transit, but nothing came of that. The street remains lined with single- and two-story homes and businesses.

Stuyvesant Avenue residents got their just deserts. The nearby Lafayette Avenue elevated line was taken down in 1950, and the street is now in a transit lacuna.

Proposals for a Utica Avenue line surfaced again in 2015 and 2019.

QUEENS SUPER EXPRESS.

Another appealing proposal involved a super express IND line from 21st Street–Queensbridge on the F line directly to Forest Hills, using the Long Island Railroad's right of way. This would have been in addition to the E and F expresses, which make only one stop between Long Island City and Forest Hills.

LAGUARDIA AIRPORT.

Why, oh why, does the Astoria line (N, W) not stretch to the roughly two and a half miles from its terminus to the airport? It's not for lack of proposals.

In the Board of Transportation's 1929 plan for the IND "second system," the Astoria line would have come under the IND and it would have been extended east along Ditmars and Astoria Boulevards, bringing it adjacent to the site where the air terminal was later built. In the 1939 iteration, a second subway line through Long Island City and Astoria would have reached the airport via the Ditmars–Astoria route. The Depression and World War II put an end to those plans. Robert Moses, who controlled much of the region's infrastructure construction for decades, consistently opposed building rail lines along his new highways, foreclosing that possibility.

Into the 21st century, plans were still alive for a subway extension, but neighborhood groups and their elected officials objected to elevated trains.

In 2015, Governor Andrew Cuomo announced plans to build a dedicated connection from the airport terminals to the subway and Long Island Railroad station at Willets Point, to the southeast of LaGuardia. But that has been criticized because it would be a more indirect route to Manhattan, and passengers would have to transfer. Moreover, it relies on the Port Washington branch of the Long Island Railroad, which does not reach eastern parts of Long Island and has relatively infrequent service.

The 1939 proposal added an IND line west of the BMT Astoria line (N, W). The new line, in yellow, was slated to turn east along Ditmars and Astoria Boulevards, bringing it close to LaGuardia Airport, which opened that year.
• OPPOSITE: IND extensions in a 1939 Board of Transportation plan stretched farther into northeast Queens, and the Staten Island line was rerouted farther east in Brooklyn, connecting with what is now the F line.

TRAIN SUBSTITUTES

Bold proposals were not limited to conventional subway lines. At various times, "people movers" were proposed for crosstown routes in lieu of rail transit.

Max Schmidt, who had built a continuous loop of small cars for Chicago's 1893 Columbian Exposition, first proposed building "moving platforms" on crosstown streets in 1904, and in 1912, finally won approval for one underneath 34th Street from Second to Ninth Avenues. Riders would first step on a rubber platform moving at three miles an hour, then hop to a second belt moving at six miles an hour, and from there to one of his small cars running in a continuous loop at nine miles an hour. Passengers could board a car anyplace along the line because the platforms would extend the full length of the route. His idea was soon scrapped, however, because the tunnel threatened to complicate construction of the BMT's Dual Contracts line up Broadway (N, Q, R, W).

The concept persisted, however, and in 1920, the Transit Commission's chief engineer proposed "river to river" moving platforms on 14th, 42nd, and 57th Streets.

The Goodyear Tire & Rubber Company put forward a similar concept in 1951, offering it as a replacement for the Times Square–Grand Central shuttle. Goodyear envisioned a moving sidewalk of rubber that ran at 1.5 miles per hour alongside small cars traveling at the same speed. The cars, with facing benches and transparent bubble covers, would accelerate to 15 miles an hour between stations. The system, built in collaboration with the Stephens-Adamson Manufacturing Company, was "the result of more than three years of study to apply the belt conveyor to mass transportation of people rather than bulk materials," Goodyear said.

The Transit Authority placed an order for Goodyear's "Carveyor" system in 1953, but soon had second thoughts. The TA eventually opted instead to experiment with automated trains. The transit unions fought that, however, and the prototype train was destroyed in a fire. After that, the authority gave up on automation. Today the shuttle operates as it has since 1918, with regular, manned trains.

Plans for people movers resurfaced again in 1970, when the MTA mulled the use of some form of them—perhaps moving sidewalks—to bring people from the periphery of the financial districts to subway stations.

OPPOSITE: Max Schmidt's plan for a "river to river" people mover across 34th Street in the early 1900s consisted of continuously moving cars that riders would hop off and on.

AUXILIARY PLATFORM Speed 3 Miles an Hour

1ST MOVING PLATFORM Speed 3 Miles an Hour

2ND MOVING PLATFORM Speed 6 Miles an Hour

3RD MOVING PLATFORM Speed 9 Miles an Hour

In the 1950s, Goodyear proposed to replace the Times Square–Grand Central Shuttle with a people mover called a Carveyor. A moving sidewalk would bring passengers up to the speed of the moving cars, which would slow down at the station and then accelerate in the tunnel. The small cars would run in a continuous loop between the two stations.

KNOW TRAINS AT A GLANCE
BY THE LARGE LETTERS
ON FRONT & SIDE SIGNS

M   - NASSAU ST. EXPRESS
N   - SEA BEACH EXPRESS
Q   - BRIGHTON EXPRESS
Q B - BRIGHTON LOCAL VIA BRIDGE
Q T - BRIGHTON LOCAL VIA TUNNEL
R R - 4TH AVE. LOCAL
T   - WEST END EXPRESS
T T - WEST END LOCAL

Q: **Why are there lettered and numbered lines?**

A: These are the legacy of the three original systems—the Interborough Rapid Transit (IRT), Brooklyn-Manhattan Transit (BMT), and the Independent Subway System (IND). The numbered trains—1 through 7—run on what was the IRT system. The A through G lines run mainly on IND tracks, while lines from J on down the alphabet are primarily old BMT routes. Some lines begin on what were originally BMT tracks and end on IND routes.

Before the modern lettering and numbering system was adopted, local trains on the BMT and IND lines were assigned double letters—e.g., AA, GG, RR, and QJ—while single letters denoted express lines. QJ stood for the Q line running to Jamaica. QT meant a train that ran through the Montague Street (R) tunnel from Brooklyn to Manhattan, while QB ran over the Manhattan Bridge.

Near-Death Experience

12

The subway began to collapse in the 1970s, and the city with it.

"You have to look as if you're the one with the meat cleaver."

That was the advice given to the writer Paul Theroux when he set out to tour the subway for a 1982 article. The subway was at its nadir. Muggings and assaults were everyday occurrences. Nearly 8,300 passengers were robbed in 1986, and there were 20 murders in the system that year, up from just 78 robberies and a single murder in 1966. It became sport to knock out windows—120,000 a year in 1981. Every square inch in most of the cars was covered with graffiti.

Crime took off in the 1970s, leading the Transit Authority to put cops on all trains in the evening and wee hours. Things were so bad in 1979 that the Guardian Angels, a volunteer civilian patrol, was formed to patrol trains. There were 1,145 token booth robberies in 1974, or about three a day. In 1979, two token booth clerks were killed when gasoline and a lit match were pushed through the coin slot.

At the same time, the infrastructure went to hell. Car doors didn't open. Lights were often out on cars. Wheels broke in two, sending trains off the rails and into concrete walls. Motors fell off axles. Steel beams under elevated lines cracked, causing tracks to sag. A 20-foot-long, 20-ton chunk of concrete fell on a 7 train under East 42nd Street, killing one passenger, hospitalizing another 10, and trapping 1,000 passengers in a smoky, 115-degree tunnel for more than an hour.

By the 1980s, one third of the car fleet was out of service on any given day, and many other cars were running with dangerous defects. Twenty-five-hundred cars caught fire one year. Riders were so fed up that they sometimes refused to get off trains when they were taken out of service, and the Transit Authority chairman received death threats when he proposed a fare increase.

Riders were surrounded by graffiti inside and outside cars in the 1970s and 1980s.

It took decades to reach this point, decades of the "lethal, silent mischief" of neglect. As early as the 1930s, maintenance was deferred and new car orders were canceled. During World War II, steel went to tanks and ships, not new subway cars, and the subway lost money again after the war. Doubling the fare to a dime in 1948 didn't begin to cover the backlog of needs. Twenty percent of the car fleet in the 1960s dated to World War I or earlier.

Meanwhile, under Robert Moses, the region's powerful infrastructure and parks czar, the city and state steered investment to highways, tunnels, and bridges to serve the spreading suburbs. Moses never held elected office but wore multiple hats and held sway over governors and mayors because he controlled hundreds of millions of dollars of spending. He was city parks commissioner for 26 years, chairman of the Triborough Bridge and Tunnel Authority from 1934 to 1981, and he ran the City Planning Commission from 1942 to 1960. He bequeathed the region a network of parks, but he was a champion of the car and highways over public transportation. Fare increases were the solution for the subway, he successfully argued, not increased property or sales taxes.

As the head of several city and state entities, Robert Moses steered hundreds of millions of dollars toward highways and bridges rather than public transit.

As his biographer Robert Caro wrote:

> Public resources would be poured with a lavish hand into improving the transportation system used by people who could afford cars.... Only a dribble of public resources would go into a transportation system used by people who could not.... While the city and state were providing car users with the most modern highways, they would be condemning subway users to continue to travel on an antiquated system utterly inadequate to the city's needs.

These policies starved public transportation and facilitated the flight of the white middle class from the city to the suburbs. That migration, and rising crime, helped send the city and the subway into a downward spiral. New York City's population, which leveled off after 1950, fell precipitously in the 1970s. The city lost 800,000 residents, a 10 percent drop. That cut steeply into city tax revenue and helped bring the city to the brink of bankruptcy in 1975.

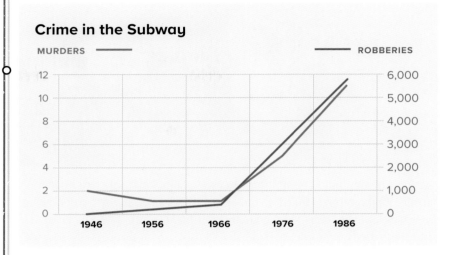

Crime in the Subway

MURDERS ——————   —————— ROBBERIES

The subway, which historically had been fairly safe, was plagued with violent crime beginning in the 1970s.

The falloff in subway ridership was even more dramatic: 21 percent fewer riders in 1982 than in 1970. By 1977, ridership was just half the levels of the late 1940s. It was back to the 1918 level—before the IND lines were built, and before many of the Dual Contracts lines in Brooklyn and Queens were completed.

You didn't need statistics to know how bad things were. If the graffiti didn't make it clear, the token suckers did. These thieves jammed the slots in turnstiles so tokens wouldn't drop and release the gate, forcing passengers to pay a second time at another gate. "Then from the shadows, the token sucker appears like a vampire, quickly sealing his lips over the token slot, inhaling powerfully and producing his prize: a $1.50 token." One frustrated token booth clerk sprinkled hot pepper powder on the slots, giving one sucker a surprise.

If that was the most disgusting sign of the times, the graffiti was the most alarming. It coated walls, floors, and windows, inside and out. It was an unavoidable visual message that no one was in control. Along with muggings, subway graffiti was *the* symbol of the city's decay.

Some saw graffiti in a different light, as a colorful gift to a sooty city that was down at its heels. The simple squiggles that covered interior walls had few defenders, but the mural-like paintings on the exteriors of many cars were "perhaps the most important art movement of the late twentieth century," the art critic Joe Austin declared. They were the work of a handful of young men who labored over these works for hours in the subway yards. The best known, like "Dondi," had distinctive styles. Novelist Norman Mailer teamed

up with a photographer to produce *The Faith of Graffiti* (1974), extolling their virtues. Photographers Martha Cooper and Henry Chalfant honored them in their book *Subway Art* (1984) and filmmaker Manfred Kirchheimer created a stunning visual and musical celebration of the painted trains, *Stations of the Elevated* (1981).

But theirs was a minority view. "Even if graffiti, understood properly, might be seen as among the more engaging of the annoyances of New York," the sociologist Nathan Glazer wrote, "I am convinced this is not the way the average subway rider will ever see them, and that they contribute to his sense of a menacing and uncontrollable city."

As early as 1972, Mayor John Lindsay launched a campaign against it, but it was a losing battle. Budget cutbacks during the city's financial crisis prevented progress, and things kept deteriorating. In a 1983 pilot program, some cars were cleaned and painted all white as a declaration that the Transit Authority could get graffiti under control. But that proved to be "a virtual invitation to an army of graffiti vandals who took full advantage of a fresh canvas," the MTA later conceded.

Restoring the essential infrastructure—cars, tracks, signals, stations—after decades of neglect required a monumental effort. First, political support had to be built to spend the money. The point man was Richard Ravitch, a real estate developer, whom Governor Hugh Carey named chairman of the MTA in 1979. From his work on subsidized housing and his turnaround of a troubled state development agency, he had learned the ins and outs of city, state, and federal politics and finance. In his four years as chairman, he mustered support among state and federal officials, business leaders, and newspaper editorial boards for a long-term rescue plan, including funding.

Ravitch struck backroom deals with politicians to raise fares and with union officials over wages, and then cheerfully took the heat when they attacked

A handful of ambitious painters did more than spray their initials. Some, like Blade (aka Steven Ogburn), created elaborate designs and executed them carefully across entire cars, like this one with the artist's name. Note that the windows are painted over.

him publicly over the concessions he proposed—which they had agreed to in private. He reached accords with legislative leaders without the knowledge of the governor, his patron, who didn't object because that preserved deniability for him. When Ravitch needed support from Republican legislators, he convinced David Rockefeller, the chairman of Chase Manhattan Bank, and two other corporate CEOs to take a 5 a.m. tour of decrepit stations and repair shops. The executives conveyed the message to Republicans in Albany that the subway needed more money urgently.

From the outset, Ravitch said that fare increases might be necessary—an idea that was taboo among elected officials. On the eve of a 1980 MTA board meeting where an increase from 50 cents to 75 cents was up for a vote, Ravitch wasn't sure if he had enough support, so he invited directors to dinner at the private Century Association club, where he hoped to win them over. Informed by lawyers that such a gathering would violate the state's open meetings laws, he booked a second table at the nearby Yale Club and

Richard Ravitch, MTA chairman from 1979 to 1983, drew on his political experience as a real estate developer to persuade the state and federal governments to provide billions of dollars to restore the subway.

sent half the board there so neither table would have a quorum and thus would be exempt from the rules. He then shuttled between the clubs until he was sure he would have the votes in the morning. Fares doubled from 50 cents to a dollar in steps between 1980 and 1986.

In 1981, Ravitch won funding in Albany and Washington for a $7.9 billion, five-year capital improvement plan, a bit more than half of what the MTA's engineers estimated would be needed over 10 years. That paid for 1,775 new cars and the overhauls of another 3,900, allowing the last cars from the 1940s to be scrapped. Stations were refurbished, and many behind-the-scenes fixes were made to cables, switches, power stations, and the like. This laid the groundwork for a full turnaround.

Robert Kiley, a onetime CIA manager, oversaw the rebuilding of the system in the 1980s as MTA chairman and clashed with the system's unions.

Much of the hardest work in restoring the subway fell to Ravitch's successor, Robert Kiley, the MTA chairman from 1983 to 1990, and David Gunn, who headed the New York City Transit division of the MTA under Kiley. Kiley, a former high-level Central Intelligence Agency official, had headed the Boston area's transit system.

Kiley and Gunn had to confront colossal internal problems. As an organization, the subway suffered from layer after layer of management, most of them unionized. In effect, the organization was run by the unions, which made it impossible to implement changes. It was not uncommon for car repairmen to work only three hours of their eight-hour shifts. The Coney Island shop "is quieter than the main reading room at the New York Public Library," the *Daily News* reported. Kiley and Gunn took a confrontational approach, disciplining workers and winning state legislation to eliminate more than a thousand unionized management positions, replacing them with managers accountable to the top brass. The workers' response? They hurled bolts at Gunn when he toured the repair shops. The fusillade aimed at a productivity analyst included wrenches.

Not that the authority was blameless. Spare parts were chronically in short supply, so working cars had to be cannibalized, and the shops were in miserable condition. Some were unheated in winter. Those conditions, too, had to be fixed.

Eliminating graffiti required its own strategy, a five-year program. Most of the paint was applied in the train yards, so they were ringed with razor wire fences and stocked with guard dogs. (The New York Zoological Society objected to Mayor Koch's suggestion in 1980 that the MTA employ wolves instead.) A squad of 34 undercover cops was assigned to catch spray-painters in the act. If a car was "tagged" while in service, the train was sent to a shop immediately for cleaning, sometimes with a solution based on orange juice, whose acid dissolved marker pen ink. After five years, in 1989, the MTA declared the system graffiti free. In truth, graffiti has never gone away. In the 1990s, vandals took to scratching windows and even stainless steel interior walls—damage that was very hard to repair. Painting, too, continues. More than 750 cars were hit in 2018, but they were quickly yanked from service and cleaned, so few passengers are aware of how common the problem still is.

Over time, the changes and the investment paid off dramatically. The average distance a car traveled without a breakdown ("mean distance between failures," or MTBF) soared from a dismal 6,640 miles in 1981 to 58,000 by 1995 as newer cars hit the rails and preventive maintenance was increased. In 2003, it was 140,000 miles. (It slipped back to 112,000 by 2016.) As service improved and crime levels fell both in the subway and aboveground, riders returned. The system carried 1.4 billion people in 2002, 40 percent more than in 1991. In 2013, it passed 1.7 billion. By the late 2010s, there were 90 percent fewer robberies than in the 1970s and some years there were no murders on the subway.

Kiley was hailed as a savior and was hired to head London's transport system.

Stations remain a work in progress. Nearly 40 years after the 1982 capital plan was approved, many have had their tiling replaced and digital displays installed. But many others are still delapidated and few are accessible to the handicapped. Only half have been refurbished in the last 30 years.

The subway is frightful looking. It has paint and signatures all over its aged face. It has been vandalized from end to end. It smells so hideous you want to put a clothespin on your nose, and it is so noisy the sound actually hurts. . . . It is a gift to any connoisseur of dubious superlatives: It has the filthiest trains, the most bizarre graffiti, the noisiest wheels, the craziest passengers, the most macabre crimes. . . . People waiting for the bus have a special pitying gaze for people entering the dark hole in the sidewalk that is the subway entrance. It is sometimes not pity, but fear; often they look like miners' wives watching their menfolk going down the pit.

—PAUL THEROUX, "SUBWAY ODYSSEY," *NEW YORK TIMES MAGAZINE*, 1982

From Horror Shows to Sitcoms

13

In 1949, Gene Kelly, playing a sailor on shore leave, fell in love with a woman he spotted in a poster on the subway in *On the Town*. *The Seven Year Itch* in 1955 gave the world the iconic image of Marilyn Monroe's skirt being lifted up by a draft from the Lexington Avenue line.

In those days, the city was still an exciting, safe place to visit. In the 1970s, the subway symbolized the fear that pervaded life in Gotham. By then, nothing good happened underground.

Woody Allen made light of it in *Bananas* (1971). Riding the 42nd Street shuttle, Allen blithely reads his intellectual journal as two thugs, one played by a young Sylvester Stallone, rough up an elderly woman on crutches sitting next to him.

There was little humor in most subway scenes of that era, however. *Death Wish* (1974) featured Charles Bronson, who rides the train with a pistol, waiting to shoot anyone who tries to mug him. They do and he does, nonchalantly exiting at the next station. It was an eerie foreshadowing of the real-life Bernhard Goetz, the so-called "subway vigilante," who shot what he claimed were assailants on a train a decade later.

In *The Taking of Pelham One Two Three*, released the same year, a train is hijacked and ransom demanded for its passengers. Mayhem is the order of the day in the gang wars flick *The Warriors* (1979), a cult classic, much of which takes place on trains or in subway stations, including a strangely graceful, stylized fight scene in a restroom. (Oddly, the cars in these movies are free of graffiti.)

Two of the best subway film scenes ever occur in *The French Connection* (1971). In one, Detective Popeye Doyle (Gene Hackman) is tailing "Frog One" (Fernando Rey), the bad guy in chief, on the 42nd Street shuttle platform in Grand Central. In a cat-and-mouse game, Frog One hops on and off the train, with Doyle always one step behind. Eventually Frog One gives Doyle the slip, then waves out the window mockingly at Doyle on the platform as the train pulls away.

This famous image of Marilyn Monroe was the result of a draft from the Lexington Avenue subway.

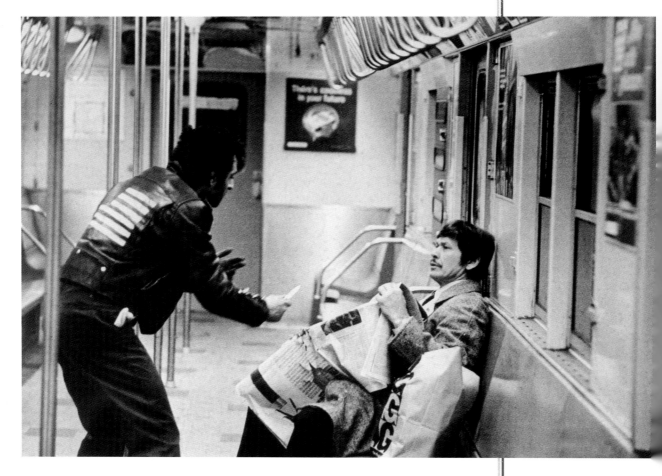

A legendary, and harrowing, car chase later in the movie has a jaw-dropping backstory. Doyle is at the wheel, maniacally following a hijacked train on elevated tracks above, weaving between girders, dodging other vehicles and pedestrians. Remarkably, the scene was filmed without a permit from the city and without closing off streets to traffic. But it took two takes on successive days.

The director, William Friedkin, was unhappy with the first take and told the stunt driver, Bill Hickman, that the chase wasn't exciting enough. Hickman, miffed that his skills were being questioned, told Friedkin to get in the car and take over from the cameraman. Hickman then took off for 26 blocks along Stillwell Avenue near Coney Island (D) at speeds up to 90 miles an hour. Miraculously, no one was hurt—or arrested. Friedkin also tells how he obtained permission to film scenes on a train, including several shootings, by

In *Death Wish*, Charles Bronson played an armed vigilante, waiting to be attacked. It foreshadowed the later case of Bernhard Goetz.

In the 1974 thriller *The Taking of Pelham One Two Three*, kidnappers take hostages on a 6 train and demand $1 million in ransom.

bribing a transit official with $40,000 in cash and a one-way ticket to Jamaica.

The subway's image, and the city's, had improved markedly by 1986, when the romantic comedy *Crocodile Dundee* was released. In the final scene, Sue Charlton (Linda Kozlowski), an American reporter who has fallen for the Australian safari leader Michael Dundee (Paul Hogan), spots him at the far end of a packed platform, but he can't hear her calling. The rush-hour hordes come to her rescue, relaying her message down the platform:

Charlton: "Don't leave. I'm not going to marry Richard."

Dundee: "Why not?"

Charlton: "Tell him I love him. I love you!"

Dundee then walks over the shoulders of the supportive crowd. And with that, the seventies were over.

OPPOSITE FROM TOP: Abbi and Ilana, the central characters on the Comedy Central show *Broad City*, met in the subway. • Violence returned to the subway in several terrifying scenes in the 2019 psychological thriller *Joker*.

By the late nineties, *Seinfeld* episodes revolved around encounters with strangers on the train, and the subway was fit for a family outing on *The Simpsons*. Encountering mentally ill and homeless people on the Flushing line, Bart Simpson decides to imitate them in the 1997 episode, "The City of New York vs. Homer Simpson." Shaking a cup for donations, he claims he was born without taste buds and demonstrates by licking a pole. But the taste was too much, even for Bart.

Broad City, the long-running web and TV sitcom, began with a chance meeting in the subway, when Abbi and Ilana, the lead characters, give each other MetroCard swipes. In a later episode, while walking from car to car on a train, they encounter an array of odd people and phenomena—a catalog of the unfortunate aspects of the subway. They squeeze between enormous backpacks and dodge gymnasts and leering and sweaty men. Finally, they arrive at a car full of Orthodox Jewish men in black coats who avert their glances from the women. Abbi smacks one on the rear as she hops off the train.

Q: **How many friends does Pizza Rat have?**

A: Pizza Rat became famous when the video of him (her?) dragging a large slice of pizza went viral in 2015. No one knows how many rats there are in the system, but a study by the City Department of Health and the Transit Authority in 2010 found that garbage collection areas were the biggest draw for rodents, and recommended that they be better sealed. If it's reassuring, researchers using statistical methods have estimated that the rat population of the entire city is only about 2 million, and not the 8 million (one per human) often supposed.

How to Get There

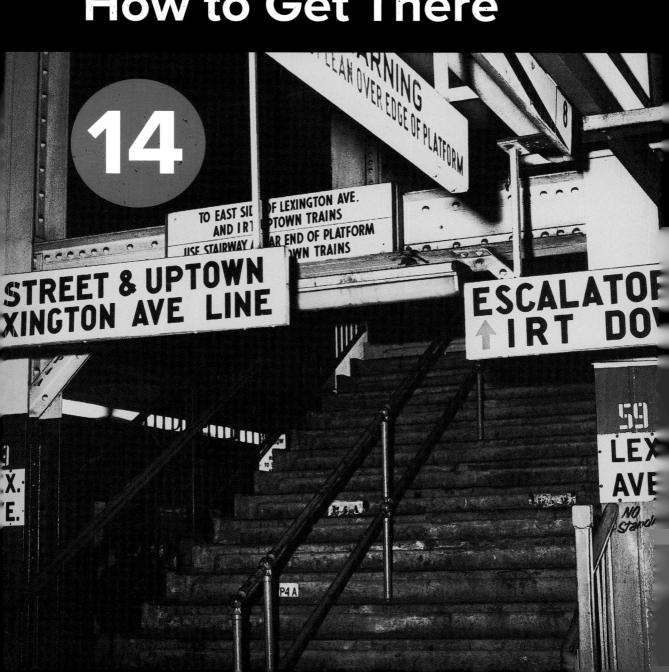

14

It took transit officials two decades to come up with a map design that worked.

Explaining the subway visually is a daunting task.

The system is uniquely complex because so many lines converge to share tracks and then diverge again, plus there are local and express trains in much of the city, and some routes don't run at all times. Generations of designers have struggled to come up with maps that riders could decipher. Simply finding the right platform at labyrinths such as the Times Square and Atlantic Avenue–Barclays Center stations is a challenge. Clear signage is essential.

Things were simpler before unification in 1940. The IRT, BMT, and IND discouraged passengers from taking competitors' lines, and there were few free transfers, so each company's maps showed its lines only. If you wanted a map showing all lines, you had to buy it from an independent publisher. And there was no need for signs telling IRT passengers how to transfer to, say, IND trains because they couldn't.

In theory the three systems were unified in 1940, but it took the Board of Transportation three years to issue an official map showing all lines—a conventional street map designed by a commercial printer with transit routes superimposed. Colors were used to indicate which lines were formerly IRT, BMT, or IND—essential information because their stations hadn't been integrated.

In 1958, the New York City Transit Authority adopted a radical new approach to its map, borrowing European design concepts.

Most modern subway maps around the world trace back to London's. In 1933, Harry Beck, a young draftsman at London Transport, on his own initiative, came up with a diagram of London's Tube routes. It was simple, abstract, and brightly colored. It dispensed with geographic reality, placing some stations out of position relative to others for the sake of simplicity and elegance.

In 1966, when Massimo Vignelli's firm was hired to come up with new, clearer signage, riders were confronted with a confusing array of signs with no consistent style, as shown in this photo at the Lexington Avenue–59th Street station.

With updates, it remains the basic guide for the London Underground today, and a lasting symbol of London. Resembling a circuit diagram more than a map, it is the touchstone for transit cartographers worldwide.

Beck's abstract, diagrammatic approach caught on in other countries in the mid-20th century, but not in America. It took George Salomon, a German-born typographer, to bring the abstract approach to New York. He had trained in England with Eric Gill, who created the typeface for the official version of Beck's map. Unsolicited, Salomon submitted a plan to the Transit Authority in 1955 to revamp station signs and the subway map, and to rationalize the naming of routes. Borrowing from Beck, as well as from Berlin's subway maps, he proposed distinct colors for individual lines.

The Transit Authority didn't accept his color proposal, but it did hire him to design a new map. His work, released in 1958, adopted Beck's convention of placing all lines at 45-degree or 90-degree angles, with geography distorted for simplicity and surface elements omitted. Land masses were in beige and there were just three somber colors—black, dark green, and dark red—to designate IRT, BMT, and IND lines. Unlike Beck's cheery creation, the palette of the Salomon diagram was drab.

Simplification came at the cost of functionality. Where different routes ran along the same street, his diagram didn't indicate which trains stopped at which stations, and it was difficult to trace a line to its destination. With an influx of tourists expected for the World's Fair of 1964–1965, the Transit Authority came under pressure from directors at the Museum of Modern Art and others to clean up its visual image and improve navigation tools.

In 1964, the authority held a contest to solicit new map ideas. Stanley Goldstein, a Hofstra University professor, and Dante Calise, the art director at a map printer, took ideas from one of the winners, Raleigh D'Adamo, and produced a new design. Drawing on Salomon's basic style, it remained fairly abstract, but added parks, route colors, and boxes indicating which trains stopped at each station. The result, handed out to the public in 1967, had more information but it was overly cluttered and difficult to interpret. It would prove short-lived.

At the same time the map was undergoing its makeover, the Transit Authority decided it was time to fix the visual mishmash it had inherited in stations, the legacy of the three systems and changes in architectural and design tastes over four decades of construction. Black-and-white enameled signs mixed typefaces willy-nilly, and they clashed with nearby tile and mosaic signs.

OPPOSITE: Before unification, each of the three systems issued its own maps, omitting rivals' lines. This 1925 BMT map shows a number of features that no longer exist, including shuttle trains over Brooklyn Bridge as well as the Lafayette Avenue and Myrtle Avenue elevated lines in Brooklyn. The latter were demolished after the IND crosstown line (G) was built. The Fifth and Third Avenue elevated line in Brooklyn, a block away from the new Fourth Avenue subway on this map, was demolished in 1940.

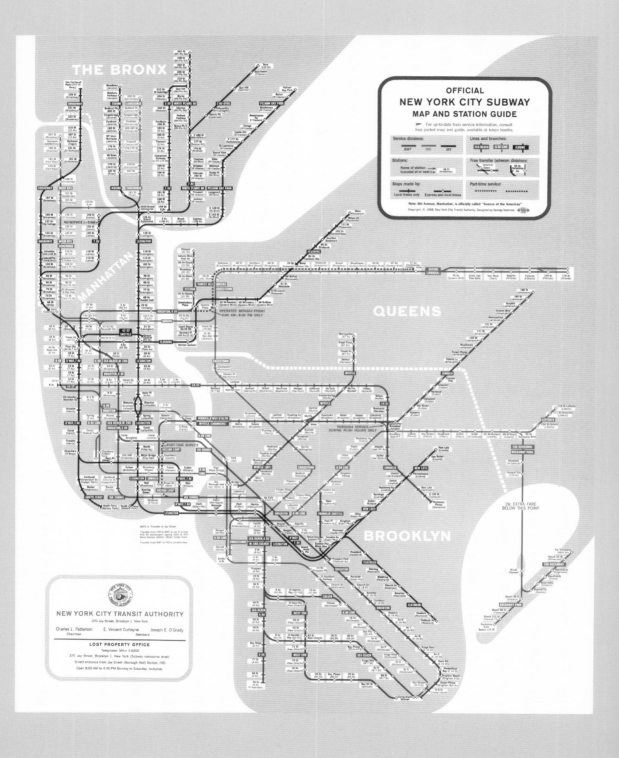

INTERBOROUGH RAPID TRANSIT COMPANY.
UPTOWN TO WOODLAWN.
DOWNTOWN VIA LEXINGTON AND 4TH AVENUES TO GRAND CENTRAL, CITY HALL, SOUTH FERRY AND BROOKLYN. CHANGE AT 149TH STREET FOR TIMES SQUARE, PENN. STATION, SO. FERRY, WALL ST. AND B'KLYN VIA B'WAY AND 7TH AVE. TO SOUTH FERRY VIA 6TH AND 9TH AVENUE ELEVATED.

OPPOSITE: In the late 1950s, the Transit Authority commissioned George Salomon to design a system map. Like the 1967 and 1972 maps that followed, it borrowed key design concepts from London's Underground diagram, such as putting all lines at 45- and 90-degree angles to one another.

In 1966, the TA hired the corporate design firm Unimark International to make sense of the signage. Unimark partner Bob Noorda spent days studying passenger movements in four busy transfer points to determine where signs were needed. He and his Italian partner, Massimo Vignelli, then wrote detailed specifications for new signs. The sans-serif face Standard Medium, very close to Helvetica, was chosen because it could be read easily at different angles—glancing out a car window, looking up a flight of stairs, as well as head-on. It was a stripped-down style more common in Europe than America at the time.

The implementation did not go well. The TA's sign-making shop interpreted a line in Unimark's specifications showing where the sign should be mounted as part of the design. When the signs emerged from the shop, they bore a superfluous black rule across the top. In addition, the lettering was created by hand instead of photographically, so the spacing and alignments looked amateurish. In the end, the damage was limited, though, because relatively few of the signs were installed before the budget ran out.

Eventually, more money was found, work resumed, and the Noorda-Vignelli signs began showing up across the system. To ensure that their graphic diktats were followed, Vignelli and Noorda codified their principles in a hulking, 356-page *Graphics Standards Manual*, which spelled out type sizes, the precise spacing between letters, exact heights of signs in stations, and so on. This time they oversaw production. (In a nod to fortuity, Unimark adopted the unintended line, which survives to this day.) The 1970 *Manual* is such a classic of modern design that a private publisher reissued it in 2015.

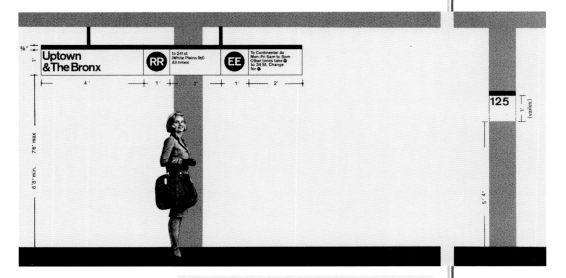

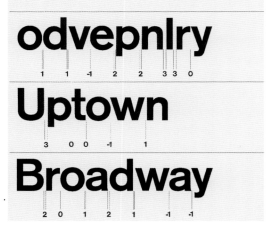

The black-on-white Unimark style was later reversed, so lettering and the unintended line are white on a black background, after it was discovered that it was more readable. But otherwise, Unimark's guidelines are still largely followed today.

While the replacement of old signs was underway, the Transit Authority engaged Vignelli and Unimark to devise a map to complement the signs. The 1967 Goldstein-Calise map was hard to use, and it was at odds with Unimark's decluttered vision for station signs.

The bold route chart that Vignelli came up with became famous and controversial.

Unimark's 1970 *Graphics Standards Manual* for the subway specified every letter, space, and location precisely, as well as the precise height of each station sign. **OPPOSITE:** The 1967 map, an adaptation of George Salomon's 1958 design, added information about routes and transfers, but the result was cluttered and difficult to decipher.

New York City Rapid Transit Map and Station Guide

THE BRONX

MANHATTAN

QUEENS

BROOKLYN

STATEN ISLAND

NEW JERSEY

* SEE STRIP MAPS ON OTHER SIDE FOR MORE SERVICE INFORMATION.

SPECIAL RUSH-HOUR SERVICE

HUDSON RIVER

EAST RIVER

HARLEM RIVER

RIKERS ISLAND

RANDALLS ISLAND

PELHAM BAY PARK

FLUSHING MEADOW

FOREST PARK

JAMAICA BAY

ATLANTIC OCEAN

THE NARROWS

GOVERNORS ISLAND

CENTRAL PARK

EXTRA FARE SOUTH OF THIS POINT

N

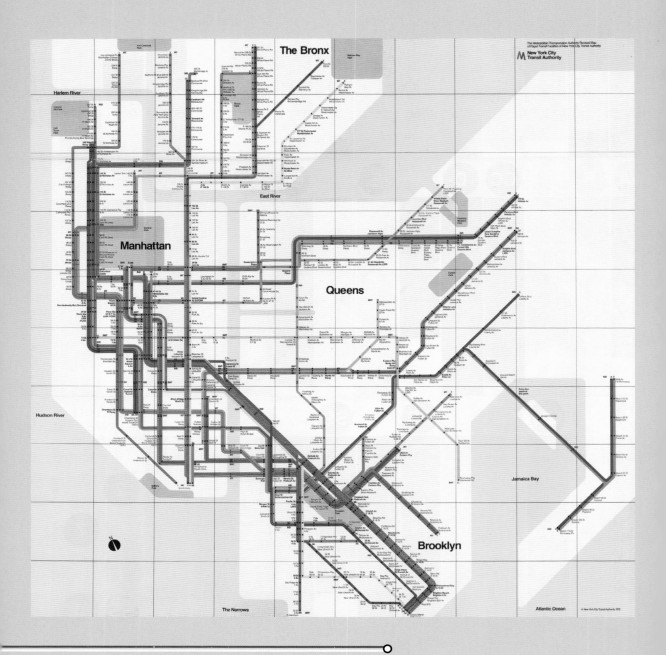

Massimo Vignelli's 1972 design was a radical simplification and more colorful than any before or since. It was admired by many, but its abstraction and geographic distortions frustrated many riders.

Like Beck, Salomon, and Goldstein, Vignelli was less interested in map-making than with design. The city at the street level was irrelevant to him. He was creating a *diagram* of rapid transit, with all lines running straight, at 45- and 90-degree angles. The few landmarks he deemed worry of mention—large bodies of water and major parks—were radically distorted for simplicity. At the TA's insistence, each route was given a bright color, 22 shades in all, a palette that resembled the psychedelic posters of the era.

Vignelli's work, officially adopted in 1972, was justly hailed as a brilliant piece of design, imposing order and simplicity on the twisted, knotted tracks beneath the streets, and it eventually won a place in the Museum of Modern Art's collection. The catch was that it, too, was hard to read. With its rainbow of minutely differentiated colors running side by side, it was difficult to tell which line ran where.

New Yorkers didn't know what to make of this innovative new look. They complained that its parks were gray, not green, and that Central Park had been rendered square. Many were irked by the fact that Vignelli put the station at 50th Street and Broadway (1) west of the 50th Street station on the Eighth Avenue line (A, C, E) to preserve the elegance of the design. His work "enchanted aesthetes and baffled straphangers," as his obituary said.

Vignelli was unapologetic. "Of course I know Central Park is rectangular and not square," he told an interviewer in 2006. "Of course I know the park is green, and not gray. Who cares? You want to go from Point A to Point B, period. The only thing you are interested in is the spaghetti [of lines]."

New Yorkers begged to differ. In London, where streets retrace Roman and medieval roads and taxi drivers spend years developing mental maps of the city, Beck's distortions may have been a welcome simplification. But New Yorkers internalize Manhattan's rigorous grid. Vignelli messed with the natives' most basic frame of reference.

Just three years after the Vignelli map went up in stations and in cars, the Transit Authority formed a committee to draw up an easier-to-read replacement. John Tauranac, an author and historian who wrote guides for the TA, was put in charge, overseeing the work of Michael Hertz Associates, a design firm. Draft versions were issued and public feedback was reflected in the final map, which was introduced in 1979.

John Tauranac, a writer and historian, chaired the committee that developed the map that supplanted Vignelli's in 1979. With updates and tweaks, it has been used ever since.

An aerial photo shows how the current map widens Manhattan, the south Bronx, and Downtown Brooklyn so the dense tangles of lines in those areas can be represented more clearly. But the map stays much closer to geographic reality than the 1958, 1967, and 1972 maps.

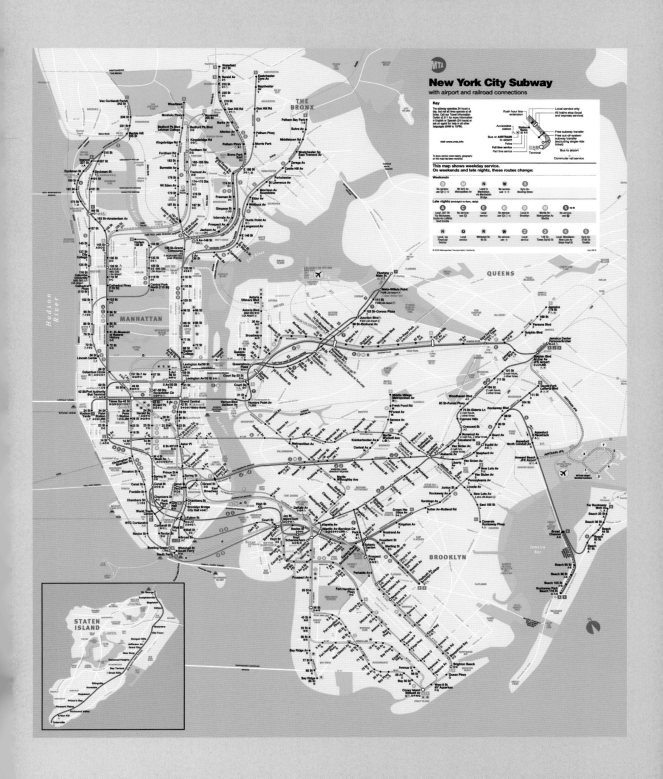

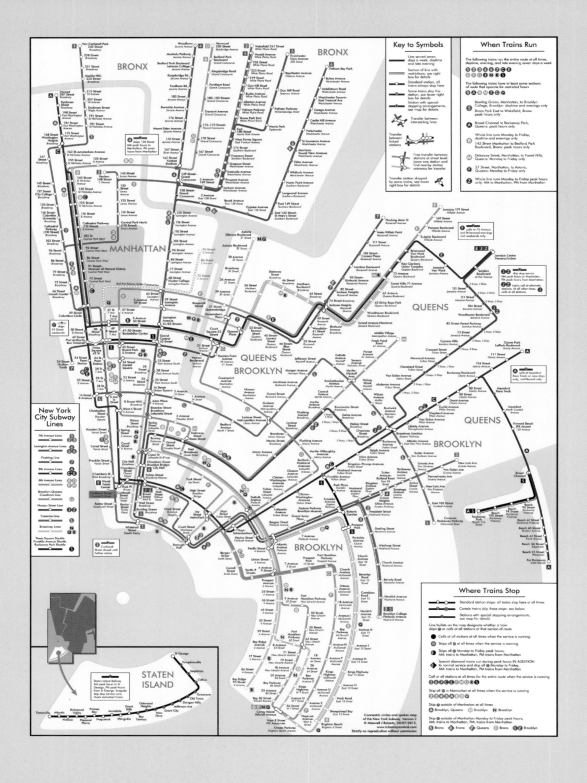

This time it was a map, not a diagram. In Tauranac's words, it restored "cartographic verities." Where stations are far apart in real life, they were widely spaced on the map. Some distortion was allowed. Manhattan, for instance, was widened to make lines that are in close quarters easier to trace, but the map was close enough to reality to use for navigation at street level. Landmarks and neighborhoods were named—the kind of detail designers like Salomon and Vignelli shunned as distracting.

The city's system of rapid transit, technical marvel that it is, has been for years under the aegis of administrators whose sole purpose, it would seem, has been to deny the public any sense of information about where they are going. It is no exaggeration to say that there is no subway system in the world with a more inadequate and confusing system of signs and maps than New York's. . . . Placing maps on platforms is too logical and sensible an idea, and no doubt was vetoed years ago by the Transit Authority's Committee in Charge of Public Confusion.

—PAUL GOLDBERGER, "DESIGN NOTEBOOK," *NEW YORK TIMES*, 1978

OPPOSITE: London-based transit cartographer Max Roberts riffed on the official map in his own way, envisioning all the lines radiating out from the Battery and Downtown Brooklyn.

Though the Hertz-Tauranac map included information Vignelli left out, in other ways it was simpler. Instead of assigning a color to each route, Tauranac's committee assigned a color to each "trunk line" in Manhattan. For example, the B, D, F, and M trains share the same orange hue because they run on Sixth Avenue, while the 4, 5, and 6 are green because they share tracks from City Hall to the South Bronx. The Transit Authority resisted because the existing route coloring scheme was not only used on the Vignelli map but throughout stations and on trains themselves. Tauranac eventually won an audience with the TA's chairman, who agreed to override the staff and reassign colors to the lines, even though that required train and station signs to be changed across the system. No longer would lines sharing the same trunk route have different colors.

Vignelli's design still has its passionate supporters, and the Transit Authority uses his format sometimes for special purposes, such as detours for construction. But what the Hertz-Tauranac map lacked in simplicity and sheer beauty, it made up for in practicality. After decades of missteps, this map has endured—for more than 40 years now.

THE MAN WHO INTRODUCED NEW YORK TO HELVETICA— OR SOMETHING LIKE IT

Massimo Vignelli left a lasting mark on New York.

"The life of a designer is a life of fight," said Massimo Vignelli. "Fight against the ugliness. The visual disease is what we have around, and what we try to do is cure it somehow with design."

For a half-dozen years, beginning in the late 1960s, the Italian-born graphic designer waged successful campaigns against his enemy in the subway, first with clear, consistent signage and then with a bold but polarizing map.

Vignelli, a passionate, loquacious, charismatic man, made a career of reshaping corporate images. He designed logos for American Airlines (the twin A's in red and blue, used from 1968 to 2013), the furniture maker Knoll (just the name in block letters), and the simple green rectangle for United Colors of Benetton. The signature brown shopping bags of the Bloomingdale's department store were also his work.

His corporate symbols were always spare, typically just sans-serif type. He once said he would relish cleaning up the Vatican's corporate identity. "I would go to the pope and say, 'Your holiness, the logo is O.K.'"—referring to the cross—"'but everything else has to go.'" If he'd had his way, the stylized eagle would never have been part of the American Airlines logo, but the company insisted. Chairs and dishes he designed also had simple, modern lines.

Many of his logos employed Helvetica or a typeface close to it, and that was his first choice for the subway. But Helvetica wasn't readily available in the United States in the late 1960s, so he and his firm used Standard Medium, which is indistinguishable to the untrained eye. The project earned Vignelli the title "the man who introduced New Yorkers to Helvetica," even though it wasn't actually Helvetica. (In 1989, the TA adopted the true Helvetica.)

When he died in 2014, Vignelli was a legend in the design world. "To get to the office, I rode in a subway with Vignelli-designed signage, shared the sidewalk with people holding Vignelli-designed Bloomingdale's shopping bags, walked by St. Peter's Church with its Vignelli-designed pipe organ visible through the window," a former employee recalled. Modernist cups that Vignelli created reflected his personality, wrote an admirer: "strong and encouraging and smiley and animated."

It always stung that the Transit Authority had tossed aside his map, and he continued to defend it decades later. He and John Tauranac, who helped create the replacement, debated their approaches publicly on several occasions.

Tauranac acknowledged that Vignelli's design might be the prettiest ever, and said it deserved its place in the Museum of Modern Art's design collection. But he called it "geographically disorienting," adding, "Mapmaking isn't for someone who sits in an ivory tower and thinks abstractly."

Vignelli thought Tauranac's 1979 replacement was a travesty. "Look what these barbarians have done," he said in 2006, waving at it. "All these curves, all this whispering-in-the-ear of balloons. It's half-naturalist and half-abstract. It's a mongrel."

OPPOSITE: The charismatic Italian graphic designer Massimo Vignelli brought a clean, modern, European-influenced look to the subway.

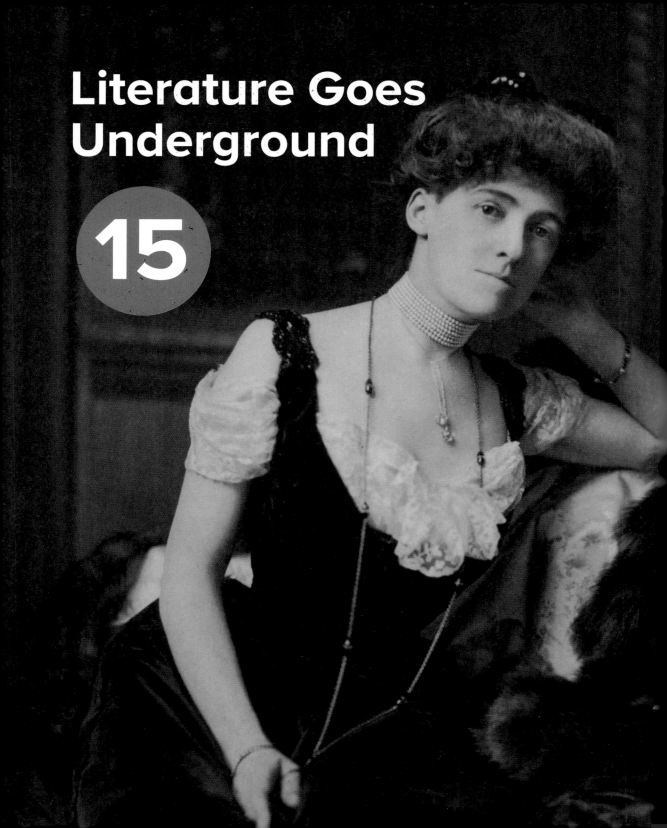

Literature Goes Underground

The subway served as both setting and subject for authors.

Inevitably, underground transit made its way into fiction about the city. Whether a character was being wedged between sweaty strangers or simply observing fellow passengers, there was a deep vein of human experience to tap.

Edith Wharton set a poignant scene in her 1913 novel *The Custom of the Country* in the subway. Ralph Marvell's wife ran off to Paris, abandoning him and their young son, but he had managed to keep her divorce suit in South Dakota a secret. One day, reading a newspaper over the shoulder of the man next to him, he is mortified to see a story about their split:

> His eye was caught by his own name on the first page of the heavily head-lined paper which the unshaved occupant of the next seat held between grimy fists. The blood rushed to Ralph's forehead as he looked over the man's arm and read: "Society Leader Gets Decree," and beneath it the subordinate clause: "Says Husband Too Absorbed In Business To Make Home Happy."

Wharton conveys not only Ralph's shame, but his disdain for the other passenger and his downmarket reading material.

The indignities a young woman faced on her commute to the office were vividly portrayed by Sinclair Lewis in his 1917 novel *The Job*. Women still did not have the vote at the time:

OPPOSITE: In Edith Wharton's *The Custom of the Country*, a character finds his divorce on the front page of the newspaper of the passenger next to him.

> Una stood with a hulking man pressing as close to her side as he dared, and a dapper clerkling squeezed against her breast. Above her head, to represent the city's culture and graciousness, there were advertisements of soap, stockings, and collars. At curves . . . she was flung into the arms of the grinning clerk, who held her tight. She, who must never be so unladylike as to enter a polling-place, had breathed into her very mouth the clerkling's virile electoral odor of cigarettes and onions and decayed teeth.

Playwright Elmer Rice, who had toured the subway as a 12-year-old shortly after it opened, later waxed poetic about it in *The Subway*, first performed in 1929, calling it "the entrails of the city" and "a monster of steel with flaming eyes and gaping jaws," "the beast of the new Apocalypse."

Thomas Wolfe demonstrated his ear for native conversational rhythms in "Only the Dead Know Brooklyn," a 1935 short story in the *New Yorker,* which consisted of a lengthy exchange on a Brooklyn platform about the best route to a particular destination:

"Sure," I says. "It's out in Bensenhoist. Yuh take duh Fourt' Avenoo express, get off at Fifty-nint' Street, change to a Sea Beach local deh, get off at Eighteent' Avenoo an' Sixty-toid, an' den walk down foeh blocks. Dat's all yuh got to do," I says.

"G'wan!" some wise guy dat I neveh seen befoeh pipes up. "Whatcha talkin' about?" he says—oh, he was wise, y'know. "Duh guy is crazy! I tell yuh what yuh do," he says to duh big guy. "Yuh change to duh West End line at Toity-sixt'," he tells him. "Get off at Noo Utrecht an' Sixteent' Avenoo," he says. "Walk two blocks oveh, foeh blocks up," he says, "an' you'll be right deh." Oh, a *wise* guy, y'know.

The excitement ordinary people felt riding to Coney Island was celebrated by an uncredited essayist in a 1938 issue of *Fortune.* It portrays the melting pot of the train and the carnival atmosphere at the Brooklyn shore, with carousel organs and sidewalk barkers:

Into this fluid mass the subway pours the people of New York and its visitors—young girls with firm high breasts and pretty legs and shrill, discordant voices—hat-snatching adolescents and youths on the make—children in arms and children underfoot and children in trouble—harried, scolding mothers and heavy-suited, heavy-booted fathers—soldiers and sailors and marines-virgins and couples in love and tarts—Gentiles and Jews and the in-betweens—whites and blacks and orientals—Irish and Italians and Poles and Swedes and Letts and Greeks—pushing, plodding, laughing, jostling, shrieking, sweating, posing—shedding their identities with their inhibitions, in the voice, the smell, the color of Coney Island.

Early on in *V.*, Thomas Pynchon's 1963 debut novel, his protagonist, Benny Profane, lying on his flophouse bed, resolves "on a whim to spend the day like a yo-yo, shuttling . . . back and forth" on the 42nd Street shuttle. Which he does.

> The shuttle after morning rush hour is near empty, like a littered beach after tourists have all gone home. In the hours between nine and noon the permanent residents come creeping back up their strand, shy and tentative. . . . Now sleeping bums and old ladies on relief, who have been there all along unnoticed, re-establish a kind of property right, and the coming on of a falling season.

Three decades later, the graffiti artist–narrator in Don DeLillo's 1997 *Underworld* finds himself riding a car covered in his own work:

> Every car tagged with his own neon zoom, with highlights and over-lapping letters and 3-D effect, the whole wildstyle thing of making your name and street number a kind of alphabet city where the colors lock and bleed and the letters connect and it's all live jive, it jumps and shouts—even the drips are intentional, painted super-sharp to express how the letters sweat, how they live and breathe and eat and sleep, they dance and play the sax.

The subway continues to hold the fascination of novelists. *X-Files* star David Duchovny titled his 2018 novel *Miss Subways* in reference to his protagonist's daily commute. Another 2018 work of fiction, Susie Orman Schnall's *The Subway Girls*, centers on a 1940s winner of the Miss Subways contest.

Q: Why do many subway entrances have colored globes by the entrance?

A: The globes were introduced in 1982 as a safety feature so passengers wouldn't be mugged descending stairs where there was no token clerk or entrance. Green indicates an entrance with a 24-hour clerk. Red means the entrance is closed at night. Originally, there were yellow globes for stations with part-time token booths. White bottoms are simply lights for illumination, with no meaning.

Q: Why can't you change across the platform between local and express trains at Penn Station and Atlantic Avenue–Barclays Center? Why do you have to cross under the tracks?

A: The stations were built that way to discourage quick dashes across the platform between trains because these stations, which are interchange points with mainline railroads, are particularly busy.

Promises, Promises

16

The Second Avenue subway is a symbol of all the thwarted ambitions for new transit lines.

Governors and mayors had been promising it since 1929. They mugged for the cameras at three ceremonial groundbreakings in the 1970s. Yet it took 45 more years before headlights were visible in the tunnels. It was "the most famous thing that's never been built in New York City," as rider advocate Gene Russianoff put it in 1981. The Second Avenue subway was a victim of the city's financial woes in the 1930s and the 1970s, compounded by overly rosy projections and overpromising politicians.

It was also a victim of New Yorkers' contentiousness.

Three things make the Second Avenue line unique among all the hoped-for subway lines that never materialized: The elevated line it was intended to replace was torn down before money was lined up for a replacement; four short segments built in the 1970s have lain unused beneath the streets for 45 years; and a short part of the line did actually open in 2017.

The first serious proposal for a subway on Second Avenue came in 1929, as construction of the first stage of the IND was underway and the city was looking toward the next round of expansion. The Board of Transportation projected a line from Wall Street, heading north the length of Manhattan, that would tie into an existing Bronx line and add two new branches there. The plan reappeared in 1932 with a tweak—a crosstown branch across 34th Street to 10th Avenue. Later in the 1930s, the board planned a tunnel to Brooklyn at the southern end. The Depression brought an end to big thinking, however. It was all the city could do to finish the Sixth Avenue subway in 1940.

The city nonetheless went ahead and demolished the Second Avenue elevated line. By then the els were reviled and seemed outdated, but the demolition was a case of hope outrunning reality. Despite protests, service ended north of 57th Street in 1940, and Mayor Fiorello La Guardia personally commenced the demolition of that section in 1941. Trains stopped running south of 57th the following year and the steel structure was dismantled.

A new class of car, the R-11, was designed with the Second Avenue subway in mind. Ten prototypes, the system's first stainless-steel cars, were delivered in 1949. They were the only ones built.

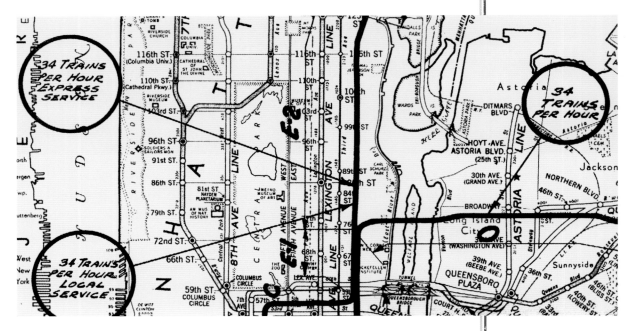

The country was at war and needed scrap metal for tanks and warships, but that was little consolation to those on the east side of the island. Now there was no rapid transit east of Third Avenue, and the Third Avenue el, too, was removed in Manhattan between 1950 and 1955, leaving only the Lexington Avenue–Park Avenue IRT (4, 5, 6) to serve the eastern flank of Manhattan.

By the late 1940s, the city was losing millions each year on the subway. Still, the dream of the Second Avenue subway wouldn't die. In 1948, Mayor William O'Dwyer made the politically unpopular decision to raise fares from a nickel to a dime. His justification: The money would help fund the Second Avenue subway. Shiny new stainless-steel R-11 prototype cars were commissioned for the future route, complete with a ventilation system designed to provide "95 percent germ-free air."

In truth, the fare increase wasn't enough to cover the system's operating shortfall, let alone build new lines. No real progress was made toward a second East Side subway. Still, the promises flowed. In the 1950 mayoral race, the Democrat, Ferdinand Pecora, made it a central plank of his campaign. "I promise you that the steam shovels will start to dig the day the [state budget cap] amendment becomes effective," he proclaimed.

Pecora lost to the acting mayor, Vincent Impellitteri, who tried to push plans forward. The next year, voters approved a $500 million bond measure

A 1951 plan for the Second Avenue subway called for a tunnel to Queens across 76th Street on the Upper East Side instead of the 63rd Street route eventually chosen. Trains were to run every two minutes or even more frequently at peak hours on both the local and express lines.

for the Second Avenue subway. It was sold to them as the funding for a massive six-track trunk line from 149th Street in the Bronx to Grand Street on the Lower East Side.

The measure passed, but then a funny thing happened. The fine print in the measure did not require that the money be spent on the new line. It allowed the Board of Transportation to divert the funds to repair existing lines, and it did just that—without advertising the fact. Rosy cost projections for the Second Avenue construction were not panning out, and after 30-odd years of underinvestment and extremely heavy usage during the war years, the system was badly run-down. Many of the cars were 30 and 40 years old. Most of the bond proceeds went to new cars and extending the last short platforms on the original IRT lines.

It took several years before the board's bait and switch came to public attention. When it did, the Transit Authority's chairman replied: "The expenditure of every penny of these funds is a matter of public record, documented in the files of the Transit Authority, the Board of Estimate and the Controller's office." But, since the board never announced the diversion, voters had been snookered, just as they had been when Mayor O'Dwyer promised that increasing fares would pay for the line.

After that, the plans languished until 1967, when Republican governor Nelson Rockefeller—laying the groundwork for a presidential run the following year—announced a bold plan for new roads and public transportation across the state. A subway would be built from 34th Street up Second Avenue to 126th Street, he announced. In November that year, voters approved $2.5 billion of new state borrowing to cover the costs of his scheme, $600 million of which was slated for city transit.

Rockefeller's projected construction costs were almost absurdly optimistic, though, and he misled the public about financial backing from the federal government. Moreover, when details of the Second Avenue subway came out, it was greeted with hostility in two neighborhoods along the route.

Residents of the Lower East Side complained that the line was too far west for their area. (The old Second Avenue el ran down First Avenue south of 23rd Street, bringing it closer to the heart of the area.) The Metropolitan Transportation Authority eventually caved in and agreed to build a costly loop out to Avenue C between Houston Street and 14th Street, allowing the main line to continue on its original path straight down Second Avenue.

Then the Upper East Side and East Harlem were up in arms when a state assemblyman got ahold of detailed plans that showed only two intermediate stops north of Midtown—at 86th and 106th. There would be a 29-block gap between the 57th and 86th Street stations, and 20- and 19-block gaps north of there. The much-touted new East Side line would speed right by most of the residents of the area. Eventually, the MTA acquiesced and added stations at 72nd and 96th Streets, pushing up construction costs still further.

Finally, the moment came that all the elected officials had been waiting for: a groundbreaking. Rockefeller and Mayor John Lindsay presided over the ceremony at 103rd Street on October 28, 1972. "Whatever is said about this project in the years to come, certainly no one can say that the city acted rashly or without due deliberation," Lindsay quipped.

Governor Nelson Rockefeller, third from left, and Mayor John Lindsay, fifth from left, led the groundbreaking for the Second Avenue subway at 103rd Street in October 1972.

A year later, Lindsay led a second ceremony near the western foot of the Manhattan Bridge at Canal Street for the southern section of the line. Not to be outdone, the next summer, Lindsay's successor, Abe Beame, staged his own groundbreaking in July 1974, posing with a jackhammer on Second Avenue above Houston.

By then, however, the cost forecasts were skyrocketing—estimates had tripled from Rockefeller's optimistic numbers six years earlier—and the city was inching toward bankruptcy. In November 1974, the MTA called off work on the project so what little transit construction money there was could be saved for cheaper extensions in Queens.

When the plug was pulled, the city was left with four short, orphan segments, not connected to each other or to other lines. Money had run out before the two East Harlem tunnels, from 99th to 105th Streets and 110th to 120th Streets, could meet up. Another short tunnel lies below Second Avenue just above Houston Street, and the fourth is south of Canal Street.

Since 1975, the MTA has paid to maintain the tunnels, pumping water out and inspecting them regularly. In 1982, then-mayor Ed Koch suggested they be rented out—possibly to mushroom farmers. "Mushrooms need a dark interior," he observed. The MTA soon began running ads, suggesting other possible uses as well—as wine cellars, bowling alleys, or even discotheques. The tunnels would be soundproofed, an MTA official pointed out. There were no takers.

Under Republican governor George Pataki, from 1995 to 2006 the MTA prioritized commuter rail projects. But after he left office, 42 years and four mayors after work was halted in 1975, there was a fourth groundbreaking in April 2007, this time underground at 99th Street. Instead of poking at the pavement, Democratic governor Eliot Spitzer and the other dignitaries chipped away at a thin, temporary wall created for the occasion. In 2005, voters had approved a $2.9 billion borrowing that included $450 million earmarked for the Second Avenue subway, and the MTA finally had rounded up the rest of

Equipment on the wall of the 72nd Street station of the Second Avenue line includes a button for the T—the letter the Transit Authority has reserved for the day when trains run down Second Avenue to Wall Street.

the money needed. The much-promised line would be built from 63rd Street to 96th, with two stops in between.

A tunnel was already in place across 63rd Street. Two tracks in it opened in 1989, bringing trains from Sixth Avenue to Queens (F). Two other trackways adjacent to those were constructed from Seventh Avenue (Q) to Second Avenue. North of 63rd Street, the new line had to be built from scratch, bored through deep bedrock in order to minimize disruption and avoid undermining the foundations of the large buildings that had sprouted along the avenue over the decades.

When the line finally opened on New Year's Day 2017, years behind schedule, riders were treated to enormous stations with vaulted ceilings and artwork—trappings residents in other cities around the world had taken for granted for decades.

Next up is Stage 2, an extension from 96th Street of the Metro-North Railroad commuter rail station to 125th Street and Park Avenue, which will incorporate the two stretches of tunnel built in the 1970s. A 116th Street stop, not in the original plans, will now be built. Funding has not been finalized, but the MTA hopes the extension can be completed by 2029.

South of 63rd, the Second Avenue line remains a distant dream. The hope still is to build it to Hanover Square in the financial district, as sketched in 1929. The MTA has even reserved the T designation for the route and assigned it its own shade of blue. The engineers of the 2017 portion demonstrated their optimism: On the station walls, where motormen punch buttons to indicate the destination of their trains to align switches, there are T as well as Q buttons.

Plans call for the Second Avenue line to be extended north to 125th Street in the 2020s. One day it may run south from 63rd Street to Hanover Square, near South Ferry. • **OPPOSITE**: The cavern for the 86th Street station and tunnels during construction in 2013.

CALAMITIES

A short list of the subway's worst disasters,
natural and man-made.

ACCIDENTS

For such a large system, the subway has been relatively safe over its history, but there have been some deadly lapses.

The worst by far was the Malbone Street crash in Flatbush, Brooklyn, in 1918, during a strike by subway workers (see chapter 8). A fill-in motorman ran too quickly around a bend, and the train derailed, killing more than 90 people as the wood-bodied cars split

The drunken motorman who caused a deadly crash at Union Square in 1991 was convicted of manslaughter. • **OPPOSITE:** Wooden-walled cars shattered in the Malbone Street wreck of 1918. More than 90 passengers were killed.

up like matchsticks. All subsequent cars were constructed entirely of steel. The accident was so notorious that a month after the accident, Malbone Street was renamed Empire Boulevard.

Two major accidents in the 1990s prompted changes in procedures and equipment.

In 1991, five people were killed and more than 200 were injured when a motorman who had been drinking approached the Union Square station at 40 miles per hour, four times the speed limit, and derailed his train. The motorman was convicted of manslaughter and sentenced to up to 15 years in prison. The incident led to random blood and alcohol testing of transit workers.

In June 1995, a Manhattan-bound J train ran into an M train stopped ahead of it on the Williamsburg Bridge, killing the motorman in the second train and injuring 54 passengers. Federal investigators concluded that the dead motorman, who was at the end of an overnight shift, fell asleep and ran a red light at high speed, but the fail-safe automatic braking system hadn't engaged. The Transit Authority also concluded that the ancient signal system couldn't halt a train in time because it was designed for slower, lighter cars. That proved to be a system-wide problem. The Transit Authority responded by installing equipment to reduce speeds, cutting the maximum on straightaways from 55 miles an hour to 40.

TERRORISM

When the twin towers of the World Trade Center were destroyed in September 2001, parts of the building collapsed through the roof of the Cortlandt Street–World Trade Center station on the 1 line, which lay below the complex. Service had to be suspended on the line between South Ferry and Chambers Street for a year, and restoration work on the Cortlandt station was not completed until 2018. R train service was also suspended for a year because of damage at Cortlandt Street on that line.

HURRICANES

The damage from Hurricane Sandy in October 2012 cost billions of dollars to repair, and the work isn't finished. The storm filled seven East River tunnels with salt water and knocked out the trestle for the A train across Jamaica Bay to Far Rockaway.

Another casualty was the new South Ferry station (1) that had opened just three years earlier, replacing the original 1918 station. Sitting at the very tip of Manhattan, the new station was vulnerable to the storm surge, and it filled with harbor water. It took

ABOVE: Water reached the top of the escalators at the South Ferry (1) station during Hurricane Sandy in 2012. **OPPOSITE:** Parts of the World Trade Center twin towers collapsed into the Cortlandt Street station on the 1 line in the September 11, 2001, terror attacks.

almost five years to repair the nearly new station. In the meantime, the old loop station, whose platforms only fit five cars, was restored to service.

In the river tunnels, the flooding wreaked havoc with signals and power systems, and the salt water corroded reinforcing steel in the tunnel walls and track beds. The Montague Street Tunnel (R), also at the Battery, was closed for a year, and others were shut for months at a time, or for long stretches on weekends, as electrical equipment and concrete were repaired. Work on the 14th Street tunnel for the L train began only in 2019.

In the 1960s, the Central Intelligence Agency conducted secret tests to determine how vulnerable the subway would be to a germ warfare attack. A team of agents fanned out through the system. Walking between cars while they were moving, the agents dropped bulbs of an unidentified substance on the tracks, where they burst. Other spooks carried monitors to see how far the substance traveled. Neither the city nor the Transit Authority was notified of the tests, which only came to light in 1975. The agency concluded that the germs would spread rapidly through tunnels.

"It apparently has not occurred to the C.I.A. that New York subway riders have a natural immunity to lethal gases and deadly diseases," wrote columnist Russell Baker. "As Harry Truman once said, 'If you can't stand the bubonic plague, stay out of the subway.'"

Q: Wasn't there a guy who hijacked a subway train in real life?

A: There were two, actually.

Darius McCollum became something of a legend in 1980 when, at age 15, he impersonated a motorman and drove a crowded E train six stops. McCollum, who was later diagnosed with Asperger's syndrome, was obsessed with subways and buses and eventually racked up more than two dozen arrests for driving Greyhound and transit buses without authorization and pretending to be a subway employee.

In 1993, another teenager, Keron Thomas, took an A train and drove it around the system for three hours before he was caught.

PARTY DOWN

Now that the subway is cool, it's the place to party.

It's dark, grimy, dank, and filled with rats. Not the first place you'd think of throwing a party. But the subway has become a popular social venue.

The Transit Authority itself got the ball rolling. In 1962, as part of a clean-up-the-subway campaign, it hosted a champagne party on the 1 train. "Claret"-colored curtains were hung on one car, carpet was laid on the floor, bouquets were placed in cups by the windows, and a bar was installed. Only privileged invitees and a half-dozen Miss Subways could board the car, which ran from Times Square to South Ferry just once.

How'd that work out?

A car on the 1 train was outfitted with carpet and velvet curtains in 1962 for a champagne party to publicize a campaign to keep the subways clean. When the festivities were over, the floor was covered with pretzel pieces and litter.

Well, there was a small problem. Each time the local train lurched to a halt, champagne sloshed out of the glasses.

At the end of the line at South Ferry, the bar was removed and the curtains taken down. "All that remained of the dream train was a carful of flower petals, pretzel crumbs, papers and dirt—and dozens of posters reminding that 'This subway is yours. Help keep it clean,'" *Newsday* reported. The headline was "Subways Are Not for Sipping."

After that, passengers took the initiative. Japanese performance artist Yayoi Kusama had made a name for herself organizing "hit-and-run nudity attacks on Manhattan's bourgeoisie." In 1968, she and a group of sympathizers met at the 14th Street station on the 1, 2, and 3 lines and proceeded to disrobe. As they did, they noticed a dwarf circling them. Finally, the group realized he was an undercover cop, and they made a run for it. The cop bolted upstairs to a waiting police car, hopped in, and he and two other cops tried unsuccessfully to catch up with the perpetrators.

The tradition of unauthorized fêtes continues. Friends of a 16-year-old decorated a car with balloons, tinsel, and streamers for her birthday in 2017, enlisting other riders to help. They strode into the car with their decorations several stops ahead of the station where the birthday girl was waiting with another friend. When the doors of that car opened in front of her, she was completely surprised. Naturally, the whole thing was posted to YouTube.

The No Pants Subway Ride began as a prank in 2002 but is now an annual event and has spread to other cities. As explained by Improv Everywhere, the organizer:

> Random passengers board a subway car at separate stops in the middle of winter without pants. The participants behave as if they do not know each other, and they all wear winter coats, hats, scarves, and gloves. The only unusual thing is their lack of pants.

Some social events are impromptu. When a dinner reservation for Amber Asaly's birthday dinner fell through in 2018, the Los Angeles photographer and friends packed a folding table, wine, lobster, and spaghetti onto a J train and dined there in style. Their photos soon found their way to the *New York Post*. In 2019, a couple brought a small Ping-Pong table onto the 6 train and began playing.

Arguably the most audacious unauthorized event was an underground party in 2013 with some 200 people and live music in an unused station, organized by impresario Jeff Stark.

CLOCKWISE FROM TOP: A stage was set up and bands hired for a 2013 party in an unused station. • For Amber Asaly's birthday in 2018, she and friends dined on lobster and spaghetti on a J train. • No Pants Day is held every January in underground rail systems around the world.

Epilogue and Prologue

17

Temper your expectations, sit back, and take in the show.

Passengers who descend the long escalators or elevators to the deep stations along Second Avenue find enormous, bright, vaulted spaces—a reminder of how cramped and primitive most of the system's stations are.

It would be nice to end with a summary of the wonderful advances straphangers can look forward to—hyperfast maglev trains, new lines to the outer corners of the city, that sort of thing.

But the truth is, the city long ago gave up its dreams for the subway. If one had to pick a date, it was 1940, when the city took full control. America's entry into World War II the following year brought a halt to new construction, and the city's money went to cover operating losses after the war, not new lines.

After that, it was a station here, a station there, and occasionally a fancy connection of existing lines (e.g., Chrystie Street and Long Island City). By the 1970s, it was all the Transit Authority could do to scrub off the new graffiti every day and to keep the trains from breaking down midway through their runs.

The stupendously expensive extensions of the 2010s—the 7 train to Hudson Yards and the Second Avenue line—added a grand total of four stations. There would have been five, but a stop at 41st Street and 10th Avenue for the 7 train was cut out of the budget late in the planning, just as 60- and 70-story apartment towers were sprouting up there. That sort of short-sighted cost cutting was typical.

Still, there are things to look forward to. With a little luck, the Second Avenue line will make it to 125th Street by 2030 or so, which could transform East Harlem, currently a transit dead zone. A new fare system is replacing the dated, temperamental MetroCard. Eventually, some kind of electronic signaling system like those on the L and 7 lines will be installed citywide. Potentially, that could have a very noticeable impact on service. When the conductor says, "There is a train immediately behind," it could actually be true.

The subway competes with the suburbs for transportation funding, and with the Hudson Yards extension and the first Second Avenue stations complete, the MTA's focus has shifted to commuter rail projects. The East Side Access tunnel will bring Long Island Railroad trains to Grand Central, and the

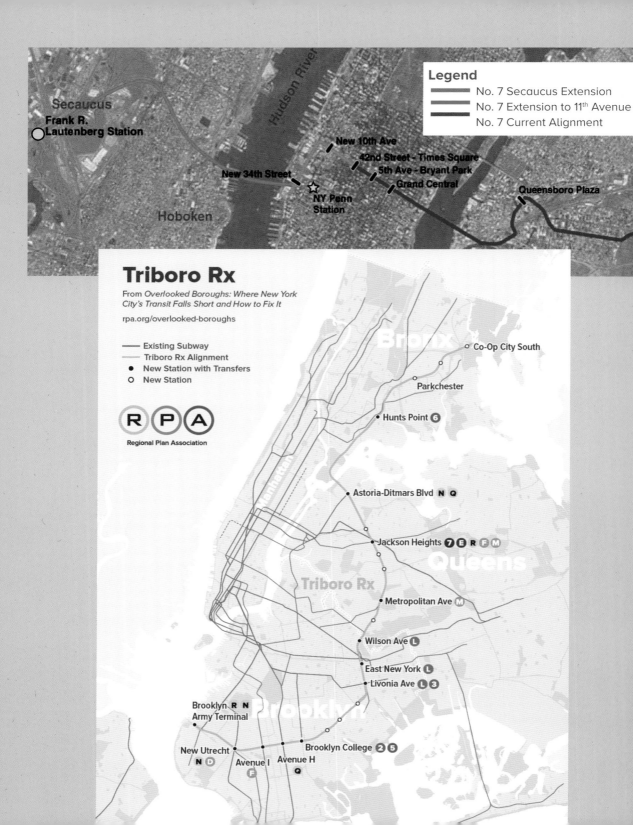

Legend
No. 7 Secaucus Extension
No. 7 Extension to 11ᵗʰ Avenue
No. 7 Current Alignment

Secaucus
Frank R. Lautenberg Station
Hudson River
New 10th Ave
New 34th Street
42nd Street - Times Square
5th Ave - Bryant Park
Grand Central
NY Penn Station
Queensboro Plaza
Hoboken

Triboro Rx

From *Overlooked Boroughs: Where New York City's Transit Falls Short and How to Fix It*

rpa.org/overlooked-boroughs

— Existing Subway
— Triboro Rx Alignment
● New Station with Transfers
○ New Station

R P A
Regional Plan Association

Bronx
Co-Op City South
Parkchester
● Hunts Point 6
● Astoria-Ditmars Blvd N Q
Jackson Heights 7 E R F M
Queens
Triboro Rx
● Metropolitan Ave M
● Wilson Ave L
● East New York L
● Livonia Ave L 3
Brooklyn Army Terminal R N
Brooklyn
New Utrecht N D
Avenue I F
Avenue H Q
Brooklyn College 2 5

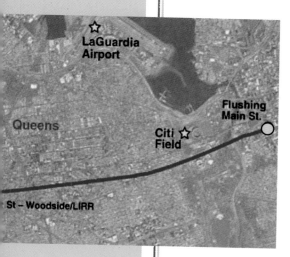

LaGuardia
Airport

Queens

Citi
Field

Flushing
Main St.

St – Woodside/LIRR

Visionary ideas for expansion have been few and far between in recent decades. An extension of the 7 line to Secaucus, New Jersey, explored in a study commissioned by the city under Mayor Michael Bloomberg, went nowhere. The Regional Plan Association recommended a subway line from the Bronx across Queens to southwest Brooklyn.

Gateway Program would mean two new tunnels from New Jersey to Manhattan, doubling capacity across the Hudson River for New Jersey Transit and Amtrak. The proposed AirTrain from LaGuardia Airport would help air travelers but not Queens residents.

Cost is one reason New York has so lagged other megacities in maintaining and expanding its transit. Depending on how you calculate it, underground rail construction in New York costs two to seven times as much per mile as the average in other major cities. In part, that's because work must be done in narrow streets with large structures nearby, and because new tunnels have to be bored through Manhattan bedrock using mining techniques. But those who have studied the problems also point to poor contracting practices, a lack of incentives for contractors to control costs, and padded union payrolls that politicians are loath to tackle. Well into the 20th century, corruption made construction in New York City "a sadistic orgy of whippings by organized crime."

It makes you long for the days when private companies, the IRT and BMT, built lines for a fixed price and delivered them on time.

Other great cities have done better. London has built several new Tube lines since the 1960s, plus a tricky 13-mile Crossrail commuter rail tunnel across Central London that threads through other buried tunnels and infrastructure. (To be fair to New York, the London project ran over budget and fell years behind schedule.)

But the fundamental reason for New York's failure to expand its system is that no one in government has advanced a grand vision for the subway since the 1960s, when Governor Nelson Rockefeller's new MTA laid out a wish list of new lines. Most politicians have distanced themselves from the subway, which seems like a no-win issue. A 10-foot pole isn't long enough.

In theory, the MTA was designed to be insulated from politics, but it was also "specifically designed to insulate the politicians from responsibility," as Mario Cuomo, governor from 1983 to 1994, candidly put it. Governors appoint nearly a majority of the MTA's directors and name the chairman, giving them effective control, but when things go wrong, they can deny that they call the shots because the city and surrounding counties hold a small majority. "I have representation on the board," said Governor Andrew Cuomo, Mario's son, minimizing his role during a crisis in 2017. On the city's side, when pressed for more city money to

Greetings from NYC

fix the problems, Mayor Bill de Blasio replied, essentially, "Not my problem." A headline summed it up: "Angry About Subway Delays? De Blasio Says Blame Cuomo, and Vice Versa."

By design, no one is responsible, for problems or for a long-term vision. Governors and mayors alike can join in that favorite local sport, bashing the Transit Authority. "No one ever lost votes in New York shaking a fist at the people in charge of the subways," as journalist Jim Dwyer put it in 1991.

While riders wait for a new era of civic-mindedness like the one that gave birth to the IRT, and a new generation of courageous, far-sighted politicians, they'll have to content themselves with a system that, on its good days, is still pretty inspiring. Take a ride from Jamaica to Midtown on the E, or from Yankee Stadium to Greenwich Village on the 2, 4, 5, or D and you're reminded of how fast New York's express lines are. Get out at 125th Street on the 1 train and take a look from the street at the enormous Manhattanville viaduct, as graceful now as it was in 1904. Or take the F or G and soak up the views of Brooklyn from the Smith–Ninth Street station, high above the Gowanus Canal. Pause a minute to

Riders must learn to grin and bear it, like the passenger in this 1980 postcard photo by Teri Slotkin.

MANHATTAN VIADUCT NEW YORK.

The 125th Street viaduct on the 1 line was an elegant solution to an engineering problem—the deep valley between Columbia University and Washington Heights.

appreciate the ceramic crests from the early lines—the ferries at Fulton Street, the stockade fence at Wall Street—that harken back to the city's early history.

Okay, so the subway smells in summertime. So does a lot of the city aboveground. Some stations seem decrepit? So are many neighborhoods. This is New York's subway, after all, and the natives were long ago inoculated against despair due to neglect and decay.

The subway still ranks as one of the greatest shows on earth, whether it's the foresighted innovations of William Barclay Parsons and Frank Sprague that are still used today or Madison Avenue's creativity, which is on display overhead in ads coaxing you to buy a mattress or a bedbug inspection. And it is unsurpassed for people watching. Are some of the riders a bit weird? Taciturn? A little too gymnastic? Hey, come on! It's New York. Somehow they coexist in this rumbling subterranean cage, mostly calmly, mostly courteously, on occasion showing surprising kindness, and generally going on their way with a sense of humor.

Enjoy the ride! Thank you for using MTA New York City Transit.

ARCHAEOLOGY:
A SELF-GUIDED TOUR

The subway is filled with long-shuttered stations, vestiges of old lines, and the beginnings of branches never built. Here's a brief guide to some artifacts you can glimpse if you know where to look:

- The original City Hall station, with its glorious vaulted ceiling, is there for the viewing. Just stay on the southbound 6 train after its last stop at the station now called City Hall—Brooklyn Bridge and ride it around the loop to pass through what was the starting point of the first line. The MTA's Transit Museum periodically offers tours to the public, as well.

- At 18th Street and Worth Street on the 4, 5, and 6 lines, you can see stations that were abandoned when nearby stations were lengthened. The five-car platforms show the scale of the original local stops.

- Abandoned five-car platforms of the 91st Street station on Broadway can be seen from the 1, 2, and 3. It was closed when the 96th Street station was lengthened

- to the south and the 86th Street station was lengthened to the north.

- At the City Hall station for the R, you can peek down stairs to see an unused lower platform where trains are sometimes stored.

- The wide pedestrian passageway between the 42nd Street shuttle platforms at Grand Central and the Lexington Avenue platforms (4, 5, 6) was built as a two-track terminus for the shuttle in 1918. But it quickly became apparent that two tracks were not enough, so three tracks of the original 1904 station were adapted for the shuttle and the trackways of the never-used terminus were covered over to create a walkway.

- Originally, Times Square was a local stop only, with just two platforms on the outside. When the West Side IRT was extended down Seventh Avenue, new platforms were built under the avenue. The old local stop became the end point for the 42nd Street shuttle. The three-track shuttle station was improvised by covering one track with a platform. The shuttles come to a halt along the curve where the original IRT line turned uptown onto Broadway, and two of the shuttle tracks still connect to the uptown local (1) tracks at the west end. Metal plates there can be lifted off when cars need to be removed for servicing. The southmost track is connected to the southbound 6 tracks at the Grand Central end.

- The New York Transit Museum in Downtown Brooklyn is located in the former Court Street station of the IND, a terminus used from 1936 to 1946. The unused fifth and sixth tracks on the outside of the nearby Hoyt-Schermerhorn station run to the museum station.

- From the Queensboro Plaza station on the 7, N, and W, you can see the steel superstructure for tracks that once ran over the 59th Street Bridge to intersect with the Second Avenue elevated line.

- Similarly, at the Myrtle Avenue station on the J, M, and Z, you can see where the Myrtle Avenue el ran south to Downtown Brooklyn, and the aboveground portions of the Broadway Junction station (J, L, and Z) afford views of long-abandoned elevated tracks.

- The narrow underpass between the uptown and downtown local platforms toward the south end of the 59th Street station on Lexington Avenue (4, 5, 6) was originally built as an eastbound train tunnel for the BMT to Queens (N, R, W) under 59th Street. After it was constructed, plans changed and it was decided to place those tracks alongside the Manhattan-bound tracks under 60th Street. The original tunnel has been substantially narrowed by the addition of equipment rooms.

JUST THE FACTS, MA'AM

ROUTES: 22

ROUTE MILEAGE: 262

STATIONS: 472, 60 percent underground

BUSIEST STATIONS:

➊ Times Square–42nd Street—(A, C, E, N, Q, R, S, W, 1, 2, 3, 7)—62 million passengers annually

➋ Grand Central (S, 4, 5, 6, 7)—43 million

➌ 34th Street–Herald Square (B, D, F, M, N, Q, R, W)—37.1 million

DEEPEST STATION: 191st Street (1), 180 feet below the surface

HIGHEST STATION: Smith–Ninth Street (F, G), on a viaduct over the Gowanus Canal, 88 feet above street level

UNDERWATER TUNNELS: 14

NUMBER OF CARS: 6,585 (2018)

EMPLOYEES: 35,913 (2018)

RANK IN THE WORLD BY RIDERSHIP: 7th (behind Beijing, Tokyo, Shanghai, Seoul, Guangzhou, and Moscow)

AVERAGE WEEKDAY PASSENGERS: 5.4 million (2018)

ANNUAL RIDERSHIP: 1.68 billion (2018)

LONGEST RIDES:

➊ With no change of trains: the A from 207th Street in Manhattan to Far Rockaway in Queens (31+ miles)

➋ With a transfer: the 2 line from 241st Street in the Bronx, transferring to the A to Far Rockaway (38+ miles)

GALLONS OF WATER PUMPED OUT OF THE SYSTEM ON A DRY DAY: 13 million

ANNUAL PASSENGER FATALITIES: 48 (2016)

MURDERS: 1 (2018)

ROBBERIES: 484 (2018)

PEOPLE ON THE TRACKS OR HIT BY A TRAIN BECAUSE THEY WERE TOO CLOSE TO THE EDGE OF THE PLATFORM, ANNUALLY: Nearly 900 (2017)

SUICIDES AND ATTEMPTS: 43 (2017)

TIMELINE: 1863–2019

1863 First London Underground sections opened using steam engines.

1865 New York State legislature approves plan for Hugh B. Wilson's subway system, but proposal is vetoed by the governor under pressure from Boss Tweed and New York City's transit interests.

1867 Charles Harvey tests cable-driven elevated train line along Greenwich Street in Lower Manhattan.

1869 Harvey's elevated line reaches 29th Street and Ninth Avenue, near 30th Street pier.

1881 Elevated lines along Second, Third, Sixth, and Ninth Avenues in Manhattan have been completed to Harlem.

1883 Brooklyn Bridge opens.

1885 Elevated line opens from Fulton Street Ferry in Brooklyn five miles east to Rockaway Avenue.

1888 Richmond, Virginia, electrifies its trolley lines using technology developed by Frank Sprague.

1890 London's first electrically propelled underground line opens under River Thames from Stockwell to city's financial center.

1897 Boston begins running electric trolleys underground.

1898 Brooklyn, Queens, Staten Island, and unincorporated portions of the Bronx merge with New York City, which then consisted of Manhattan and western portions of the Bronx.

1900 John B. McDonald wins bidding to build and operate first subway. He allies with August Belmont Jr.'s Interborough Rapid Transit Company (IRT), and ground is broken at City Hall. Paris Metro debuts with electric power.

1901 Boston debuts subway with full-sized cars.

1902 Berlin's U-bahn subway debuts.

1903 IRT gains control of all elevated lines in Manhattan and the Bronx.

1904 IRT subway opens from City Hall to 145th Street and Broadway.

1908 IRT tunnel from Manhattan to Brooklyn opens, ending at Atlantic Avenue terminus of Long Island Railroad.

1913 Dual Contracts agreed to between city, IRT, and Brooklyn Rapid Transit Company (BRT), launching a new wave of subway construction.

1915 BRT line opens from Coney Island in Brooklyn up Fourth Avenue to Manhattan Bridge and Chambers Street near City Hall (D, N, R, Q). IRT line from Grand Central completed to Corona, Queens (7).

1918 IRT Seventh Avenue line opens south from Times Square, Lexington Avenue IRT line opens north from Grand Central, and 42nd Street shuttle is created. Crash near Malbone Street, Brooklyn, kills more than 90 passengers.

1919 BRT Broadway line (N, Q, R, W) is completed from Manhattan Bridge to 59th Street and Lexington Avenue.

1925 Construction of Eighth Avenue IND line (A, B, C, D) begins in Harlem.

1928 IRT Queens line (7) extension to Main Street, Flushing, completed.

1932 Eighth Avenue IND line opens from Chambers Street to 207th Street in Manhattan.

1932 IRT goes into receivership after years of losses.

1933 Queens Boulevard IND line (E) opens from 50th Street and Eighth Avenue in Manhattan to Roosevelt Avenue in Queens.

1936 Construction of IND line down Sixth Avenue (B, D, F) begins in Midtown.

1936 • Lower East Side IND line (F) tunnel opens to Brooklyn, where it meets Eighth Avenue IND lines (A, C).

1940 • Sixth Avenue IND line (B, D, F) opens from West Fourth Street to 50th Street–Rockefeller Center, with local tracks only south of 34th Street.

1940 • Unification: BMT (successor to the BRT) and IRT are consolidated with IND under city control. Second Avenue el line ceases operation north of 57th Street, and demolition begins.

1942 • Service ceases on rest of Second Avenue el, and tracks are taken down.

1948 • Fare raised from five cents to 10 cents, first increase in 44 years.

1953 • Subway tokens introduced when fare is raised to 15 cents and can no longer be paid with one coin. New York City Transit Authority established to replace Board of Transportation.

1955 • Third Avenue elevated line closes in Manhattan.

1955 • Connection is opened between former BMT 60th Street tunnel in Manhattan and IND Queens Boulevard line, allowing Seventh Avenue–Broadway trains (R) to travel on IND lines in Queens.

1967 • Chrystie Street Connection opens, allowing trains from former BMT lines on the Manhattan Bridge to run on the IND Sixth Avenue line, in addition to their existing routes along Broadway and Center Street. New Sixth Avenue IND express lines completed between West Fourth and West 34th Streets.

1968 • Metropolitan Transportation Authority formed as new parent for New York City Transit Authority.

1971 • City buys Staten Island Railroad from Baltimore & Ohio Railroad and makes it part of transit system.

1972 • Mayor John Lindsay declares first war on subway graffiti.

1973 • Service ends on Third Avenue el in the Bronx.

1975 • First production trains with air-conditioning enter service, and retrofitting of AC to older trains begins.

1988 • Archer Avenue line opens in eastern Queens, adding three stations and joining E and J lines.

1989 • Graffiti is declared to be eliminated.

1994 • Construction of connection between 21st Street–Queensbridge station in Long Island City (F) and Queens Boulevard lines begins. First MetroCard electronic fare card machines installed.

1997 • Installation of MetroCard fare system is completed.

2001 • 63rd Street tunnel (F) is connected to Queens Boulevard lines in Long Island City, increasing capacity between Queens and Midtown. September 11 attacks on World Trade Center destroy Cortlandt Street station on 1 line, cutting off service to South Ferry.

2002 • IRT service to South Ferry restored.

2003 • Tokens phased out.

2004 • Full subway service returns to Manhattan Bridge for first time since 1986, when rust and other deterioration of 1909 structure forced its closure for repairs.

2007 • Construction begins on one-mile extension of 7 train from Times Square to Hudson Yards, and work recommences on Second Avenue subway on Upper East Side.

2015 • Flushing line (7) opens to Hudson Yards at 10th Avenue and 34th Street, near Javits Convention Center.

2017 • Second Avenue subway opens from 63rd Street to 96th Street.

2018 • Cortlandt Street station (1), destroyed on September 11, reopens.

2019 • Installation begins of OMNY fare collection system, which will replace MetroCard.

THE STRAPHANGER'S ESSENTIAL LEXICON

Transit employees and subway buffs employ acronyms and historical terms that may puzzle the ordinary rider. Here's a quick guide to some terms used in transit-savvy circles.

Abbreviations, Acronyms, and Technical Terms

A Division = The numbered lines, formerly IRT routes.

B Division = The lettered lines, a combination of the former BMT (roughly today's J to Z) and IND routes (roughly the A to G).

BMT = Brooklyn Manhattan Transit Company, the successor to the Brooklyn Rapid Transit Company (see BRT), beginning in 1923. Today's lines J through Z run mainly on what were originally BMT tracks.

BRT = Brooklyn Rapid Transit Company, the company that began as an operator of elevated lines in Brooklyn, and later operated subways in Manhattan (see chapter 6). It filed for bankruptcy in 1918 and was reorganized and renamed in 1923. See BMT.

CBTC = Communications-Based Train Control, an electronic signaling system to replace the electromechanical systems used since 1904 (see chapter 4).

Dwell time = The time a train remains in a station; crucial to maintaining schedules.

IND = The city-built, city-owned system begun in the 1920s to compete with the private IRT and BMT. Formally known as the Independent City-Owned Subway System but referred to as the Independent Subway System or the IND, it operated what today are the A through G lines.

IRT = Interborough Rapid Transit Company, the company that, with affiliates, built and operated the original subway. Today's numbered lines were originally IRT lines.

MDBF = Mean Distance Between Failures, the average distance a subway car travels before suffering a breakdown. A crucial measure of reliability that declined dramatically in the 1960s and 1970s and slumped again in the late 2010s.

Metropolitan Transportation Authority (MTA) = A state body created in 1968 as the parent for the New York City Transit Authority, the suburban commuter rail lines, and the body that controls bridges and tunnels (see chapter 9).

Motorman = The former term for the person who sits in the cab at the front of the train and controls the power. The gender-neutral "train operator" is now preferred.

SAS = Second Avenue subway.

SMS = Scheduled Maintenance System. Preventive maintenance practices designed to avoid breakdowns; generally skimped on in periods of austerity and budget cuts.

TPH = Trains per hour, a measure of capacity, which on some lines is lower than it was a century ago.

Transit Authority (TA) = Shorthand for the New York City Transit Authority, formed by the state in 1953 to oversee subways and city buses. When the MTA was created, the TA became one of its divisions. Transit Authority can also be shorthand for the MTA. The MTA now uses MTA New York City Transit as a synonym for New York City Transit Authority.

Geographical Designations

Brighton Line = Former BRT/BMT line that originally terminated at Brighton Beach, the aboveground portions of the B and Q routes.

Chrystie Street Connection = Tracks that connect the north tracks of the Manhattan Bridge (B, D) and the Williamsburg Bridge tracks (M) to the Sixth Avenue line.

Culver Line = F line along McDonald Avenue in Brooklyn, named for Andrew Culver, who built a steam-powered surface line along this route that was later rebuilt as an elevated line by the BRT. It was incorporated into the IND when the IND's underground line across Park Slope came aboveground near Church Avenue and connected to the existing elevated tracks.

Clark Street Tunnel = Route of the 2 and 3 from Wall Street to Clark Street in Brooklyn Heights.

Cranberry Street Tunnel = IND tunnel for the A and C lines from Fulton Street in Manhattan to High Street in Brooklyn.

GCT = Grand Central Terminal. The fastidious emphasize that it is a terminal, not a station, because trains do not run through it; they end there, in contrast to Pennsylvania Station.

Joralemon Street Tunnel = The first subway tunnel to Brooklyn, now carrying the 4 and 5 from Bowling Green in Manhattan to Borough Hall, Brooklyn, under Joralemon Street on the Brooklyn side.

Montague Street Tunnel = The first BRT/BMT tunnel under the East River, today carrying the R from Whitehall in Manhattan to Court Street in Downtown Brooklyn.

Sea Beach Line = Today's N route through southern Brooklyn. The portion east from Fourth Avenue along 61st Street was built under the Dual Contracts to connect the Fourth Avenue line with an existing BRT/BMT elevated line east of New Utrecht Avenue.

Steinway Tunnel = Tunnel from East 42nd Street in Manhattan to Long Island City, originally built to carry trolleys from Long Island City to Manhattan, though it was never used for that. Acquired by the IRT and adapted for use by the 7 line to Flushing, Queens. Named for William Steinway, whose piano factory was in Astoria and who promoted construction of the tunnel.

Uptown/Downtown = Used for trains and geography in Manhattan. Uptown is north- or Bronx bound; downtown is south- or Brooklyn bound.

West End Line = The former BRT/BMT elevated tracks over which the D runs in Brooklyn, connecting to the Fourth Avenue subway at 36th Street.

Other Important Expressions

"Passenger in need of medical assistance." = A reason for train delays. Can be a euphemism for someone being struck by a train.

"Stan klih close dure." = "Stand clear of the closing doors" in conductor speak.

Straphanger = Subway or elevated train passenger; derived from the overhead leather straps that riders could hold on to in early cars.

Subway surfing = Standing on top of a moving train. Not advisable.

"There's a train immediately behind." = Announcement that in some senses is always true but arouses suspicions because it does not disclose how far behind the next train is. Used by conductors who want to get their trains moving to persuade passengers on the platform that it's not worth their while to push their way onto a jam-packed car.

"We're delayed because of train traffic ahead. We'll be moving shortly." = All-purpose announcement used when a train remains stationary in a tunnel for no apparent reason.

FREQUENTLY CITED SOURCES

Baker, Ray Stannard. "The Subway Deal," *McClure's Magazine*, March 1905, available at https://www.nycsubway.org/wiki/The_Subway_Deal_(1905).

Belmont, Eleanor Robson. *The Fabric of Memory.* New York: Farrar, Straus and Cudahy, 1957.

Brobrick, Benson. *Labyrinths of Iron: Subways in History, Myth, Art, Technology & War.* New York: Henry Holt, 1994.

Caro, Robert A. *The Power Broker: Robert Moses and the Fall of New York.* New York: Alfred A. Knopf, 1974.

Cudahy, Brian J. *Rails Under the Mighty Hudson.* New York: Fordham University Press, 2004.

———. *Under the Sidewalks of New York.* Rev. ed. New York: The Stephen Greene Press, 1988.

Derrick, Peter. *Tunneling to the Future: The Story of the Great Subway Expansion That Saved New York.* New York: New York University Press, 2002.

Dougherty, Peter. *Tracks of the New York City Subway.* Self-published, 2017.

Dwyer, Jim. *Subway Lives: 24 Hours in the Life of the New York City Subway System.* New York: Crown, 1991.

Gardner, Fiona, and Amy Zimmer. *Meet Miss Subways: New York's Beauty Queens 1941–1976.* Kittery, ME: Seapoint Books, 2012.

Historic American Engineering Record of the Heritage Conservation and Preservation Service (HAER), National Park Service, Department of the Interior, Survey Number HAER NY-122 (1979). Available at http://cdn.loc.gov/master/pnp/habshaer/ny/ny0300/ny0387/data/ny0387data.pdf.

Hood, Clifton. *722 Miles: The Building of the Subways and How They Transformed New York.* New York: Simon & Schuster, 1993.

Malcolm, Tom. *William Barclay Parsons: A Renaissance Man of Old New York.* New York: Parsons Brinckerhoff, 2010.

Raskin, Joseph B. *The Routes Not Taken: A Trip Through New York City's Unbuilt Subway System.* New York: Fordham University Press, 2014.

Roess, Roger P., and Gene Sansone. *The Wheels That Drove New York: A History of the New York City Transit System.* New York: Springer, 2013.

Walker, James Blaine. *Fifty Years of Rapid Transit, 1864–1917.* New York: Law Publishing, Co., 1918; reprinted by facsimile reprint, Ann Arbor: University of Michigan University Library, 2008.

NOTES

CHAPTER 1
Horse-Drawn Gridlock and Dreams of a Subway

7   *Its streets were clogged . . . according to one observer: Facts and Figures 1979*, Public Affairs Department, New York City Transit Authority, p. 4, http://www.laguardiawagnerarchive.lagcc.cuny.edu/FILES_DOC/WAGNER_FILES/06.021.0058.060284.11.PDF

7   *By 1880 . . . scooping it up for fertilizer*: Clay McShane and Joel A. Tarr, *The Horse in the City* (Baltimore: John Hopkins University Press, 2007), pp. 22, 64–65; Jennifer 8. Lee, "When Horses Posed a Public Health Hazard," *New York Times*, June 9, 2008.

8   *The political barrier . . . many levers to use against rivals*: Clifton Hood, *722 Miles: The Building of the Subways and How They Transformed New York* (New York: Simon & Schuster, 1993), p. 43; Peter Derrick, *Tunneling to the Future: The Story of the Great Subway Expansion That Saved New York* (New York: New York University Press, 2002), pp. 27–28. "Tweed, William Marcy," Biographical Directory of the United States Congress, http://bioguide.-congress.gov/scripts/biodisplay.pl?index=T000440; Allen J. Share, "Tweed, William M(agear) 'Boss,'" in Kenneth T. Jackson, ed., *The Encyclopedia of*

New York City (Yale University Press, 1995), pp. 1205–1206.

8   *As early as 1863 . . . attack Harvey's structure*: Hood, *722 Miles*, p. 43; James Blaine Walker, *Fifty Years of Rapid Transit, 1864-1917* (Law Publishing Co. 1918, reprinted by University of Michigan), p. 85, citing *The New York Herald*, June 5, 1877.

8   *When Tweed was jailed . . . and the ferry landings*: Walker, *Fifty Years*, p. 111; Derrick, *Tunneling*, pp. 29–30.

8   *The els were far faster . . . "aerial nuisances"*: Hood, *722 Miles*, p. 53–54.

13   *Charles Harvey...steam locomotives*: Roess and Sansone, *Wheels*, pp. 100–105.

14   *Others put their faith in...waiting area;* Ibid., pp. 100–105; Hood, *722 Miles*, pp. 42–48.

15   *Dr. Rufus Gilbert...downhill by gravity*: Roess and Sansone, *Wheels*, p. 105.

CHAPTER 2
Men, Mules, and Dynamite: Building the IRT

17   *A thousand police . . . . to join Van Wyck:* "Rapid Transit Tunnel Begun," *New York Times*, March 25, 1900, p. 2.

17   *That was the photo opp . . . . directly along the line:* "Actual Work on the Big Tunnel Begun," *New York Times*, March 27, 1900, p. 14.

17   *On Parson's recommendation . . . while digging continued:* Hood, *722 Miles*, pp. 76, 82–83; Wallace B. Katz, "The New York Rapid Transit Decision of 1900," in Historic American Engineering Record of the Heritage Conservation and Preservation Service, National Park Service, Department of the Interior, Survey Number HAER NY-122 (1979) (hereafter HAER), p. 66; Charles Scott, "Design and Construction of the IRT: Civil Engineering," in HAER, pp. 238–240, 243–244.

19   *South of what was then Lafayette Place . . . was created over the line*: Christopher Gray, "Along Lafayette Street, Some Very Odd Lots," *New York Times*, June 17, 2010, p. RE6.

19   *There were many other obstacles . . . grand town houses*: Scott, "Design and Construction of the IRT: Civil Engineering," in HAER, pp. 248, 249, 251, 537.

19   *It's almost inconceivable today . . . on upper Broadway*: Ibid., pp. 243, 252; "Progress in the Subway," *New York Times*, August 10,

1902, p. 20; Roger P. Roess and Gene Sansone, *The Wheels That Drove New York: A History of the New York City Transit System* (Springer 2013), pp. 213, 243, 252, 269; Hood, *722 Miles*, p. 85.

21   *Eight mules . . . so it could be sent below*: "Some Imaginary Beasts of the Subway," *New York Times*, January 11, 1903, p. 28; "Song of a Subway Mule Blocks Broadway," *New York Times*, August 7, 1904, p. 9.

21   *Remarkably, McDonald . . . wrote another chronicler of the work*: Ray Stannard Baker, "The Subway Deal," *McClure's Magazine*, March, 1905, available at https://www.nycsubway.org/wikiThe_Subway_Deal_(1905); Walker, *Fifty Years*, p. 171; S. L. F. Deyo, "Enormous Difficulties That Were Overcome In Subway Construction," *Evening World*, Special Subway Souvenir, October 27, 1904, p. 2.

21   *The scale of the disruption . . . "on his knees as if in prayer"*: Baker, "Subway Deal"; *New-York Tribune Illustrated Supplement*, November 1, 1903, p. 3.

21   *There were real dangers . . . into the construction site and survived:* Ibid.; "Charles F. Allaire Injured," *New York Times*, September 7, 1902, p. 11.

26   *Others weren't so lucky . . . eleven days later:* "Death in Tunnel Dynamite Explosion," *New York Times*, January 28, 1902; Walker, *Fifty Years*, p. 182. ; Charles Scott, "Design and Construction of the IRT: Civil Engineering," in Historic American Engineering Record of the Heritage Conservation and Preservation Service, National Park Service, Department of Interior, Survey Number HAER NY-122 (1979), available at http://cdn.loc.gov/master/pnp/habshaer/ny/ny0300/ny0387/data/ny0387data.pdf, pp. 267–268. "Major Shaler Crushed Under Fall of Rock," *New York Times*, June 18, 1902; Hood, *722 Miles*, p. 88.

26   *By the time the work . . . the price of such an undertaking:* Scott, "Design and Construction," p. 268; Hood, *722 Miles*, p. 90.

28   *In 1900, when work began . . . Europe and Appalachia:* "Actual Work on the Big Tunnel Begun," *New York Times*, March 27, 1900, p. 14. "Miners Flock to New York," *New York Times*, April 28, 1901, p. 17.

28   *The subway was first and foremost . . . blocked the view of drivers:* David J. Framberger, "Architectural Designs for New York's First Subway," in HAER, pp. 366–367; "City Asked to Raze Old Subway Kiosks," *New York Times*, October 12, 1951, p. 25.

29   *While Parsons and his engineers . . . gleaming subway stops:* New York Transit Museum and Andrew Garn (photographer), *Subway Style: 100 Years of Architecture and Design in the New York City Subway* (New York: Stewart, Tabori & Chang, 2004), pp. 7, 121.

30   *To the credit of McDonald . . . what is now the 4 and 5:* "Twenty-Five Years of the New York Subway," *New York Times*, October 27, 1929, p. 188; Baker, "Subway Deal"; Wallace B. Katz, "The New York Rapid Transit Decision of 1900," *Historic American Engineering Record of the Heritage Conservation and Preservation Service*, National Park Service, Department of Interior, Survey Number HAER NY-122 (1979) (hereafter HAER NY-122), p. 116; Walker, *Fifty Years*, pp. 179, 190.

32   *Opening day . . . names were mentioned:* "Our Subway Open: 150,000 Try It," *New York Times*, October 28, 1904; "Exercises at

City Hall: Mayor Declares Subway Open; Ovations for Parsons and McDonald," *New York Times*, October 28, 1904, p. 1.

32   *Observers gushed . . . "arranged in forms of beauty":* Bassett Staines, "World's Greatest Effort to Solve City Transportation Problem," *Times-Dispatch* (Richmond, VA), October 9, 1904, p. 3; Baker, "Subway Deal."

32   *New York was late . . . "will be the greatest city in the world":* Hood, *722 Miles*, p. 93; Walker, *Fifty Years*, p. 202.

33   *When the original route...the IRT was awarded the contract:* Walker, *Fifty Years*, pp. 119; 176–180.

33   *This so-called Contract 2 project...inserted as permanent tunnel walls:* "One Battery Tunnel Cut Through at Last," *New York Times*, December 9, 1906.

33   *The air in the front chamber...pressure they were subjected to:* "Under the East River to Brooklyn," *New York Times*, June 11, 1905.

33   *"Pooh! Pooh!...a fine view of the city":* "Worker Shot Skyward from Under River Bed," *New York Times*, March 28, 1905; "Blown Through River," *New-York Tribune*, March 28, 1905.

35   *When the IRT...morning till night":* "Brooklyn Joyful over Its Tunnel," *New York Times*, January 8, 1908.

35   *The new line...all for a nickel:* "Our First Subway Completed at Last," *New York Times*, August 2, 1908.

37   *New York employed...East Side to West Side:* Hood, *722 Miles*, p. 98.

37   *Reinforced concrete...to limit its use:* Scott, "Design and Construction of the IRT: Civil Engineering," in HAER, pp. 228, 266–267.

37   *Fittingly for a city of immigrants...until 1991:* Alan Riding, "In a Class by Itself, and Now, Dear Paris, Classless," *New York Times*, August 3, 1991.

37   *Innovation continued...survived unharmed:* Hood, *722 Miles*, p. 222; "Frank Hedley, 91, of I.R.T. Is Dead," *New York Times*, July 17, 1955.

CHAPTER 3
The Forgotten Mogul

39   *The man with the money . . . Rothschild banking family of Europe:* Ron Chernow, *The House of Morgan: An American Banking Dynasty and the Rise of Modern Finance* (New York: Atlantic Monthly Press, 1990), pp. 73–75.

40   *Belmont's father . . . cementing his social position:* David Black, *The King of Fifth Avenue: The Fortunes of August Belmont* (New York: Dial Press, 1981), pp. 20–25, 39–40, 60–68.

40   *By the time the elder Belmont . . . Louisville & Nashville Railroad:* Walker, *Fifty Years*, pp. 167–168; Maury Klein, *History of the Louisville & Nashville Railroad* (Lexington, KY: University of Kentucky Press, 2013), p. 242.

40   *When the subway opened . . . a list of Wall Street evildoers:* "Mr. Belmont and the City," *New York Times*, December 24, 1905, p. 6; Eleanor Robson Belmont, *The Fabric of Memory* (Farrar, Strauss, and Cudahy, 1957), p. 101.

41   *Nothing in Belmont's nature . . . a haughty ring:* Black, *King of Fifth Avenue*, p. 666.

42   *Today we would call Belmont . . . said one good friend:* Belmont letter to John B. McDonald, October 13, 1904, and Belmont letter to E. P. Bryan, IRT vice president, November 14, 1904, August Belmont Jr. papers, Manuscripts and Archives Division, New York Public Library (hereafter NYPL); "Funeral Tomorrow for August

Belmont," *New York Evening Post*, December 11, 1924, p. 1; "Antique Staplers & Other Paper Fasteners," Early Office Museum, http://www.officemuseum.com/staplers.htm; Belmont, *Fabric*, p. 100.

42 *At times, however . . . on the man's behalf*: Belmont letter to Frank Hedley, April 30, 1912, in August Belmont Jr. papers, NYPL.

42 *Among those he considered equals . . . magazine reported*: Baker, "Subway Deal"; Robert M. Coates and Geoffrey Hellman, "Soup of the Evening," in *The Fun of It: Stories from The Talk of the Town*, ed. Lillian Ross (New York: Modern Library, 2001). This was originally a *New Yorker* item published in 1930.

42 *The term "conspicuous consumption" . . . walls of the main house*: "Yacht Syndicate Names," *New York Times*, November 22, 1900, p. 1; Belmont, *Fabric*, pp. 104–105, 119–120; "August Belmont's Great Nursery for Fast Horses," *Los Angeles Herald*, January 5, 1896, p. 1.

43 *Belmont also had the mogul's sine qua non . . . hunt moose*: Belmont, *Fabric*, p. 89; Dwyer, *Subway Lives*, pp. 132–133.

43 *These pleasures were easy . . . abandoned banking*: Letter from Frank Hedley, President of the Interborough Rapid Transit Co., to Holders of the Three Year Secured Convertible 7% Gold Notes of the Interborough Rapid Transit Co., December 20, 1921, and letter from Frank Hedley, President of the Interborough Rapid Transit Co., to Manhattan Railway Stockholders, July 20, 1922, in August Belmont Jr. papers, NYPL; "Elevated Rent Cut About Half for I.R.T.; Receiver

Averted," *New York Times*, April 7, 1922, p. 1; "Belmont's Estate Put at $20,000,000," *New York Times*, December 17, 1924, p. 1.

43 *He faced a second crisis . . . who anted up $500,000*: Belmont, *Fabric*, p. 125.

43 *On Belmont's death . . . where his mansion once stood*: "Belmont's Seat on Exchange Sold," *New York Times*, June 12, 1925; Belmont, *Fabric*, p. 119; "Belmont's Estate"; author's telephone interview of Mary Cascone, Town of Babylon historian, February 9, 2018.

44 *His private subway car . . . volunteers*: Email to author from William Wall, Shoreline Trolley Museum, March 9, 2018.

45 *New Yorkers adored...dandruff and constipation*: Hood, *722 Miles*, p. 96.

49 *Guardians of the city's aesthetics...get in the way*: "Architectural League Condemns Subway 'Ads,'" *New York Times*, November 2, 1904; "'Ads Arouse Art Society," *New York Times*, November 2, 1904.

50 *2 A.M. in the Subway...provoke the police*: See youtube.com/watch?v=90puwKMIUp8.

51 *In the popular 1927 film...president of the subway*: See imdb.com/title/tt0017439/.

51 *The jam-packed...take their seats*: See youtube.com/watch?v=C-CxHT139opM.

CHAPTER 4
The Engineers Who Made the Subway Possible

55 *Sprague worked briefly . . . capacity was limited*: William D. Middleton and William D. Middleton III, *Frank Julian Sprague: Electrical Inventor and Engineer* (Bloomington, IN: Indiana University Press, 2009), pp. 39–40, 56, 91–98; Hood, *722 Miles*, pp. 79–82.

56 *For a while in the early 1890s . . . Boston and other cities*: Middleton and Middleton, *Sprague*, pp. 91–98, 111–132.

57 *"The true parent of the subway" . . . great-grandparent of both*: Baker, "Subway Deal."

57 *When Sprague died . . . with their ingenuity*: "Father of the Trolley Car," *New York Herald Tribune*, October 26, 1934, cited in Middleton and Middleton, *Sprague*, pp. 267–268.

57 *Sprague was also a shrewd businessman . . . additional elevator inventions*: Middleton and Middleton, *Sprague*, pp. 86, 104, 135, 147, 258, 259.

57 *Parsons (1859–1932) was just 35 . . . tunneling through the rock*: Tom Malcolm, *William Barclay Parsons: A Renaissance Man of Old New York* (Parsons Brinkerhoff 2010), pp. 12–13; Roess and Sansone, *Wheels*, pp. 162, 164; Hood, *722 Miles*, p. 83.

58 *Soon after his appointment . . . transmission lines, and electric motors*: Wm. Barclay Parsons, *Report to the Board of Rapid Transit Railroad Commissioners in and for the City of New York on Rapid Transit in Foreign Cities* (1894), pp. 59–63, available at babel.hathitrust.org/cgi/pt?id=mdp.39015021057891.

58 *The monumental task . . . said August Belmont Jr.*: Walker, *Fifty Years*, p. 183; Malcolm, *Parsons*, pp. 39–47, 64; Arthur Goodrich, "William Barclay Parsons: The Chief Engineer of the Great Subway System of New York City—His Personality and Method of Working," *World's Work*, May 1903, p. 3470; "Belmont Denies Row with John B. McDonald," *New York Times*, November 23, 1904, p. 12.

59 *Parsons was a blue-blooded . . . their friends and relatives*: Hood, *722 Miles*, p. 77; Malcolm, *Parsons*, pp. 7, 47–48; Goodrich, "William Barclay Parsons," p. 3470.

59 *Like Sprague . . . he refused to retreat*: Malcolm, *Parsons*, pp. 23–26; Benson Brobrick, *Labyrinths of Iron: Subways in History, Myth, Art, Technology & War* (New York: Henry Holt, 1994) p. 213–214.

60 *"It undoubtedly took"... on the subway's centennial in 2004*: Randy Kennedy, "The Rumble That's Lasted for 100 Years," *New York Times*, March 19, 2004, p. E31.

60 *When the first stage ... sometimes under artillery fire*: Malcolm, *Parsons*, pp. 99–116.

61 *The engineering firm ... republished in 1968*: William Barclay Parsons, *Engineers and Engineering in the Renaissance* (1939; reprint, Cambridge, MA: MIT Press, 1968).

61 *"A militant genius of the city age"*: "William Barclay Parsons," *New York Times*, May 10, 1932, p. 20.

62 *Behind those...go slow*: Dougherty, *Tracks*, pp. xii–xvii.

62 *It's old-fashioned...as long as 1,000 feet*: Hannah Frishberg, "New York Subway 101: A Guide to the Signal System: Understanding the Subway's Signals Helps You Understand How the Subway System Functions," *Curbed New York*, February 27, 2019.

62 *Block signaling...imposes unnecessarily long gaps*: William Neuman, "For Less Crowding on L Train, Think 2010, Report Says," *New York Times*, May 22, 2007.

62 *Capacity on one line in London...fell 40 percent*: Stephen J. Smith, "Advanced Signaling Makes the Most Out of Old Subways, But Can New York Handle It?" *Next City*, May 2, 2014.

62 *New York is late to adapt the technology, which has been installed in Europe for decades*: *Moving Forward: Accelerating the Transition to Communications-Based Train Control for New York City's Subways* (New York: Regional Plan Association, 2014).

62 *The L line...Paris Metro since 1998*: Dougherty, *Tracks*, p. xvii.

62 *The 7 line...is still many years away*: Paul Berger, "New York City Transit Chief: Subway Signal Overhaul Could Be Done in 10 to 15 Years," *Wall Street Journal*, March 29, 2018.

64 *There's another way...pass a red signal*: Richard Perez-Pena, "Inquiry Links Subway Crash to Signals," *New York Times*, June 16, 1995.

64 *Over time...the speed limit was 20*: Dan Rivoli, "Byford Vows to Speed Up Trains," *Daily News* (New York), July 22, 2018; Dan Rivoli, "MTA Tests Subway Signals, Plans Fixes to Get Trains Moving Faster," *Daily News* (New York), October 29, 2018; and Adam Pierce, "How 2 M.T.A. Decisions Pushed the Subway into Crisis," *Daily News* (New York), October 29, 2018.

65 *The original method...inserted a nickel in a slot*: Hood, *722 Miles*, pp. 221–222; Dwyer, *Subway Lives*, p. 140; and "The Wall Street Station's Wooden Token Booth," *Ephemeral New York*, August 2, 2010.

68 *That worked...for the subway*: "15c Fare Starts; Lines Form to Buy Tokens in Subways," *New York Times*, July 25, 1953.

68 *As fares increased...cheaper tokens wouldn't work*: "Tickets, Tokens and MetroCards," MTA, and "Fare Collection in the Subway," nycsubway.org.

68 *The swipe...2.27 miles per hour*: James B. Fishman, "Metropolitan Diary: Speed of a MetroCard Swipe," *New York Times*, June 15, 2016, p. A16.

68 *In 2019...commuter rail lines, as well*: "Say Hello to Tap and Go, with OMNY," MTA, and Caroline Spivack, "A Guide to OMNY," *Curbed New York*, May 22, 2019.

69 *With the MetroCard...facility in Queens*: Dwyer, *Subway Lives*, p. 59; Michelle Young, "The MTA's Special Armored Money Train That Ran from 1951 to 2006 in NYC," *Untapped Cities*, February 12, 2016; Jeff Vandam, "Cash and Carry," *New York Times*, December 31, 2006.

69 *The deepest station...below St. Nicholas Avenue*: "MTA Facts and Figures, Subways".

69 *The nearby 190th Street station...protected from cosmic rays*: Dwyer, *Subway Lives*, pp. 170–171.

69 *Stone removed...in 1905 and 1906*: "Ellis Island Chronology," National Park Service.

69 *...and schist tunneled for the Second Avenue subway provides the contours at Ferry Point Park and the golf course there*: Ferry Point Park, "New York City Department of Parks."

CHAPTER 5

Defects in the New Marvel

71 *The system was designed ... that all local stations were lengthened*: Walker, *Fifty Years*, p. 185; Paul Crowell, "Platforms Added at 32 IRT Stations," *New York Times*, September 14, 1949, p. 29; "City Approves Contract for Subway Projects," *New York Times*, April 24, 1963, p. 19.

71 *The idea of running longer trains ... open at the next station*: "MTA Selects 8 Winners, 2 Honorable Mentions of MTA Genius Transit Challenge," Metropolitan Transit Authority, press release, March 9, 2018.

71 *Loading and unloading ... reducing station delays*: "Subway a Year Old; What It Has Done," *New York Times*, October 27, 1905; Hood, *722 Miles*, p. 114.

71 *Out of safety concerns ... two or three trains per hour*: William Barclay Parsons, "Subway Embodies All Up-to-Date Ideas for Handling Passengers," *Evening World*, Special Subway Souvenir, October 27, 1904, p. 3; Clifton Hood, "The Impact of the IRT on New York City," in HAER, pp. 166–167.

72 *Then, as now, stations . . . reduced the temperature only slightly*: "Electric Fans Put in Subway at the Bridge," *New York Times*, June 29, 1905, p. 8. "Trains Will Pump Out the Bad Subway Air," *New York Times*, May 19, 1905, p. 20; "Three Parks Cut into for Subway Ventilation," *New York Times*, June 6, 1905, p. 7; David J. Framberger, "Architectural Designs for New York's First Subway," in HAER, p. 386; Walker, *Fifty Years*, p. 206.

72 *The glass ceiling bricks . . . more heat in the tunnels*: "Three Parks Cut into for Subway Ventilation"; Framberger, "Architectural Designs," pp. 385–386.

73 *The IRT began installing fans . . . he observed*: "Electric Fans for All Subway Fans," *New York Times*, August 11, 1910, p. 6; "A Hotter Subway," *New York Times*, August 10, 1910, p. 6.

73 *Things got much worse . . . when it was only 86 degrees outside*: Aaron Gordon, "Prepare Yourselves, There Is No Immediate Fix for Hot Subway Stations," *Village Voice*, August 16, 2018, https://www.villagevoice.com/2018/08/16/hot-subway-stations-mta-climate-change/.

73 *Unfortunately, air-conditioning . . . air-cooling systems*: James Barron, "So You Think It's Hot Above Ground," *New York Times*, July 27, 1989, p. B3. "Cortlandt Street Subway Station Reopens," Spectrum New NY1, September 8, 2018, https://www.ny1.com/nyc/all-boroughs/news/2018/09/08/cortlandt-street-subway-station-reopens; Eric Jaffe, "A Brief History of Air-Conditioning on the New York Subway," CityLab, August 15, 2012, https://www. citylab.com/transportation/2012/08/brief-history-air-conditioning-new-york-subway/2952/.

74 *Stations smelled . . . "ozone of the subway does me good"*: Framberger, "Architectural Designs," p. 386; "Finds Subway Air Good, But Sanitation Bad," *New York Times*, February 28, 1906, p. 16; "Electric Fans Put in Subway at the Bridge," *New York Times*, June 29, 1905, p. 8

74 *The smells never went away . . . a water main broke years earlier*: Milton Esterow, "Subway Sniffer Leads Mole's Life, Hunting Aromas on 247-Mile Beat," *New York Times*, July 25, 1950, p. 29; Dwyer, *Subway Lives*, p. 15.

74 *Many found the subway . . . the ear muscles, he said*: "Some Subway Ifs and Don'ts," *New York Times*, October 28, 1904; "Relief for 'Subway Eye,'" *New York Times*, January 8, 1905, p. 4; Dr. A. S. Atkinson, "New Senses Developed by Subway Travel," *New York Times*, December 30, 1906, p. 22.

75 *"In the Bronx subway"...New York Times, 1912*: Hood, *722 Miles*, p. 116.

75 *"Had I treated German prisoners"...Transit Commision, 1924*: Cudahy, *Rails Under the Mighty Hudson*, p. 93.

75 *"We do not get a civilized ride"...Board of Estimation and Apportionment, 1927*: Brobrick, *Labyrinths of Iron*, pp. 269–270.

76 *At its worst..."a violation of the laws of decency"*: Hood, *722 Miles*, p. 118.

CHAPTER 6

The Lost Decade and the Dual Contracts

81 *The delay stemmed, . . . commissions that controlled the subways*: Hood, *722 Miles*, pp. 148–149.

81 *Only two other short new lines . . . to Bay Ridge Avenue in 1915*: "BMT Nassau Street—Jamaica Line," nycsubway.org, https://www.nycsubway.org/wiki/BMT_Nassau_Street-Jamaica_Line; "BMT 4th Avenue Line," nycsubway.org, https://www.nycsubway.org/wiki/BMT_4th_Avenue_Line.

81 *The slow buildout . . . would bid for the latter*: "Twenty-Four Subways In Committee's Plan," *New York Times*, March 31, 1905, p. 1; Derrick, *Tunneling*, pp. 49–52; Hood, *722 Miles*, pp. 120–121; Walker, *Fifty Years*, p. 196.

82 *Belmont protested . . . a city official retorted*: "Has Right to Subways, Asserts Interborough," *New York Times*, March 29, 1905, p. 1.

82 *The commission's ambitious plan . . . overplaying his hand in 1905*: Hood, *722 Miles*, p. 126; Walker, *Fifty Years*, pp. 207–208.

82 *Belmont's hand was forced . . . Belmont confided years later*: Walker, *Fifty Years*, pp. 193–199; Derrick, *Tunneling*, pp. 53–54, 57–58; Hood, *722 Miles*, pp. 123–124; "Say City Must Finish Present Subway Plan," *New York Times*, April 1, 1905, p. 6; "Bel-mont-Ryan Think They've Got New York," *New York World*, January 25, 1906, p. 15.

84 *The 1906 gubernatorial election . . . the previous commission*: "Metz Would End 'Strap Hanging,'" *New York Herald*, March 2, 1906, p. 5; Hood, *722 Miles*, pp. 131, 137–138; Walker, *Fifty Years*, p. 208.

84 *Six months after . . . could take away at will*: Derrick, *Tunneling*, pp. 73–80, 139; Hood, *722 Miles*, pp. 136–145; Walker, *Fifty Years*, pp. 219–221.

84 *Still, the IRT had demonstrated . . . through a tunnel to Brooklyn*: Hood, *722 Miles*, pp. 145–149; Walker, *Fifty Years*, pp. 229–230.

84 *As the driving force . . . withdrew the offer*: Derrick, *Tunneling*, pp. 141–142; William G. McAdoo, *Crowded Years: The Reminiscences of William G. McAdoo* (Boston: Houghton Mifflin, 1931), pp. 95–96; Anthony Fitzherbert, "The Public Be Pleased: William Gibbs McAdoo and the Hudson Tubes," supplement to *Headlights* (Electric Railroaders Association), June 1964, available at https://www.nycsubway.org/wiki/The_Public_Be_Pleased:_William_Gibbs_McAdoo_and_the_Hudson_Tubes; Brian J. Cudahy, *Rails Under the Mighty Hudson* (New York: Fordham University Press 2004), p. 18; Hood, *722 Miles*, p. 148.

87 *A new rival soon emerged . . . the fringe of Manhattan*: Hood, *722 Miles*, pp. 150–151.

87 *This was the negotiating lever . . . half the construction costs*: Walker, *Fifty Years*, p. 228; Derrick, *Tunneling*, pp. 153–160, 173–185; Hood, *722 Miles*, pp. 151–157; "Subway Plan Gives the City a Master Hand," *New York Times*, June 14, 2011.

87 *Once again, the IRT . . . more subways in New York*: Walker, *Fifty Years*, pp. 229–233; "Subway Delay Stirs Realty Men," *New York Herald*, January 30, 1912, p. 6.

88 *Finally, in March 1913 . . . to Pelham Bay Park (6)*: Hood, *722 Miles*, pp. 155–161.

88 *When the bulk . . . the new Bay Ridge line*: Walker, *Fifty Years*, p. 225.

89 *Perhaps the best known song...made the piece famous*: Smithsonian, "Duke Ellington and Billy Strayhorn, Jazz Composers: Take the 'A' Train," americanhistory.si.edu.

90 *Alan James Markley...synthesis*: youtube.com/watch?v=kdHxovVLMjQ.

92 *The Transit Authority refuses...third rail is there*: https://www.reddit.com/r/nyc/comments/14xvsg/ama_nyct_conductor_clarification/.

93 *Judging by signage...spitting was a major health issue*: "Raid on Spitters Catches Hundreds," *New York Times*, February 10, 1909.

93 *Even unlit cigars..."cigars in the trains"*: "Smoking in the Subway," *New York Times*, March 2, 1909.

94 *During the Great Depression..."tune to be played"*: "Subway Beggars Barred on B.M.T. Trains; Sad Tales and Serenades Held Nuisances," *New York Times*, June 8, 1933.

94 *It may come as a surprise..."solicitation of money for them"*: "Rules of Conduct & Fines," Section 1050.6(b), Transit Adjudication Bureau, MTA.

95 *The most crucial unspoken rule...Avert your glance*: Tom Vanderbilt, "Underground Psychology: Researchers Have Been Spying on Us on the Subway. Here's What They've Learned," *Slate*, November 17, 2009.

CHAPTER 7
A Very Different Subway

97 *The project was jinxed . . . sat dormant for nine years*: Walker, *Fifty Years*, pp. 284–286; Cudahy, *Rails Under*, pp. 12–14.

97 *It took William Gibbs McAdoo (1863–1941) to get the project underway again*: William G. McAdoo, *Crowded Years: The Reminiscences of William G. McAdoo* (Boston: Houghton Mifflin, 1931), pp. 64–66, 72, 75ff.

98 *It took six years . . . that were never built*: Cudahy, *Rails Under*, p. 23; Anthony Fitzherbert, "The Public Be Pleased"; Walker, *Fifty Years*, p. 287; "M'Adoo Subway Wins Fight for Franchise," *New York Times*, December 16, 1904, p. 1.

98 *Like August Belmont Jr. . . . surprised ironworkers*: Fitzherbert, "Public Be Pleased."

98 *Unlike the short, thin-skinned . . . "The public be pleased"*: McAdoo, *Crowded Years*, pp. 98, 104.

99 *He studied New York's subway . . . loading and unloading*: Cudahy, *Rails Under*, p. 20; Fitzherbert, "Public Be Pleased."

100 *H&M offered service . . . unusual at the time*: Hood, *722 Miles*, p. 119; McAdoo, *Crowded Years*, pp. 105–106.

100 *McAdoo was solicitous . . . "her neighbors' clothes"*: Fitzherbert, "Public Be Pleased"; Hood, *722 Miles*, p. 118–119; "Women's Own Cars Filled to Hoboken," *New York Times*, April 2, 1909, p. 6.

100 *In 1910, McAdoo applied . . . served until 1938*: Hood, *722 Miles*, pp. 145–149; "Gives New Banks an Early Start," *New York Times*, November 17, 1914, p. 6; "'Fine,' Says M'Adoo," *New York Times*, July 7, 1920, p. 5; "Davis Gets By Wire Congratulations of Smith and M'Adoo," *New York Times*, July 10, 1924, p. 1; "M'Adoo Defeated, Says Pension Zeal Is Peril to Party," *New York Times*, September 1, 1938, p. 1.

CHAPTER 8
The Pugnacious Mayor and the Media Baron

104 *Unlike most of the mayors . . . to work on the el*: John Francis Hylan, *Autobiography of John Francis Hylan, Mayor of New York* (New York: The Rotary Press, 1922), pp. 15–18, 24, available at https://archive.org/details/autobiographyofj00hyla/.

104 *His transit career . . . trace at least partly to that incident*: Ibid., pp. 24–25; "Hylan Tells How He Lost B.R.T. Job," *New York Times*, Dec. 31, 1924, p. 3; Hood, *722 Miles*, p. 304, fn. 21.

104 *Hylan had nearly earned his law degree . . . Hearst's attention*: Hylan, *Autobiography*, pp. 27–28; Hood, *722 Miles*, pp. 187–188.

104 *Like Hylan, Hearst (1863–1951) was an outsider . . . the city and passengers*: Michael W. Brooks, *Subway City: Riding the Trains, Reading New York* (New Brunswick, NJ: Rutgers University Press, 1997), pp. 74–77, 85–90; Hood, *722 Miles*, p. 188.

104 *Hearst served two terms . . . different visions for the nation*: Brooks, *Subway City*, pp. 75–77, 79-80.

105 *Hearst engineered Hylan's nomination . . . as a magistrate*: Ibid., p. 91; Hood, *722 Miles*, pp. 187–188; "Public Ownership of City Railways Urged By Hylan," *New York Tribune*, October 7, 1917, p. 7; "The W.R. Hearst Launched," *New York Times*, March 18, 1923, p. 22; "Hylan Adds Pinchot to Presidency List; Foresees a Revolt," *New York Times*, December 10, 1922, p. 1; Brooks, *Subway City*, p. 91; Ben Procter, *William Randolph Hearst: The Later Years, 1911–1951* (New York: Oxford University Press, 2007), p. 97.

106 *In November 1918 . . . dealings with the transit companies*: Brooks, *Subway City*, pp. 92–93; Cudahy, *Under the Sidewalks*, pp. 86–87; Hood, *722 Miles*, p. 193; "Mayor Orders 5 B.R.T. Arrests," *New York Times*, December 12, 1918, pp. 1.

107 *He blocked completion . . . coal mines that supplied the IRT*: Brian Cudahy, *Under the Sidewalks of New York*, rev. ed (New York: The Stephen Greene Press, 1988), pp. 86–87; Brooks, *Subway City*, p. 104; "Hylan Threatens to Arrest Hedley," *New York Times*, December 24, 1919, p. 1; "Hylan Committee Visits Mine Camps," *New York Times*, October 30, 1922, p. 23.

107 *Like other progressives . . . soporific speeches in full*: "Hylan Adds Pinchot to Presidency List"; "Hylan in Attack upon Untermyer," *New York Times*, November 2, 1921, p. 3.

107 *Perhaps inevitably . . . the end of Hylan's political career*: "Full Text of the McAvoy Report on the City's Transit Problems," *New York Times*, February 9, 1925, p. 1; "Report a Staggering Blow to Mayor's Chances of Wigwam Renomination," *New York Evening Post*, February 9, 1925, p. 1; Joseph B. Raskin, *The Routes Not Taken: A Trip Through New York City's Unbuilt Subway System* (New York: Fordham University Press, 2014), pp. 130–131; Cudahy, *Under the Sidewalks*, p. 93.

107 *Though Hylan always . . . to build for a fixed price*: Hood, *722 Miles*, p. 181; Derrick, *Tunneling* pp. 234–235.

107 *Liabilities from the Malbone Street wreck . . . "which we call New York City"*: "Court Puts B.R.T. In Receivership; Garrison Named," *New York Times*, Jan. 1, 1919, p. 1; Letter from Frank Hedley, President of the Interborough Rapid Transit Co., to Holders of the Three Year Secured Convertible 7% Gold Notes of the Interborough Rapid Transit Co., December 20, 1921, in August Belmont Jr. papers, New York Public Library; "Elevated Rent Cut About Half for I.R.T.; Receiver Averted," *New York Times*, April 7, 1922, p. 1; letter

from Frank Hedley, President of the IRT, to Manhattan Railway Stockholders, July 20, 1922, in August Belmont Jr. papers, New York Public Library; Roess and Sansone, *Wheels*, pp. 199–200; "I.R.T. In Receivership," *New York Times*, August 27, 1932, p. 1; Hon. John F. Hylan, "Traction and Finance," in *The Forum*, vol. 65, ed. George Henry Payne (New York: Forum Publishing, 1921), p. 258, https://books.google.com/books?id=VYAAAAAAYAAJ.

109 *Tormenting the IRT and BMT . . . victory for Hylan and Hearst*: Hood, *722 Miles*, pp. 204–205; Cudahy, *Under the Sidewalks*, p. 92.

109 *It came with one large string attached . . . the city's development*: Hood, *722 Miles*, pp. 187, 203, 207, 209; Randy Kennedy, "Tunnel Vision: An Old Rivalry, a Quiet Continuance," *New York Times*, August 21, 2001.

109 *In December 1924 . . . that were already urbanized*: Hood, *722 Miles*, p. 207; Roess and Sansone, *Wheels*, pp. 212–213.

109 *Three months later . . . with typical flourish*: Cudahy, *Under the Sidewalks*, p. 94.

109 *Over the next 15 years . . . another candidate for mayor*: "Hylan Puts His Hope in 5-Cent Fare Issue," *New York Times*, May 1, 1925, p. 1; Brooks, *Subway City*, p. 104.

110 *The IND was as remarkable . . . never inspired oohs and aahs*: Cudahy, *Under the Sidewalks*, pp. 94, 104; Hood, *722 Miles*, p. 214; Kennedy, "Tunnel Vision: An Old Rivalry."

110 *Moreover, the city still suffers . . . competitors to one another*: Derrick, *Tunneling*, p. 376 fn. 36.

110 *Just as bad . . . if the city built more lines*: Roess and Sansone, *Wheels*, p. 220; Hood, *722 Miles*, pp. 210–211, 244.

112 *By enshrining the five-cent fare . . . sewn by Hylan and Hearst*: Hood, *722 Miles*, pp. 219–223, 230–231.

112 *On some subway platforms...can cause hearing loss*: See "Decibels & Damage," HEARsmart.

112 *Transit Authority rules...kitchen blender*: "Rules of Conduct and Fines," Section 1050.6(c)(4), Transit Adjudication Bureau, MTA.

114 *More recently, the rivalry and animosity...has played out in part over the subway*: Linda Greenhouse, "For Nearly a Generation Nelson Rockefeller Held the Reins of New York State," *New York Times*, January 28, 1979.

114 *Starting in 1907...a pushover for the private operators*: Hood, *722 Miles*, pp. 126–132.

115 *When Democratic governor Al Smith...clashed repeatedly with the transit commissions*: Raskin, *The Routes Not Taken*, p. 202.

115 *Although Smith named John Delaney...a Democrat*: Roess and Sansone, *Wheels*, pp. 204–205.

115 *The TCC was short-lived...set fares*: Roess and Sansone, *Wheels*, pp. 207.

115 The city retained a veto over routes and any borrowing, but that was all: "Full Power over Fares and Franchises Given to the New Transit Commission in Bill Made Public by Gov. Miller," New York Times, February 14, 1921.

115 In another slap to Mayor Hylan, the governor appointed George McAneny: "New Transit Board Names Appraisers," New York Times, May 6, 1921.

116 In 1953, with the subways . . . chosen by the first four: Philip Mark Plotch, "Waiting More Than 100 Years for the Second Avenue Subway to Arrive," Journal of Planning History 14, no. 4 (2015), p. 316; Facts and Figures 1979, Public Affairs Department, New York City Transit Authority, p. 13, available at http://www.laguardiawagnerarchive.lagcc.cuny.edu/FILES_DOC/WAGNER_FILES/06.021.0058.060284.11.PDF

116 who negotiated...private companies: Hood, 722 Miles, pp. 193–194.

116 In 1922, Smith defeated...a campaign to take them over: Hood, 722 Miles, pp. 204–205.

116 But the losses continued...on the rail operations: Roess and Sansone, Wheels, p. 328.

116 The political result...effective control: Roess and Sansone, Wheels, pp. 328–329; "About Us," MTA; Nicole Gelinas, "Who Runs the MTA?" City Journal, June 22, 2017.

117 On Eighth Avenue...lower level east of Seventh Avenue: Clayton Guse, "MTA to Add Express Train Service to F Train in Brooklyn," Daily News, July 10, 2019.

CHAPTER 9
Unification and Demolition

121 In 1940 . . . "largely frozen in time": Derrick, Tunneling, p. 238.

121 La Guardia, a feisty . . . a newspaper strike in 1945: "A Picture of O'Brien, McKee and LaGuardia in the Heat of the Campaign, with Statements of Their Views," New York Times, October 22, 1933, p. 144.

122 A six-term Republican congressman . . . Tammany circles: Hood, 722 Miles, p. 224.

122 Even before La Guardia . . . it was losing money: "Text of LaGuardia's Address at Fusion's Final Rally in Brooklyn," New York Times, November 5, 1933, p. 3; "LaGuardia to Act at Once on Transit," New York Times, November 18, 1933, p. 9; Hood, 722 Miles, p. 230.

122 The private companies . . . break even: Hood, 722 Miles, pp. 222–223, 229–230.

123 In 1937, an election year . . . on the eve of unification: Ibid., pp. 231–234 237.

124 The Sixth Avenue el . . . by buses or nearby subways: Roess and Sansone, Wheels, pp. 284, 292–294; Cudahy, Under the Sidewalks, pp. 112, 117–118, 126.

124 In 1948, the city . . . rail lines that were repurposed: Hood, 722 Miles, pp. 246–247, 251.

124 1941: "Rail Line Is Added to Subway System," New York Times, May 16, 1941, p. 25; Cudahy, Under the Sidewalks, pp. 102, 119, 130, 132.

124 1946–1956: "Fulton Subway Opens After All-Night 'Dry Runs,'" Brooklyn Eagle, November 28, 1948, p. 3; Stan Fischler, Uptown, Downtown: A Trip Through Time on New York's Subways (New York: Hawthorn Books, 1976), pp. 244–245.

125 1956: "L.I.R.R. May Abandon Burned Beach Line," New York Times, May 9, 1950, p. 1.

125 1967: Sixth Avenue: Emanuel Permutter, "Subway Changes to Speed Service," New York Times, November 16, 1967, p. 1; "Diggers of Subway Tunnel Work 80 Feet Under Sixth Avenue," New York Times, June 16, 1962, p. 16.

126 1967: Chrystie Street: "Subway Changes to Speed Service," New York Times, November 16, 1967; "Speed Record," New York Times, May 23, 1976, p. 408.

127 1988: Kirk Johnson, "Big Changes for Subways Are to Begin," New York Times, December 9, 1988.

127 1989: Donatella Lorch, "The 'Subway to Nowhere' Now Goes Somewhere," New York Times, October 29, 1989, p. 36; "East Side Access: Project Overview," MTA, http://web.mta.info/capital/esa_alt.html.

127 2001: Sarah Kershaw, "V Train Begins Service Today, Giving Queens Commuters Another Option," New York Times, December 17, 2001, p. 71.

127 2015: Patrick McGeehan, "Subway Extension Provides a Link to Hudson Yards, Still a Work in Progress," New York Times, October 9, 2015.

127 2017: Edgar Sandoval, Dan Rivoli, and Stephen Rex Brown, "New Yorkers Take Historic First Ride on Second Ave. Subway—Experience Historic First Delay," Daily News (New York), January 1, 2017.

129 One was a manicurist who did Powers's nails at the Waldorf Astoria Hotel: Gardner and Zimmer, Meet Miss Subways, pp. 13–14.

129 Enid Berkowitz...stuffed cabbage: Robertson, "Miss Subways Reigns," New York Times, February 18, 1957.

129 As the contest gained popularity...some women themselves: Gardner and Zimmer, Meet Miss Subways, p. 14.

130 *Miss Subways..."handpainted masterpieces"*: Robertson, "Miss Subways Reigns."

130 *After 1963...father's beat*: Gardner and Zimmer, *Meet Miss Subways*, p. 14.

130 *An admirer...lemon meringue pie*: Robertson, "Miss Subways Reigns."

130 *Civil rights leaders...celebrate her selection*: Gardner and Zimmer, *Meet Miss Subways*, p. 15–18.

131 *A year earlier...armed forces, which had been segregated*: "Executive Order 9981: Desegregation of the Armed Forces (1948), Ourdocuments.gov.

131 *There was no black contestant...until 1983*: Gardner and Zimmer, *Meet Miss Subways*, pp. 16–19.

131 *In a 1976 piece..."from her ears"*: Gardner and Zimmer, *Meet Miss Subways*, pp. 19–20.

132 *Beginning in the 1970s...lower maintenance costs*: Dwyer, *Subway Lives*, pp. 164–165.

133 *When the brakes are applied...returned to the third rail*: MTA Press Release, "New Technology Train Rolled Out This Morning Along the E Line," December 22, 2008.

CHAPTER 10
How New Lines Shaped the City

137 *Manhattan's population . . . black and Puerto Rican slum*: Derrick, *Tunneling*, p. 3; Hood, *722 Miles*, p. 135. Mike Wallace, *Greater Gotham* (New York: Oxford University Press, 2017), p. 251ff.

137 *Successively tighter building codes . . . provide adequate transit*: Herbert Croly, "The New York Rapid Transit Subway, How It Will Affect the City's Life and Business," *Review*, September 1904, pp. 306–311, available at https://www.nycsubway.org/wiki/The_New_York_Rapid_Transit_Subway,_How_It_Will_Affect_the_City%27s_Life_and_Business_(1904); Calvin Tomkins, "The Desirability of Comprehensive Municipal Planning in Advance of Development" (1905), in *Empire City: New York Through the Centuries*, ed. Kenneth T. Jackson and David S. Dunbar (New York: Columbia University Press, 2002), p. 470.

137 *Reformers imagined . . . class warfare*: Wallace, *Greater Gotham*, p. 263.

138 *The elevated lines . . . rose tenfold*: Derrick, *Tunneling*, pp. 2–3; Hood, *722 Miles*, p. 138; Wallace, *Greater Gotham*, p. 280.

138 *For the real estate industry . . . "water is to the West"*: Dwyer, *Subway Lives*, p. 56.

138 *Transit-driven development . . . which remain to this day*: Peter Salwen, *Upper West Side Story: A History and Guide* (New York: Abbeville Press, 1989), pp. 64–70; Henry Morgenthau with French Strother, *All in a Lifetime* (Garden City, NY: Doubleday, Page & Co., 1922), p. 47.

138 *When planning for a subway . . . before the subway opened*: Morgenthau, *Lifetime*, pp. 47–50; "Expresses to 221st Street," *New York Times*, May 30, 1906, p. 1.

139 *As the IRT neared completion . . . and Washington Heights*: Morgenthau, *Lifetime*, pp. 87–88.

139 *An even bigger land speculator . . . once owned by Barney*: Hood, *722 Miles*, p. 1; Clifton Hood, "The Impact of the IRT," *Real Estate Record and Builders' Guide*, vol. 74, no. 1910 (October 22, 1904), p. 834; Salwen, *Upper West Side Story*, p. 126.

139 *Like many New Yorkers . . . resigned from the IRT board*: "No Tunnel Injunction," *New York Times*, August 27, 1902, p. 14; "Barney House Still Sinks," *New York Times*, February 3, 1903, p. 16.

139 *Barney came to a strange end . . . it was ruled a suicide*: "Jury Says Barney Committed Suicide," *New York Times*, November 27, 1907, p. 2; "Barney's Successor Puts All on Morse," *New York Times*, November 16, 1907, pp. 1–2.

140 *In economic terms . . . many had hoped for*: Hood, *722 Miles*, pp. 110–111, 173–178.

140 *Rather than a rush . . . their public transit connections*: Raskin, *Routes*, pp. 109–113.

140 *The IRT and BMT had been forced . . . commute to Grand Central*: Derrick, *Tunneling*, p. 79; Advertisement, *New York Times*, January 11, 1931, p. 147/RE33.

141 *Things didn't always play out . . . well short of the homes*: Raskin, *Routes*, pp. 121–129.

142 *By the time the main IND lines . . . as reformers had hoped*: Derrick, *Tunneling*, pp. 10, 231, 245–256, 267.

145 *The work left an enduring scar...until recent years*: Christopher Gray, "Along Lafayette Street, Some Very Odd Lots," *New York Times*, June 17, 2010.

145 *The cock-eyed angles...to the wrecker's ball*: "Landmarks Doomed for New Avenue," New York Times, October 5, 1913.

145 *It was plowed through four solid city blocks*: "Subway Loop Approved; Will Have Four Tracks," *New York Times*, January 26, 1907; "Bridge Loop to Open for One Line Only," *New York Times*, August 3, 1913.

CHAPTER 11

Dream On

149 *Hudson and Manhattan New York Lines*: Hood, *722 Miles*, pp. 145–149; Roess and Sansone, *Wheels*, p. 184; "M'Adoo Subway Wins Fight for Franchise," *New York Times*, December 16, 1904, p. 1; Cudahy, *Rails Under*, p. 24; "McAdoo Extension To Be Ready in 1911," *New York Times*, June 5, 1909, p. 16; "M'Adoo's Railroad Slow In Building," *New York Times*, April 9, 1914, p. 5.

150 *Staten Island Tunnel*: Raskin, *Routes*, pp. 124–126, 131, 136; "Richmond Tunnel Promised," *New York Times*, December 22, 1921, p. 5; "Staten Island Waits For Narrows Tunnel," *New York Times*, May 10, 1925, p. 12; "City Committed to Spend $4,000,000 on Narrows Tunnel," *Brooklyn Daily Eagle*, May 7, 1922, p. 27; "Staten Island Tube Started by Hylan," *New York Times*, April 15, 1923, p. 20; "Hylan Swings Pick at Shaft Opening," *New York Times*, July 20, 1923, p. 28.

152 *IND Second System*: "100 Miles of Subway in New City Project," *New York Times*, September 16, 1929, p. 1; Dougherty, *Tracks*, p. x; "Push Subway Links to Aid Brooklyn," *New York Times*, July 30, 1930, p. 12; "Eighth Av Subway Nearly Completed," *New York Times*, August 24, 1930, p. 19.

155 *Utica Avenue Line*: "Transit Expansion to Cost $827,102,344," *New York Times*, September 15, 1938; Raskin, *Routes*, pp. 109–112, 115–116; Amy Plitt, "Utica Avenue Subway Extension to Be Studied, Again," Curbed New York, April 8, 2019, https://ny.curbed.com/2019/4/8/18300459/brooklyn-new-york-subway-utica-avenue-extension.

155 *Queens Super Express*: Andrew Lynch, "Mysteries of the Queens Boulevard Subway," http://www.vanshnookenraggen.com/_index/2015/09/mysteries-of-the-queens-boulevard-subway/.

157 *LaGuardia Airport*: Emma G. Fitzsimmons, "Plans for AirTrain to La Guardia Airport Move Ahead Amid Criticism," *New York Times*, June 25, 2018; Connor Harris, "The LaGuardia AirTrain Project Is a Truly Stupendous Waste," *New York Post*, July 2, 2019.

158 *His idea was soon scrapped…up Broadway (N, Q, R, W)*: "Transit Board Favors Moving Platform Plan," *New York Times*, May 20, 1904; Rebecca Read Shanor, *The City That Never Was* (New York: Penguin, 1991), pp. 100–103; "Adopt 34th Street Moving Platform," *New York Times*, July 3, 1912.

158 *The concept persisted…on 14th, 42nd, and 57th Streets*: Daniel L. Turner, "A Report by the Chief Engineer Submitting for Consideration a Comprehensive Rapid Transit Plan Covering All Boroughs of the City Of New York," Office of Transit Construction Commissioner (1920), available at Archive.org.

158 *The Goodyear Tire & Rubber Company…Grand Central shuttle*: "Moving Sidewalk Shown," *New York Times*, July 27, 1952.

158 *The system…Goodyear said*: Goodyear News Service press release, March 23, 1951.

158 *The TA eventually opted…manned trains*: Shanor, *The City That Never Was*, p. 105.

158 *Plans for people…subway stations*: "M.T.A. Narrows Its Decision on Wall Street 'People Movers,'" *New York Times*, April 1, 1970; "A 'People Mover' Being Considered to Link Subways," *New York Times*, March 24, 1971.

CHAPTER 12

Near-Death Experience

163 *"You have to look as if"… was covered with graffiti*: Paul Theroux, "Subway Odyssey," *New York Times Magazine*, January 31, 1982; Dwyer, *Subway Lives*, pp. 34, 129; Brian Kates, Arthur Browne and Bob Herbert, "Vandals: Hound 'em Down," *Daily News* (New York), October 8, 1981, p. 7.

163 *Crime took off … pushed through the coin slot*: Anna Quindlen, "Policemen to Ride All Subway Trains on Nighttime Runs," *New York Times*, March 17, 1979, p. 7; Guardian Angels website http://guardianangels.org/about/history; Judith Cummings, "Should Subway 'Angels' Get a Halo?" *New York Times*, December 21, 1980, p. 6; Dwyer, *Subway Lives*, p. 26.

163 *At the same time, the infrastructure … . for more than an hour*: Brian Kates, Arthur Browne and Bob Herbert, "Our Subways Are Going to Hell," *Daily News* (New York), October 10, 1981, p. 3; Brian Kates, Arthur Browne, and Bob Herbert, "This Is It. The End of the Line," *Daily News* (New York), October 7, 1981, p. 19; Paul L. Montgomery, "1,000 Trapped in I.R.T. Tunnel Accident," *New York Times*, August 29, 1973, p. 1.

163 *By the 1980s … he proposed a fare increase*: Mark Seaman, Allison L. C. de Cerreño, and Seth English-Young, *From Rescue to Renaissance: The Achievements of the MTA Capital Program 1982–2004* (New York: Rudin Center for Transportation Policy & Management, 2004); Ari L. Goldman, "A Host of Problems Await Kiley at the M.T.A.," *New York Times*, October 7, 1983.

164 *It took decades … World War I or earlier*: Dwyer, *Subway Lives*, p. 45. Robert A. Caro, *The Power Broker: Robert Moses and the Fall of New York*, (New York: Alfred A. Knopf, 1974), pp. 755–757, 932.

164 *Meanwhile, under Robert Moses . . . "inadequate to the city's needs"*: "Robert Moses: Offices Held," New York Preservation Archive Project, http://www.nypap.org/preservation-history/robert-moses/#moses1; Caro, *Power Broker*, pp. 758–759, 900.

164 *These policies starved . . . in Brooklyn and Queens were completed*: "New York City, New York Population 2019," http://worldpopulationreview.com/us-cities/new-york-city-population/; "Ridership Through Time," http://web.mta.info/nyct/110Anniversary/ridership.htm.

165 *You didn't need statistics . . . giving one sucker a surprise*: Randy Kennedy, "The Kiss of Desperation: A Disgusting Practice Vanishes with the Token," *New York Times*, April 8, 2003; Dwyer, *Subway Lives*, pp. 139–142.

166 *But theirs was a minority view . . . "uncontrollable city"*: Nathan Glazer, "On Subway Graffiti," *Public Interest*, no. 54 (Winter 1979), p. 3.

166 *As early as 1972 . . . the MTA later conceded*: "Twenty-Five Years Ago Today NYCT Subways Became Graffiti-Free," press release, MTA, May 12, 2014, http://www.mta.info/news-subway-graffiti-free-graffiti-new-york-city-transit/2014/05/12/twenty-five-years-ago-today-nyct.

166 *Restoring the essential infrastructure . . . including funding*: Nicole Gelinas, "Lessons from a Transit Savior," *Politico*, May 8, 2014, https://www.politico.com/states/new-york/albany/story/2014/05/lessons-from-a-transit-savior-080025.

166 *Ravitch struck backroom deals . . . groundwork for a full turn-around.*: Richard Ravitch, *So Much to Do: A Full Life of Business, Politics, and Confronting Fiscal Crises* (New York: Public Affairs 2014), pp. 126–131, 139–141; Seaman, de Cerreño, and English-Young, *From Rescue to Renaissance*, pp. 5, 8; Citizens Budget Commission, "Getting Back on Track: Replacing and Repairing Subway Cars Will Be Expensive and Take More Than a Decade," July 18, 2018, https://cbcny.org/research/getting-back-track.

168 *Kiley and Gunn had to confront . . . included wrenches*: Brian Kates, Bob Herbert, and Arthur Browne, "The Place Where All Hope Dies," *Daily News* (New York), October 6, 1991, p. 16; Jim Dwyer, *Subway Lives*, pp. 124–126.

168 *Not that the authority . . . had to be fixed*: Kates, Herbert, and Browne, "The Place Where All Hope Dies."

168 *Eliminating graffiti . . . how common the problem still is*: "Foxy Koch Alters Wolf Story," *New York Times*, August 28, 1980, p. 25; Peter V. Leyden, "The Graffiti Wars in New York's Subway," *Chicago Tribune*, April 26, 1985; Dwyer, *Subway Lives*, p. 15; Jose Martinez, "Subway Graffiti Costs and Delays Up as New Generation Makes Its Mark," *The City*, April 8, 2019, https://thecity.nyc/2019/04/subway-graffiti-costs-and-delays-up.html.

169 *Over time, the changes . . . to head London's transport system*: Richard Perez-Pena, "Subway Cars Perform Better Even as They Age," *New York Times*, May 15, 1996, p. B1; "R36 Mean Distances Between Failures (MDBF)," R36 Preservation, Inc., http://www.coronayard.com/r36preservation/r36mdbf.html; Citizens Budget Commission, "Getting Back on Track"; Sam Roberts, "Robert Kiley, Mass Transit Chief in Boston, London and New York, Dies at 80," *New York Times*, August 9, 2016; "MTA Facts and Figures, Subways," web.mta.info/nyct/facts/ffsubway.htm.

172 *The director, William Friedkin . . . a one-way ticket to Jamaica*: "William Friedkin on the Car Chase Scene in *The French Connection*," posted by American Film Institute, YouTube, March 5, 2010, https://www.youtube.com/watch?v=YoPI0MRAVB4; "William Friedkin, on Creating the Chase Scene in The French Connection," posted by hudsonunionsociety, YouTube, March 24, 2009, https://www.youtube.com/watch?v=TXX__AR_ONo; "*The French Connection* (1971)—Permits and the Car Chase," posted by Oscars, YouTube, October 12, 2016, https://www.youtube.com/watch?v=_O71RkiV4u8.

175 *No one knows how many rats...they be better sealed*: Michael Grynbaum, "Subway Study Finds Rats Remain Wily," *New York Times*, June 15, 2010.

175 *If it's reassuring, researchers...often supposed*: Polly Mosendz, "New York Doesn't Have More Rats Than People After All," *Newsweek*, November 6, 2014.

CHAPTER 14
How to Get There

177 *Things were simpler . . . because they couldn't*: New York Transit Museum, *Subway Style: 100 Years of Architecture and Design in the New York City Subway* (New York: Stewart, Tabori & Chang, 2004), p. 159.

177 *Most modern subway maps . . . for transit cartographers worldwide*: Ken Garland, *Mr. Beck's Underground Map* (Harrow Weald, UK: Capital Transit, 1994).

178 *Beck's abstract, diagrammatic approach . . . colors for individual lines*: Paul Shaw, *Helvetica and the New York Subway System* (Cambridge, MA: MIT Press, 2011), p. 13; "Historical Maps: Berlin S- and U-Bahn Maps, 1910–1936," Transit Maps, https://www.transitmap.net/berlin-1910-1936/.

178 *The Transit Authority didn't accept . . . the Salomon diagram was drab*: Mark Ovenden, *Transit Maps of the World* (New York: Penguin, 2007), p. 32.

178 *In 1964, the authority . . . It would prove short-lived*: New York Transit Museum, *Subway Style*, p. 175.

181 *In 1966, the TA hired . . . America at the time*: Shaw, *Helvetica*, p. 29.

181 *The implementation . . . before the budget ran out*: Ibid., p. 31, fn. 27.

181 *Eventually, work resumed . . . reissued it in 2015*: Ibid., p. 95, fn. 35; New York City Transit Authority, *NYCTA Graphics Standards Manual*, eds. Jesse Reed and Hamish Smyth (New York: Standards Manual, 2014).

182 *The black-on-white Unimark style . . . largely followed today*: Author's conversation with John Tauranac, June 21, 2019.

182 *Like Beck, Salomon, and Goldstein . . . psychedelic posters of the era*: Alice Rawsthorn, "The Subway Map That Rattled New Yorkers," *New York Times*, August 5, 2012; author's conversation with John Tauranac, May 21, 2019; New York Transit Museum, *Subway Style*, p. 163.

185 *Vignelli's work . . . difficult to tell which line ran where*: Paul Goldberger, "At Last, A Usable Subway Map," *New York Times*, August 2, 1979, p. 38.

185 *New Yorkers didn't know . . . as his obituary said*: Ovenden, *Transit Maps*, p. 34; New York Transit Museum, *Subway Style*, p. 164; Douglas Martin, "Massimo Vignelli, Visionary Designer Who Untangled the Subway, Dies at 83," *New York Times*, May 27, 2014.

185 *Vignelli was unapologetic . . . was introduced in 1979*: Alex Mindlin, "Win, Lose, Draw: The Great Subway Map Wars," *New York Times*, September 3, 2006.

185 *This time it was a map . . . were distracting*: Ibid.

189 *Though the Hertz-Tauranac map . . . different colors*: Author's conversation with John Tauranac, May 21, 2019.

189 *Vignelli's design still . . . more than 40 years now*: Ovenden, *Transit Maps*, p. 34; author's conversation with Amy Hausman, deputy director of collections, New York Transit Museum and a Vignelli map fan, March 29, 2019.

190 *"The life of a designer . . . somehow with design"*: Spoken in the 2007 documentary *Helvetica*, available at https://vimeo.com/ondemand/helvetica3

190 *Vignelli, a passionate, loquacious, charismatic man*: Michael Bierut, "Massimo Vignelli: 1931–2014," *Design Observer*, May 27, 2014.

190 *He designed logos...from 1968 to 2013)*: Joshua Johnson, "Check Out the New American Airlines Logo," *Design Shack*, January 23, 2013.

190 *the furniture maker Knoll...United Colors of Benetton*: Alex Bigman, "Remembering Massimo Vignelli, Modernist Master," 99designs.com.

191 *He once said..."everything else has to go"*: Douglas Martin, "Massimo Vignelli, Visionary Designer Who Untangled the Subway, Dies at 83," *New York Times*, May 27, 2014.

191 *If he'd had his way...simple, modern lines*: Bigman, "Remembering Massimo Vignelli."

191 *But Helvetica wasn't readily available...indistinguishable to the untrained eye*: Paul Shaw, *Helvetica and the New York Subway System* (Cambridge, MA: MIT Press, 2011), p. 41.

191 *The project earned Vignelli the title "the man who introduced New Yorkers to Helvetica"*: Taken from the moderator's introduction for Vignelli at a 1994 event at Cooper Union attended by the author.

191 *(In 1989, the TA adopted the true Helvetica)*: Alice Rawsthorn, "New York Subway's Long Dance with a Typeface," *New York Times*, April 3, 2011.

191 *"To get to the office...visible through the window"*: Michael Bierut, "Massimo Vignelli: 1931–2014," *Design Observer*, May 27, 2014.

191 *"strong and encouraging and smiley and animated"*: Quoted in Christopher Bonanos, "Massimo Vignelli: 5 Appreciations by 5 Design Professionals," *The Cut*, May 28, 2014.

191 *It always stung...decades later*: Andrew Hawkins, "The Great Subway Map War of 1978, Revisited," *The Verge*, October 29, 2015.

191 *But he called it...thinks abstractly"*: "Designing the New York City Subway Map: John Tauranac Speaks," posted by Peter Lloyd, YouTube, March 12, 2013.

191 *Vignelli thought..."It's a mongrel"*: Alex Mindlin, "Win, Lose, Draw: The Great Subway Map Wars," *New York Times*, September 3, 2006.

CHAPTER 15
Literature Goes Underground

194 *Playwright Elmer Rice . . . "new Apocalypse"*: Hood, *722 Miles*, p. 97; Brobrick, *Labyrinths*, p. 268.

195 *"Sure," I says . . . Oh, a wise guy, y'know*: Thomas Wolfe, "Only the Dead Know Brooklyn," *New Yorker*, June 7, 1935, https://www.newyorker.com/magazine/1935/06/15/only-the-dead-know-brooklyn.

CHAPTER 16
Promises, Promises

200 *By the late 1940s . . . "95 percent germ-free air"*: Roess and Sansone, *Wheels*, p. 296; Plotch, "Waiting More Than 100 Years," pp. 314–315; "New Stainless Steel Train for the Subway," *New York Times*, June 20, 1947.

200 *In truth, the fare increase . . . he proclaimed*: Hood, *722 Miles*, p. 251; "The Text of Pecora's Opening Campaign Address," *New York Times*, October 3, 1950, p. 25.

200 *Pecora lost . . . would pay for the line*: Paul Crowell, "$500,000,000 Voted for 2d Ave. Subway by Estimate Board," *New York Times*, September 14, 1951; Leo Egan, "Inquiry Is Sought by State Senator on 'Transit Mess,'" *New York Times*, January 17, 1957, p. 1; Caro, *Power Broker*, p. 832; Cudahy, *Under the Sidewalks*, p. 128.

201 *After that, the plans languished . . . slated for city transit*: "State Bonds Due to Help City Transit," *New York Times*, November 27, 1967, p. 49.

201 *Rockefeller's projected . . . pushing up construction costs still further*: Plotch, "Waiting More Than 100 Years," pp. 310, 318; "Lower East Side Loop Offered for 2d Ave. Subway by M.T.A.," *New York Times*, January 31, 1970, p. 1; "Board Approves Downtown Subway Route and East Side Loop," *New York Times*, March 20, 1970, p. 39; Frank Prial, "Stop Demanded at 96th St. in 2d Ave. Subway Hearing," *New York Times*, September 16, 1971, p. 85; Frank Prial, "M.T.A. Adds a Stop, 72d St., to Its 2d Avenue Subway Plan," *New York Times*, August 28, 1971, p. 29; "M.T.A. Agrees to Station at 96th on 2d Ave. Line," *New York Times*, October 4, 1971, p. 1.

202 *Finally, the moment came . . . Second Avenue above Houston*: "Rockefeller and Lindsay Break Ground for 2d Avenue Subway," *New York Times*, October 28, 1972, p. 35; "Beame and Wilson Man the Jackhammers to Start 4th Segment of 2d Ave. Subway," *New York Times*, July 26, 1974, p. 10.

203 *By then, however, . . . There were no takers*: Edward C. Burks, "2d Ave. Subway Faces New Delay," *New York Times*, December 14, 1974, p. 17; Greg Sargent, "The Line That Time Forgot," *New York Magazine*, March 26, 2004, p. 25; Ari L. Goldman, "FOR RNT BY M.T.A.: 2 TUNLS, NEED WRK, NO VU," *New York Times*, August 2, 1982, p. 4.

203 *Under Republican governor George Pataki . . . with two stops in between*: Plotch, "Waiting More Than 100 Years," p. 320; William Neuman, "Was There a Ghost? No, Just a Tunnel at the Latest Subway Groundbreaking," *New York Times*, April 13, 2007.

205 *Next up is Stage 2 . . . completed by 2029*: J. K. Dineen, "E. Harlem Demands Subway," *Daily News* (New York), April 17, 2001.

208 *All subsequent cars were constructed entirely of steel*: Hood, *722 Miles*, p. 192.

208 *The accident was so notorious...renamed Empire Boulevard*: Sam Roberts, "100 Years After New York's Deadliest Subway Crash," *New York Times*, November 1, 2018.

208 *The motorman was convicted of manslaughter and sentenced to up to 15 years in prison*: Ronald Sutherland, "Motorman Gets 5 to 15 Years in Crash," *New York Times*, November 7, 1992.

208 *The incident led to random blood and alcohol testing of transit workers*: Ronald Sutherland, "Motorman Goes to Trial in Subway Deaths," *New York Times*, September 16, 1992.

208 *The Transit Authority responded...55 miles an hour to 40*: Richard Perez-Pena, "Safety Board Cites Rules Lapse in 1995 Subway Crash," *New York Times*, September 5, 1996; Clyde Haberman, "Rapid Transit Fast Becoming an Oxymoron," *New York Times*, September 18, 1998.

209 *Service had to be suspended...until 2018*: Emma G. Fitzsimmons and Winnie Hu, "Cortlandt Street Station, Damaged on Sept. 11, Reopens 17 Years Later," *New York Times*, September 8, 2018.

209 *Sitting at the very tip of Manhattan...filled with harbor water*: Matt Fliegenheimer, "Flooded Tunnels May Keep City's Subway Network Closed for Several Days," *New York Times*, October 30, 2012; Matt Fliegenheimer, "For Subway Riders, Fallout from Hurricane May Last Years," *New York Times*, October 28, 2013.

210 *The agency concluded that the germs would spread rapidly through tunnels*: Nicholas M. Horrock, "Senators Are Told of Test of Gas Attack in Subway," *New York Times*, September 19, 1975.

210 *"It apparently has not occurred to the C.I.A."..."stay out of the subway'"*: Russell Baker, "Test-Tube Nonsense," *New York Times*, September 23, 1975.

210 *In 1993, another teenager...before he was caught*: Kimberly J. McLarin, "Subway Caper Fueled by Passion for Trains," *New York Times*, May 12, 1993

212 *"All that remained of the dream train"..."Subways Are Not for Sipping"*: Robert Mayer, *Newsday*, January 18, 1962, and reproduced in Gardner and Zimmer, *Meet Miss Subways*, p. 180.

212 *After that, passengers took the initiative...catch up with the perpetrators*: James Hoagland, "Cops Spy on Nude 'Happening,' It Shifts Scene," *Florida Today*, December 8, 1968, reprinted in Tracy Fitzpatrick, *Art and the Subway: New York Underground* (New Brunswick, NJ: Rutgers University Press, 2009), pp. 158–160.

212 *Naturally, the whole thing was posted to YouTube*: "Subway Sweet Sixteen—A Surprise Birthday on the Train!" posted by Improv Everywhere, May 9, 2017.

212 *Random passengers...lack of pants*: See improveverywhere.com/missions/the-no-pants-subway-ride/.

212 *Their photos soon found their way to the* New York Post: Ben Feuerherd, "Woman Throws Impromptu Birthday Party on the J Train," *New York Post*, November 8, 2018.

212 *In 2019, a couple...began playing*: @marykarrlit, "On the 6 train tonight," Twitter, June 29, 2019.

212 *Arguably the most audacious...impresario Jeff Stark*: John Del Signore, "Photos: Inside an Illegal Party in an Abandoned Subway Station Deep Under NYC," *Gothamist*, June 24, 2013.

212 *The tradition of unauthorized fêtes . . . posted to YouTube*: "Subway Sweet Sixteen—A Surprise Birthday on the Train!" posted by Improv Everywhere, May 9, 2017, https://www.youtube.com/watch?v=ejMZdtNReH4&t=36s.

CHAPTER 17
Epilogue and Prologue

217 *Cost is one reason . . . . "whippings by organized crime"*: Brian M. Rosenthal, "The Most Expensive Mile of Subway Track on Earth," *New York Times,* December 28, 2017; Dwyer, *Subway Lives*, p. 83.

217 *Other great cities . . . years behind schedule*: "Crossrail to Be Finished Without Bond Street 'by March 2021,'" *BBC News,* April 26, 2019, https://www.bbc.com/news/uk-england-london-48054789.

219 *In theory, the MTA was designed . . . . put it in 1991*: Dwyer, *Subway Lives*, pp. 63, 79–80; Dana Rubenstein, "Cuomo Distances Himself from the State-Run MTA," *Politico,* May 18, 2017, https://www.politico.com/states/new-york/albany/story/2017/05/18/governor-andrew-cuomo-no-longer-wants-to-be-associated-with-the-mta-112163; J. David Goodman, "Angry About Subway Delays? De Blasio Says Blame Cuomo, and Vice Versa," *New York Times,* May 19, 2017; Marc Santora, "Why Does New York State Control the Subway? That's the 20-Cent Question," *New York Times*, May 19, 2017; Marc Santora, "De Blasio Says Stick to Subway (but Don't Blame Him If You Run Late)," *New York Times,* May 19, 2017.

JUST THE FACTS, MA'AM

222 Metropolitan Transportation Authority, Comprehensive Annual Financial Report for the Years Ended December 31, 2018 and 2017, pp. 148, 156; http://web.mta.info/mta/investor/pdf/2019/2018_CAFR_Final.pdf; Metropolitan Transportation Authority 2018 Annual Report Narrative, http://web.mta.info/mta/compliance/pdf/2018_annual/Annual_Report_Narrative.pdf; http://web.mta.info/nyct/facts; "Subway FAQ: Facts and Figures," nycsubway.org, https://www.nycsubway.org/wiki/Subway_FAQ:_Facts_and_Figures; Nir, Sarah Maslin. "Water, Water Everywhere in New York Subway. And with It, Problems," *New York Times,* February 12, 2018.

THE STRAPHANGER'S ESSENTIAL LEXICON

228 *GCT = Grand Central Terminal...Pennsylvania Station:* See GCThistory.com.

ACKNOWLEDGMENTS

This book traces back to Carl Oppedahl, my original subway tour guide, who enthused about the beavers and Milton Glaser plaques in the Astor Place station, pointed out abandoned platforms, and led me on a trip around the City Hall loop during visits to New York in the 1980s.

When I relocated to New York in the 1990s, I looked for a book about the subway packed with pictures and factoids to satisfy a reader with a short attention span like me. It didn't exist. I even went so far as to sketch an outline of chapters for such a work. Fast forward to 2016, when I mentioned the idea to Leah Spiro, and she thought it could sell and agreed to be my agent. Thanks to brainstorming sessions with her, and her enthusiasm and persistence, we lined up a first-rate publisher, Black Dog Leventhal. I'm deeply grateful for her support throughout.

In Lisa Tenaglia, I was blessed with a gifted editor who matter-of-factly identified simple solutions to problems that vexed me. Collaborating with her has been a pleasure. My thanks, too, to Susan Van Horn, who came up with an ingenious design to accommodate all the images (so big!) and the complex structure of subchapters. Thanks to Lisa and Susan, the book emerged in a form far, far better than anything I imagined at the outset. Mark Steven Long's careful copy editing spared me from many pitfalls, factual and linguistic.

A number of people shared suggested topics and valuable trivia early in my research: Sarah Kaufman (*Broad City, The Warriors*), D.M. Osborne (token suckers), Joe Raskin (*The Simpsons, Bananas)*, and Nate Gerstein and William Wall (*Mineola*). Diane Knox deserves a special call-out for delivering a full page of terrific ideas, including Miss Subways, which I had forgotten.

Andrew Lynch, Subutay Musluoglu, Uday Schultz, and John Tauranac read parts or all of the proposal or manuscript, made valuable suggestions, and flagged mistakes. It's mandatory to say (but no less true) that responsibility for any remaining errors is mine.

At the New York Transit Museum, archivists Rebecca Haggerty and Desiree Alden were extremely helpful, organized, and efficient.

My thanks, also, to others who helped track down historical records and photos: Joe Brennan, John Proto at the Shore Line Transit Museum; Tom Malcolm at WSP/Parsons Brinckerhoff; John L. Sprague; and Sandy Campbell of the Electric Railroaders Association.

Amber Asaly, Andrew Chaikin, Jonathan Poore of Express Watersports, Teri Slotkin, John L. Sprague, Luca Vignelli, Brian Weinberg, WSP/Parsons Brinckerhoff, and the Regional Plan Association graciously granted permission to use images of theirs. Thanks, also, to cartographers Andrew Lynch, Maxwell F. Roberts, and Cameron Booth for allowing me to include their work.

I owe a particular debt to six other authors. My understanding of the subway's creation was framed by Clifton Hood's smart and lucid *772 Miles*. The deep, original research in three other works was also invaluable: Peter Derrick's *Tunneling to the Future*; Joe Raskin's *The Routes Not Taken*; and Tom Malcolm's privately published *William Barclay Parsons*.

Two books by two journalists—Jim Dwyer's *Subway Lives* and Randy Kennedy's *Subwayland*—provided a wealth of more contemporary detail and color and reinforced my conviction that a book about the subway should capture what's outrageous and funny about the system. These books made me laugh again and again, often out loud.

Finally, I must thank all the friends who endured several years of my rambling dissertations about the subway, particularly about the remarkable duo of August Belmont, Jr. and William Barclay Parsons.

PHOTO CREDITS

INDEX

Illustrations are in **bold.**

Unimark International, 181, 182

Union Square station at 14th Street, **22–23**

    accident, **206**, 208

    temperatures in, 73

United Colors of Benetton, 190

Upper West Side real estate development, 139

uptown/downtown, 229

Utica Avenue line (proposed), 141, 152, 155

Utilities restructuring, 17

V

V. (Pynchon), 196

Van Wyck, Robert, 17

Vanderbilt, William H., 99

Vera-Ellen, **131**

Verge, The (journal), 191

Verrazzano-Narrows Bridge, 152

Vignelli, Massimo, 177, 181, 182, 184, 185, 189, **190**, 191

    various corporate images, 190

"Visions of Johanna" (song), 89

Visual assaults on senses in subways, 74

W

W line, 88, 125, 157, 158, 221

Waits, Tom, 90

Waldorf Astoria Hotel, 129

Walking Dead, The, (TV show) advertisements, **48**, 49

Wall Street station, 88, 126

    decoration, **28**

Warriors, The (movie), 171

Washington Heights, 21, 26

    real estate development, 138, 139

Wayside zone controller, **63**

"We're delayed because of train traffic ahead. We'll be moving shortly," 229

Wednesday Morning 3 A.M. (album), 89, **91**

Wesley-Smith, S., 74

West 181st Street real estate development, 138

West 74th Street real estate development, 138

West 75th real estate development, 138

West End line, 229

West Fourth Street station, 117, 126, 145

Westinghouse, 57

Wharton, Edith, **192**, 193

what to do if you fall on the tracks, 92

Willets Point, 157

Williamsburg Bridge, 35, 64, 126

    accident, 208

    "Bridge Loop," 81

subway lines, 145, 147, 154

Williamsburg real estate development, 142

Willson, Hugh B., 8, 12, 223

Wise Bread guide, 95

Wolfe, Thomas, **194**, 195

Wood, Harmon and Company, 140, 141, 142, 155

World Trade Center, **209**

World War I, 58, 59, 107

World War II, 121, 124, 157, 164, 200, 215

World's Fair 1964–1965, 178

Worth Street and 18th Street abandoned stations, 220–221

Worth Street line to Williamsburg (unbuilt), 152, **154**

Y

Yale Club, 167

YouTube, 90, 191, 212

Z

Z line, 88, 118, 126, 127, 145, 154, 221, 227

Zizmor, Jonathan, advertisements, **48**, 49

ABOUT THE AUTHOR

John E. Morris has been fascinated by trains and transit systems since childhood, and has indulged this passion while pursuing careers, as a lawyer and, later, as a journalist. He has worked as an editor and reporter at the *American Lawyer* magazine, *The Deal*, Dow Jones, and Bloomberg News, and he's the coauthor with David Carey of *King of Capital: The Remarkable Rise, Fall, and Rise Again of Steve Schwarzman and Blackstone*, a history of the Blackstone Group and the private equity industry. He holds an undergraduate degree in philosophy from the University of California, Berkeley, and a JD from Harvard Law School. He lives in New York.

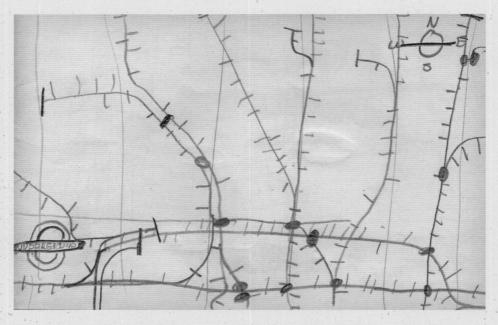

At age nine, the author tried his hand at transit cartography, drawing his own map of the London Underground.

East River Tunnel, Now